ARCHITECTURAL DETAILS FOR INSULATED BUILDINGS

Ronald Brand, Ph.D.

Carleton University
Ottawa, Ontario
Canada

 VAN NOSTRAND REINHOLD
New York

Disclaimer

When the details herein are incorporated into buildings, they must be used with care by professionals who understand the implications of what they are doing.

Copyright © 1990 by Van Nostrand Reinhold
Library of Congress Catalog Card Number 89-22477
ISBN 0-442-23674-3

Printed in the United States of America

Van Nostrand Reinhold
115 Fifth Avenue
New York, New York 10003

Van Nostrand Reinhold International Company Limited
11 New Fetter Lane
London EC4P 4EE, England

Van Nostrand Reinhold
480 La Trobe Street
Melbourne, Victoria 3000, Australia

Nelson Canada
1120 Birchmount Road
Scarborough, Ontario M1K 5G4, Canada

16 15 14 13 12 11 10 9 8 7 6 5 4 3 2 1

Library of Congress Cataloging-in-Publication Data

Brand, Ronald G.
    Architectural details for insulated buildings / Ronald Brand.
      p.   cm.
    ISBN 0-442-23674-3
    1. Insulation (Heat) 2. Building—Details. I. Title.
  TH1715.B66 1989
    693′.83—dc20   89-22477
                                                                  CIP

ARCHITECTURAL DETAILS FOR INSULATED BUILDINGS

Contents

Preface

This is a book of architectural details for building envelopes. It is intended to be used as a desk manual by architects, architectural technologists, students, and builders. It has a Prolegomenon which contains the material one should know if the book is to be more than superficially useful. The Prolegomenon is followed by eight series of details and seven chapters that explain the science and technology behind those details.

With two exceptions, the details include most of the currently popular construction types. The first exception is wood-frame construction. Wooden houses work quite well, but no one seems to know exactly why. The empirical rules are not readily transferred to noncombustible construction.

The second exception is the popular use of metal studs and gypsum board to support brick veneer. In spite of the fact that the system does not stand up to engineering analysis in respect to stiffness, it does seem to be performing adequately. The most useful current guidelines are in *Technical Note 28B,* second revision, published February 1987 by the Brick Institute of America, 11490 Commerce Park Drive, Reston, Virginia 22091. Because the system, as commonly designed and supervised, bears so little resemblance to these guidelines, it has not been included in the details.

Acknowledgments

The argument for construction details based on building science was first put forward by Jean Claude Perreault in a submission to the National Research Council of Canada (NRCC). It was he who made it possible to observe, first hand, the problems besetting the construction industry; problems caused by architects who do not know how to design watertight insulated buildings.

I am grateful to Professor Colin H. Davidson, former Dean of the Faculté de l'aménagement, Université de Montréal, for his supervision of the original manuscript.

The climate of Alberta, Canada, provides one of the severest tests of building envelope design. For that reason the original detail designs were sent to the Alberta Building Envelope Council. The suggestions of Malcolm Johnston, Terry Christoff, Barry Dennis, Christopher Makepeace, and Jean Claude Perreault, president and members of that council, have been incorporated in this book.

A review by G. Adaire Chown, who has an eye for technical detail and logical argument, is largely responsible for the coherence and clarity of the text.

It will be obvious when reading this book that most of the building science comes from the Institute for Research in Construction, formerly the Division of Building Research, NRCC; from Max Baker, Kirby Garden, J.K. Latta, R.G. Turenne, and particularly from G.O. Handegord and N.B. Hutcheon through their book "Building Science for a Cold Climate."

I am pleased to acknowledge the work of Peter Mill and his associates at Public Works Canada, who have provided the most coherent assessment available of the state of Canadian public buildings.

Finally, I wish to thank my wife Annette who helped me, encouraged me, then composed and typed this manuscript many times.

RONALD G. BRAND

ARCHITECTURAL DETAILS FOR INSULATED BUILDINGS

Prolegomenon
or
"Stuff You Should Know"

Building envelope failures are far more widespread and serious than most architects suspect:

- Claims for "facade failures" have increased from 15% of all claims in 1960 to 33% of all claims in 1980 (Shand, Morhan and Company 1981).
- A recent report (Zabas 1983) states that nearly two-thirds of high rise condominium buildings have experienced major parking garage problems. The biggest problem has been water leakage, followed by concrete deterioration. One corporation spent $850,000 on garage repairs.
- One quarter of all high rise condominiums have roofing problems. The cost for each incident has averaged $45,000. The accountants reporting on frequency and costs say "those twenty year roofs should really be called convertible six year roofs." The report also states that 40% of townhouse roofs have needed repairs costing on average $24,000.
- Three-quarters of high rise condominiums and 65% of townhouses experienced water leakage through the walls.
- Repair costs varied between $4,000 and $150,000. Of the corporations suffering these difficulties, half of the corporations have taken, or are taking, the developer to court to recover costs.

During the years 1983 to 1985, the exterior walls of four of the two dozen major buildings on the Carleton University campus in Ottawa had failed to the extent that they had to be replaced. The buildings, ranging between five and fifteen years old, were designed by prominent Canadian architects and received very favorable critical acclaim at the time of their design and construction. Repairs will cost the university over $5,000,000. Another very large building on campus is having similar problems and similar repairs are anticipated. In one case, the university is suing the architect. This situation is not unique to Carleton University nor to Canada.

Although the frequency of lawsuits is increasing, they are fewer than might be expected given the extent of failures. Delays and the difficulty of assessing blame seem to be the main reasons that redress was not sought more often. However, that may no longer be the case. Using infrared thermography, it is now quite possible to detect potential failures before the buildings are completed. It is also possible to assess blame at this stage, a fact that should be of great concern to architects.

CAUSES OF FAILURE

Over the last decade, building scientists at Public Works Canada have turned the lenses of their infrared cameras on a wide range of their own buildings. They have found that only 3% of the building enclosures were working as well as they should. Their studies show the following deficiencies. These deficiencies are discussed in more detail in Chapters 1, 2, and 3.

- No air barrier.
- Air barrier material not airtight—many buildings leak air because brick and block masonry are thought to be reasonably airtight.
- Air barrier not continuous—it should be possible to trace a continuous plane of airtightness through any detail of the building envelope.
- Air barrier not flexible at joints—such techniques as parging make a tremendous improvement in airtightness but, because of its brittle nature, parging is no good at all where any movement may occur.
- Air barrier not well supported—in some buildings, polyethylene film was expected to withstand wind forces.
- Air barrier not insulated to prevent condensation and frost. The use of insulation to improve comfort and to reduce energy consumption is well known. Its role in keeping the air barrier warm is not so well understood.
- Insulation not tight to air barrier—a 4 mm space between insulation and its backup can reduce the effectiveness of the insulation by 40%.
- Thermal bridging—in cavity wall construction, some steel must penetrate the insulation to provide support for the cladding. Where these penetrations are relatively modest in size, the heat loss will not be excessive and will, in most circumstances, help to dry and preserve the steel supports. Continuous steel and aluminum supports, however, will conduct large quantities of heat through the insulation. Thermal bridging also occurs when insulation is placed between metal studs.
- No air space behind cladding—in rainscreen construction, this space provides a path for most of the water to run safely down behind the cladding until it can be drained to the outside. It is also the best place to accommodate some of the inaccuracies in construction.
- No positive cavity drainage—water penetrates most claddings to some extent. A single wythe of brick masonry leaks very badly. The situation can be improved if the water is led out from the cavity by flashings and weep holes.
- Cladding improperly supported—many buildings have cladding supports that are subject to corrosion; others form serious heat bridges. Few take into account the serious consequences of the normal inaccuracies in building frames.
- No allowance for creep and deflection—in buildings with steel and concrete frames, neither the cladding nor the backup panel walls are normally designed to take superimposed loads. Thus a clearance space must be left to allow beams and columns to deflect without putting loads on the nonbearing walls beneath them. Quite often the elastic deflections of a steel structure are acknowledged, but the larger, permanent creep deflection of concrete is not.
- Vapor barrier needed.
- Cladding caulked for airtightness and watertightness.

At the Institute for Research in Construction (IRC), a part of the National Research Council of Canada (NRCC), it is estimated that over 80% of the inquiries they receive are from individuals and organizations looking for assistance with building malfunctions that occur after completion and occupancy. Only a small group of architects regularly seek NRCC advice during the design stage of their projects.

Many of the failures are blamed on poor workmanship. However R.L. Quirouette's study (Quirouette 1982) and the author's reports to Public Works Canada in 1980 show this is seldom the case. As Quirouette states:

> Many of the problems of the building envelope are caused, not by the builder, but by those who prepare the architectural or engineering drawings. The cause of many facade problems, for example, originates in the way in which materials are specified to be put together and the type of materials chosen for various parts of the envelope. Either from lack of appropriate information about the construction sequence or from incorrect assumptions of end performance, unsuspected weaknesses appear first in architectural and engineering drawings, are carried through to shop drawings and are eventually "built in" by the construction team.

A CASE FOR MODEL DETAILS

Masons laying out a square corner, often do so by using a triangle with sides in the ratio 3, 4, and 5. They find the system useful and dependable, whether or not it is recognized as a particular case of Pythagoras' theorem. Architects use it too, and in spite of the fact that many have forgotten the proof, it is still used with confidence.

Mathematicians have thousands of these equations (or models) that free them for more creative work. The equations range from $2+2=4$ to $E=mc^2$. It is hard to imagine the development of mathematical thought if, at each step, mathematicians were required to revert to first principles. As it is, they use equations or models, once they have been convinced of their validity.

Most of the problems that architects are experiencing could be avoided by using soundly based model details. If this is so, it is puzzling that most of an architect's building information is fragmented, more or less in the form of first principles, as though assembling it into useful models was infringing on the designer's prerogatives. It is a point of view that does not stand up to examination. For instance, if a designer, when choosing a window, were to research all the factors that might affect the type, size, and position of a window, it would turn out to be a life's work rather than a finite step in design. On the other hand, several model details of window installations would allow the technical details to be resolved quickly and would free the designer to concentrate on refinements, position, proportion, context, and imagery.

It is true that the model details would subsume some of the design decisions, but it is instructive to see how mathematicians handle a similar problem. For instance, they find that $2+2$ always equals 4. They cannot make it equal 5, for they are unable to change the inexorable laws of mathematics. Neither can architects change the inexorable laws of nature, although the first paragraphs of this Prolegomenon record some of the best efforts to do so.

How would model details fare in the drafting room? It would be naive to think that a designer's dreams can be converted to reality without some adjustment. However, that adjustment is particularly harsh when designers and their technical associates are working at cross purposes. At times these associates seem to take pleasure in subverting the design for practical reasons. However, if the designer and his associates share images of simple model details, these destructive differences could be overcome. One would hope that each office might refine the details for their own use and thus establish their own conventions; conventions that the designers, draftsmen, and builders would all understand.

The model details offered here, and the principles behind them, will be readily understood by most builders. This will be helpful in two ways. First, if the builder and designer share an image of what is to be achieved, the thousands of specific instructions included in the contract documents will become more coherent and understandable. More than that, the mutual comprehension of goals will allow the builder to make confident, independent decisions. For example, builders are seldom able to schedule the work in the most desirable sequence. The decisions that they make in that regard often result in seemingly minor changes to the assemblies, but such changes have had serious effects on enclosure performance. This is less likely to happen if the builder understands the basic model from which the design has been generated.

It is an appealing idea that dependable models might free architects for more creative work. In fact, that seems to be exactly what happened in Greek and Gothic architecture. Not only did the designers have model forms to follow, but they had highly developed traditional means of achieving them. Through the model forms they achieved a level of order and meaning that has never been surpassed. Through the model details they achieved an exquisite refinement of form as well as a longevity that puts present technology to shame. For those who look askance at any sort of restraint, it is comforting to be reminded that although the essential models remained remarkably constant during the centuries in which these buildings were built, there was no lack of originality in the evolution and refinement that took place.

REQUIREMENTS FOR BUILDING ENVELOPES

Model details should respond to the requirements for building envelopes in your climate. This book is concerned with building envelopes in climates where cold winters make insulation necessary. The following requirements have been identified by Dr. Neil Hutcheon in the *Canadian Building Digest—CBD 48* (Hutcheon 1963):

1. control heat flow;
2. control air flow;
3. control water vapor flow;
4. control rain penetration;
5. control light, solar and other radiation;
6. control noise;
7. control fire;
8. provide strength and rigidity;
9. be durable;
10. be aesthetically pleasing; and
11. be economical.

Examinations of many building problems have shown that it is requirements 1, 2, 3, 4, and 9 that are most in need of solutions. Solutions to the other requirements are either more readily found or are outside the scope of this book.

Based on the frequency and types of failures noted above, the following eight rules are proposed as the basis for the detail designs presented here. These rules also form an excellent "catechism" to test any detail, new or old.

THE RULES

1. Enclose the building in a continuous air barrier.
2. Provide continuous support for the air barrier against wind loads.
3. Ensure that the air barrier is flexible at joints where movement may occur.
4. Provide continuous insulation to keep the air barrier warm and to conserve energy in the building.
5. Keep the insulation tight to the air barrier.
6. Protect the insulation with a rainscreen/sunscreen supported out from the structure in a way that does not penetrate the insulation with excessive heat bridges.
7. Provide enough open space for drainage and construction clearances between the rainscreen and the insulation.
8. Drain the wall cavity to the outside.

Now is as good a time as any to get out a set of plans with a detail section showing, say, a wall-roof intersection. See if Rule 1 is observed: it can be tested by tracing the line of airtightness with a red pencil. One should not have to lift the pencil from the drawing at all. Look particularly at the joints between materials. For instance when two 2″ x 4″ are drawn touching each other, it looks as if the joint between them was airtight. One would only have to look at the real thing to know that this would not be so. Look particularly at the joints in sheet metal.

TYPICAL ARRANGEMENTS

These rules result in a few typical configurations that form the basis for all of the details in Part 1. The following schematic drawings show these typical configurations. It is essential that the relationship of the elements be maintained if the design principles are to be respected. After the basic ideas are established, the schematic elements will be filled in to show steel construction, concrete, masonry, etc. In the details presented in Part 1, the schematic representation will be replaced with more or less conventional representations of the actual materials.

WALL-ROOF INTERSECTION

Figure P–1a shows a flat roof extending out to the edge of a wall. This wall does not support the roof, an arrangement that is typical of most construction other than houses. Because the roof and its supports will deflect, a space is left between roof and wall, for the wall is not designed to take the roof load and must not be allowed to do so. When the roof edge is neat and square and aligned with the outer edge of the wall, the next step is easy.

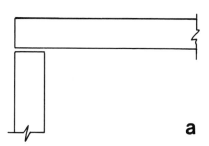

FIGURE P-I. Wall-roof schematic drawing.

Figure P–1b shows a continuous air barrier applied to the structure of Figure P–1a. The little bulge in the material at the joint between roof and wall is intended to indicate that the membrane is flexible at this joint where movement may occur. The air barrier must be well adhered to the wall and roof for it will be buffeted by both positive and negative air pressures. For the same reason, the flexible part must be quite strong.

Figure P–1c shows a continuous layer of insulation in close contact with the air barrier. It must be a little flexible where it goes over the joint between roof and wall.

Figure P–1d shows this assembly protected with a rainscreen/sunscreen which is represented schematically. The top of the wall is protected with a sort of umbrella. On roofs, it is assumed that the insulation is waterproof, so the material over the insulation serves only as a sunscreen and ballast.

INTERSECTION OF AN EXTERIOR WALL WITH AN INTERMEDIATE FLOOR

Figure P–2a shows the floor structure projecting to the outer edge of the wall, just as it did at the roof. Note that the floor structure carries the wall above it. Again, the floor will deflect and space must be left for this to happen when the wall below is not designed to carry the load of the floor.

Figure P–2b shows the air barrier membrane securely adhered to the wall and to the edge of the floor. The wall and floor edge must be neat and flush if this is to be done effectively. Again, the little bulge indicates that the membrane is flexible at this joint where movement may occur. The wall provides support for the air barrier membrane except at the joint, where the flexible part must be strong enough itself to withstand wind loads.

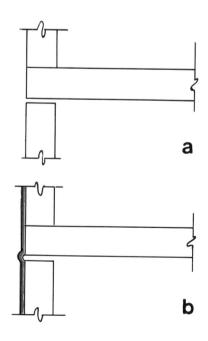

FIGURE P–2. Wall-floor schematic drawing.

Figure P–2c shows a continuous layer of insulation fastened tightly to the air barrier. Note that it, too, must be flexible at the joint where movement may occur.

Figure P–2d shows this assembly protected with a rainscreen/sunscreen, which is represented schematically. Because the rainscreen/sunscreen will be supported at each floor, it must be divided into story-height sections that can move independently, following the deflection of the floors. A membrane sealed to the air barrier drains the wall assembly to the outside.

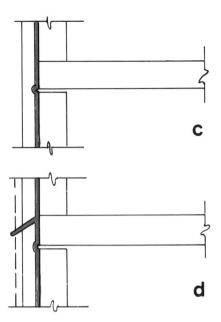

WALL-FLOOR-FOUNDATION INTERSECTION

Figure P–3a shows the wall sitting flush with the face of the foundation. This is unusual because conventionally the foundation will project out to pick up the cladding. In almost all cases, the edges of the floor will be supported on the foundation wall and not by the building frame as at other floors.

Figure P–3b shows how simple it is to apply an unbroken air barrier to this structure. If a waterproof membrane is used for the air barrier, it can be extended down to form the waterproofing on the foundation wall.

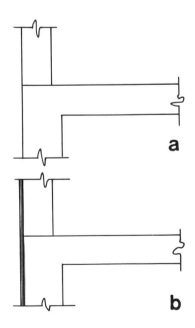

FIGURE P-3.   Wall-floor-foundation schematic drawing.

Figure P–3c shows a continuous layer of insulation applied to this air barrier. Arranging the structure as in Figure P–3a is the only way to get this layer continuous.

Figure P–3d shows a schematic rainscreen/sunscreen applied to this assembly. It is supported at the floor level, as it is at every other floor. Here the bottom can simply be left open for drainage; no cavity flashing is necessary. Earth will protect the insulation below grade. The band of insulation between grade and the rainscreen/sunscreen must be protected against sunlight, snow shovels, lawnmowers, etc. Whatever material is used in that position will be subject to very destructive climatic and other forces.

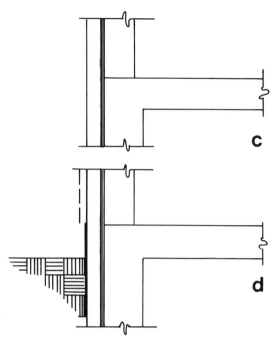

ROOF-PENTHOUSE INTERSECTION

Figure P–4a—this intersection occurs wherever a wall rises above a roof. Frequently the roof is supported on a structure that is independent of the structure supporting the wall. That separation is indicated here. The implication is that these two elements can move independently. Any connection between the two must therefore be flexible.

Figure P–4b shows the air barrier adhered to this structure. Note that some excess material is left to accommodate deflection of the deck; as might occur, for instance, with a snow load. The air barrier membrane can also serve as the roof membrane. Fortunately, there are now materials that are satisfactory for both purposes.

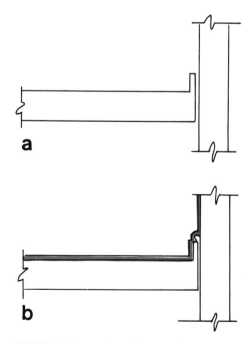

FIGURE P-4. Roof-penthouse schematic drawing.

Figure P–4c shows insulation applied to the membrane. It, too, must be flexible at the joint where movement may occur. Both wall and roof insulations must be able to withstand wetting, but the one on the roof will be wet for long periods of time and must be particularly waterproof.

c

Figure P–4d shows the same schematic representation of a rainscreen/sunscreen used on other walls. The cover on the roof serves as ballast and as a sunscreen for the waterproof insulation.

d

STRUCTURAL IMPLICATIONS OF TYPICAL ARRANGEMENTS

Until now only the general shapes of structural supports for the building envelope have been shown. In Figure P–5a, the roof shape has been detailed in concrete and the wall in concrete block masonry. Note that the center line of vertical reinforcing is shown in the wall, as are two angles that provide horizontal restraint for the top of the wall. The inner angle is placed after the wall is erected. A space is left above the masonry wall and within the angles so that the roof slab can deflect.

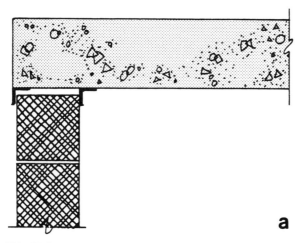

a

FIGURE P–5. Structural implications.

In Figure P–5b, the essential, simple shape of the roof edge has been achieved by wrapping the edge of the roof construction with heavy gauge galvanized sheet metal and gypsum board. In this drawing, the wall is detailed in metal studs and gypsum board. Space for deflection is provided by nesting two drywall runner channels. Half of the windload on the wall will be transmitted to the structure through these channels, so they must be selected and erected with care.

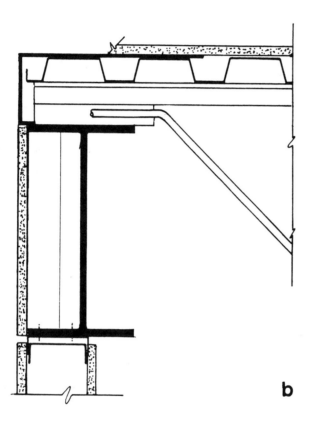

b

NOTES REGARDING THE DETAILS

Each of the building details that follows is derived from the eight rules previously stated. Except where these rules demand a particular arrangement, the detailing is simply that demanded by good practice. Occasionally, a deviation from the details may be considered. One value of the details and rules is that the nature and extent of any deviations are easy to see. The user is then aware that he/she is leaving charted ground and must be particularly careful. On such occasions, it will be useful to review the pertinent theory in the chapters that follow the details.

The building envelope details that follow are arranged in eight series, each with a particular cladding backed up by an appropriate non-bearing infill or backup wall referred to in this text as a panel wall. They include most of the combinations in common use today.

The notes on the drawings are intended to resemble the notes that may be found on an architect's working drawing. Like such notes, they do not adhere rigorously to a simple descriptive system but include notes and instructions that may make the designer's intentions clearer. To achieve maximum legibility the lines and textures on the drawings depart somewhat from standard practice. For a variety of reasons the drawings are not to scale, so they should not be traced.

The boldface numbers beside the notes on the drawings refer to paragraphs below the detail. These paragraphs offer fuller explanations of important parts of the assembly as well as references for further reading on the subject.

These references are of four kinds. Two or three numbers in brackets refer to a section in one of the chapters in Part 2; the first number always referring to the chapter. For example, (1.5.4) refers to section 1.5.4 in Chapter 1. For broader subjects, the note may refer to a whole chapter. There are also many references to Canadian Building Digests published by the National Research Council of Canada (NRCC). These are noted as CBD's, e.g., (CBD 125). They are readily available from the Council. There are a few references to other NRCC documents. These are noted NRCC followed by the publication type and number. For example, (NRCC B.P.N. 37), the B.P.N. referring to a Building Practice Note.

When using these details, the designer should consult the local building code for requirements related to fire. In many instances, particularly in multistory buildings, structural elements will require protection against excessive temperature rise due to fire.

In addition, the code may require certain fire separations, for instance between floors. To maintain the integrity of these separations, not only must duct and pipe spaces be closed against fire penetration but fire stops may be required in the wall cavity.

NOTES REGARDING THE CHAPTERS

The chapters that follow in Part 2 are intended to bring to the practitioner the basic science related to the details and to discuss the implications of this science on the design of buildings in climates where winters may be cold. Other writings on the subject are listed. Most are from the NRCC.

REFERENCES

Hutcheon, N.B. 1963. "Requirements for Exterior Walls." *Canadian Building Digests CBD 48.* Ottawa: National Research Council of Canada.

Quirouette, R.L. 1982. "A Study of the Construction Process." *Construction Canada* 24(January):28–29.

Zabas, A. 1983. "Leakage Called Big Problem." *Daily Commercial News* October 25.

Part I

The Details

Series A: Brick Cladding, Concrete Block Panel Wall

The purpose of this series of details is to show how the basic patterns developed in the Prolegomenon can be applied to walls with brick cladding, concrete block backup (panel) walls, and either steel or reinforced concrete structural frames. The vital air barrier is traced through the detail with a red line. This line is continuously insulated, as required by the rules, and the insulation is tight to the air barrier.

Where there are several ways of achieving the same ends, the details will attempt to illustrate two or three of them. For instance, Details A1 and A5, like most details, show a curb without a cant strip, since this is the preferred detail with rubberized asphalt roofing and flashing. Detail E6 shows the curb and cant strip preferred for built-up roofing.

Several ways of ballasting the roof insulation are shown. Note 5 on Detail A3 is important in this regard.

There is a discussion of through-wall flashings in 7.4.11 of Chapter 7, in which it suggests that they are not needed at every floor. Detail A5 shows a wall-floor intersection with through-wall flashing, while in Detail A2 there is none.

Insofar as sequence is concerned, all of the details have been designed to allow the roof and roof edge to be completed before the walls are built. Each detail should be carefully examined to see how continuity of the all-important air barrier has been achieved. The architect should not allow a sequence of construction that prejudices this continuity.

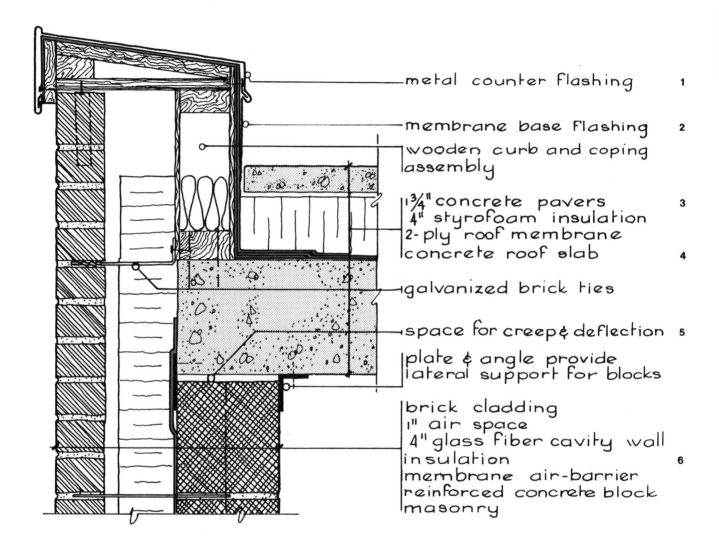

metal counter flashing   **1**

membrane base flashing   **2**

wooden curb and coping
assembly

1¾" concrete pavers   **3**
4" styrofoam insulation
2-ply roof membrane
concrete roof slab   **4**

galvanized brick ties

space for creep & deflection   **5**

plate & angle provide
lateral support for blocks

brick cladding
1" air space
4" glass fiber cavity wall
insulation   **6**
membrane air-barrier
reinforced concrete block
masonry

1. Metal is the only satisfactory material here. Your chances of making it watertight are nil, so put a waterproof membrane underneath it and put a good slope on both. Slope to the roof, or you will have dirt streaks on the face of the building. Form the metal with slip joints and hold it down with clips along the edges. Caulking or soldering the joints is wishful thinking, so is trying to join membranes to this metal. (Chapter 7)(CBD 69)

2. Any metal counterflashing here would be merely a decorative sun screen that some idiot will nail through the membrane. Use mineral surfaced roofing for a sun screen. The base flashings are rubberized asphalt, solidly "torched" in place. The base flashings and the roof membranes should be interleaved as directed by the manufacturer. One ply of the membrane is carried up and over the parapet and nailed to the outside face. Remember it's part of the roof and must be supported from the roof, not the wall. Treat the wood to prevent rot. (Chapter 7)(CBD 69, CBD 111, CBD 112)

3. To be effective even during temporary flooding, this ballast must function under water, where concrete weighs 87.5 lb/ft^3 (1400Kg/m^3) instead of 150 lb/ft^3 (2400Kg/m^3). For normal use the manufacturer recommends that 4" (100mm) of insulation be ballasted with 20 lb/ft^2 (108Kg/m)^2. Alternatives to ballasting are discussed in Chapter 6.

4. This surface must slope. 1:50 is a minimum. Light weight toppings are not strong enough to restrain a built-up membrane (CBD 181). If you want a level underside to the slab, you are faced with slabs about 6" (150mm) thicker at the edges than at the drain. Sorry.

5. Closing this joint is the most important part of this whole detail. Joints must be airtight and flexible for the life of the building. You can never get at them again. If torched-on rubberized asphalt is used as an air barrier, it will also provide airtight flexible joints. Caulking around a concrete block wall is like caulking around a sieve. (2.4.1, 2.5.4)

6. Use Fiberglas. Hold it in intimate contact with the air barrier with mechanical fasteners. Whatever you do, don't let outside air get behind the insulation. For that reason daubs of adhesive must not be used. (1.5.2)

CLADDING **BRICK**

PANEL WALL **CONCRETE BLOCK**

STRUCTURAL FRAME **CONCRETE**

detail A1

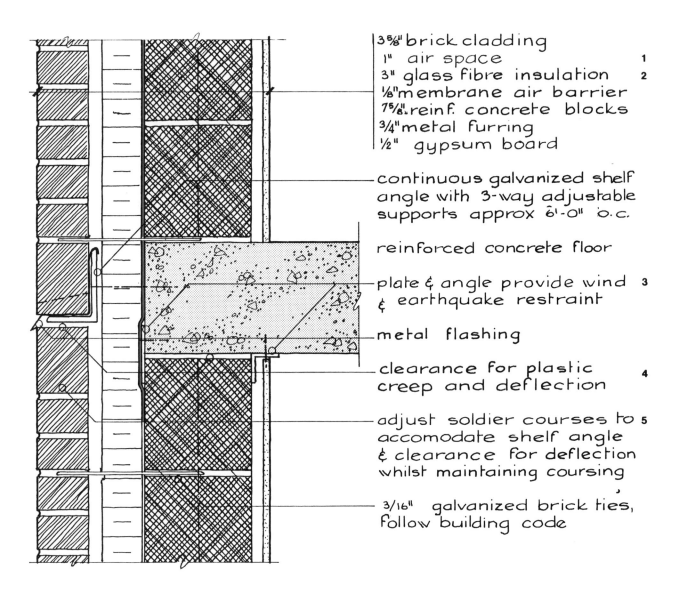

3⅝" brick cladding   1
1" air space
3" glass fibre insulation   2
⅛" membrane air barrier
7⅝" reinf. concrete blocks
¾" metal furring
½" gypsum board

continuous galvanized shelf
angle with 3-way adjustable
supports approx 6'-0" o.c.

reinforced concrete floor

plate & angle provide wind   3
& earthquake restraint

metal flashing

clearance for plastic   4
creep and deflection

adjust soldier courses to   5
accomodate shelf angle
& clearance for deflection
whilst maintaining coursing

3/16" galvanized brick ties,
follow building code

1 This cavity provides a path for water to run down and out of the wall. It should be as clean as possible but it is unrealistic to expect it to be free of mortar. Mortar bridges will carry some water across the cavity. This makes it very important that the air barrier is waterproof and intact. Note that no cavity flashing is shown in this detail. The difficulties of installing it properly override its doubtful advantages in buildings with a good air/vapour barrier. (Chapter 3)

2 This wall has a thermal resistance of R 17 (Rsi 3). Glass fiber insulation is suggested, for it can be drawn up tightly to the irregularities of the blockwork and around the not inconsiderable bumps caused where three thicknesses of membrane overlap. Mechanical fasteners are required. (1.5.2, 1.5.3)

3 This plate and angle restrain the wall against wind and earthquake loads without allowing the floor load to come down on the concrete block wall. Note that the wall is reinforced to sustain horizontal loads. Note also that the brick wythe will be lowered as the floor deflects.

4 A wythe of brickwork is not at all waterproof. Expect large quantities of water to stream down the back of the bricks. (3.1) The shelf angle, which should be galvanized, will intercept most of this water and divert it outward through the weep holes. This flashing is intended to throw it clear of the bricks and to screen the gap which was left for deflection. The flashing must be sheet zinc or heavily galvanized sheet steel, for any other metal will set up a destructive electrolytic current with the galvanized shelf angle when the joint is damp.

5 The clearance required for creep and deflection must be obtained from your structural engineer. There are many instances of severe cladding failure when inadequate clearance has been allowed. (CBD 125) It is not possible to accommodate the shelf angle and the necessary clearance in a brick joint. Caulking the joint is not only unsightly but seals the joint so that it cannot drain. Design the brickwork to respond gracefully to the situation. After all, most constraints can be turned into an opportunity.

CLADDING **BRICK**

PANEL WALL **CONCRETE BLOCK**

STRUCTURAL FRAME **CONCRETE**

detail A2

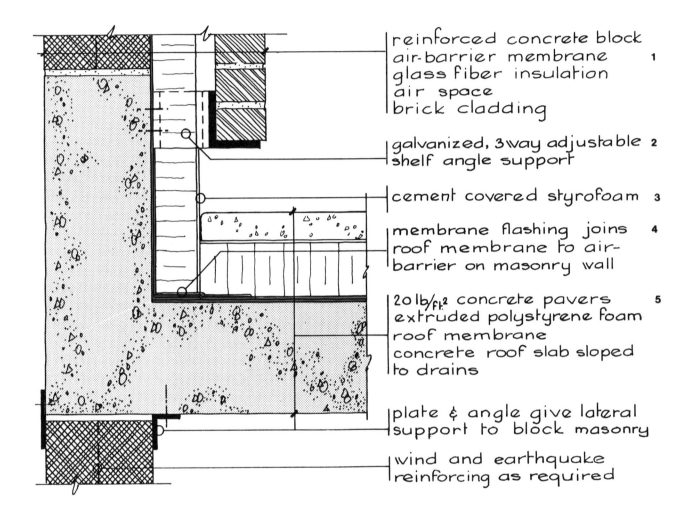

reinforced concrete block
air-barrier membrane   1
glass fiber insulation
air space
brick cladding

galvanized, 3 way adjustable 2
shelf angle support

cement covered styrofoam   3

membrane flashing joins   4
roof membrane to air-
barrier on masonry wall

20 lb/ft.² concrete pavers   5
extruded polystyrene foam
roof membrane
concrete roof slab sloped
to drains

plate & angle give lateral
support to block masonry

wind and earthquake
reinforcing as required

1. The air barrier membrane must be watertight when brick cladding is used. (6.4.4)   Self-adhering rubberized asphalt seems to adhere well when the membrane material is new and when the block and mortar are dry and reasonably warm. The best arrangement is to weld polyester reinforced rubberized asphalt to the masonry using propane torches. (4.6).

2. When the brick veneer loads are heavy and where the blockwork would not otherwise require much reinforcement, the edge of the reinforced concrete slab should be turned up to form a beam. The 3-way adjustable shelf angle support is described in Chapter 3, Figure 3-8.

3. It is very important that the air barrier be continuously insulated. This piece of styrofoam will provide that insulation and will withstand wetting. The integral cement coating will protect it from ultra-violet degradation.

4. Unlike detail A6, there is no differential movement here between roof deck and wall. This allows the roof membrane to joint the air barrier on the wall in a simple, straightforward way. A wood curb and cant strip will be needed with built-up roofing. When rubberized asphalt roofing and flashing are used, there will be two flashing plies interleaved with two roofing plies. (7.4.3)

5. The Dow Chemical Company recommends a ballast of 20 lb/ft^2 (108 Kg/m^2) of roof for 4" (100mm) of Roofmate. Concrete weighs 140 to 150 lb/ft^3 (2200 to 2400 Kg/m^3), so that a 2" (50mm) thickness weighs about 25 lb/ft^2 (115 Kg/m^2). Some building scientists would be happier if there was a ventilation space between the pavers and the insulation. In theory, that should help to prevent the accumulation of condensation in the insulation. Three $\frac{1}{4}$" (6mm) shims, 4" (100mm) wide, sawn from the length of the insulation board will work quite well. (6.3.2)

detail A3

CLADDING   **BRICK**

PANEL WALL   **CONCRETE BLOCK**

STRUCTURAL FRAME   **CONCRETE**

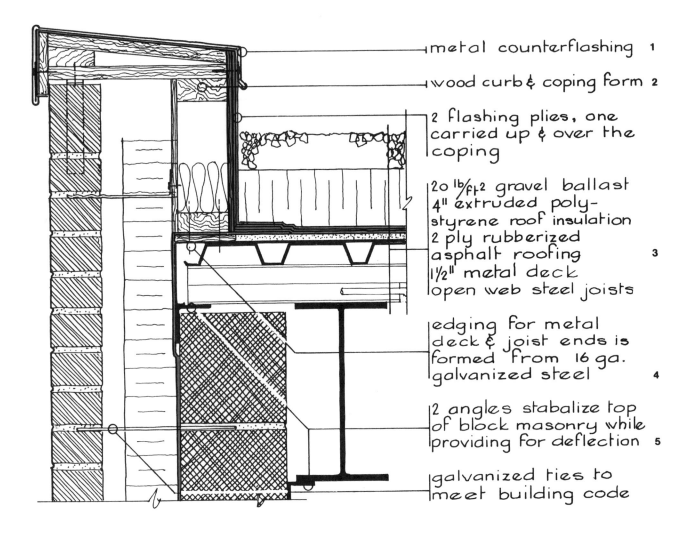

metal counterflashing **1**

wood curb & coping form **2**

2 flashing plies, one carried up & over the coping

20 lb/ft² gravel ballast
4" extruded poly-styrene roof insulation
2 ply rubberized asphalt roofing
1½" metal deck
open web steel joists **3**

edging for metal deck & joist ends is formed from 16 ga. galvanized steel **4**

2 angles stabalize top of block masonry while providing for deflection **5**

galvanized ties to meet building code

1 Metal counterflashing serves only as a decorative sunscreen. Secure it with metal clips that allow expansion and contraction. Don't carry this metal down any farther. (7.4.2)

2 This wooden assembly serves three purposes. First, it allows the roofing and flashing to be completed before the walls are erected, a great boon to construction in our climate. Second, it provides enough insulation to keep the air barrier beneath it warm. (Chapter 3) Finally, it provides a curb that allows the roof to be shaped as a shallow bowl. (6.2) This is the best shape for roofs. Note that the coping is tied to the first two rows of bricks.

3 There are two membranes here. The upper one extends from the roof up and over the parapet. It does what the metal counterflashing cannot do, that is, provide a reliable extension of the roof over the top of the wall. The exposed portions must include an integral sunscreen, such as mineral or metallic surfacing. Note the air barrier. (Chapter 3) It is continuous from roof to concrete block wall and flexible at the joint between roof and wall, where deflection occurs. It is also continuously insulated to keep it warm. It takes this rather strange route because the curb and coping assembly goes on early in the sequence of work, sometimes long before the roofing, and the gypsum board cannot be left uncovered.

4 To provide a satisfactory path for the rubberized asphalt air barrier, the roof deck must extend to the outer face of the concrete block. This is done with extended joist shoes and a purpose-formed sheet metal cover that gives a smooth edge to the deck assembly and leaves it ready to accept the air barrier membrane. The wooden curb is fastened to it. A similar channel is also required around the edges of the metal deck that are parallel to the joists.

5 In this detail, as in all others except bearing wall construction, space must be left to allow deflection without loading the walls. This must be done in a way that transfers wind and earthquake loads to the structure. It is done with a continuous plate attached to the outer face of the joists and a continuous angle at the lower flange of the beam.

CLADDING **BRICK**

PANEL WALL **CONCRETE BLOCK**

STRUCTURAL FRAME **STEEL**

detail A4

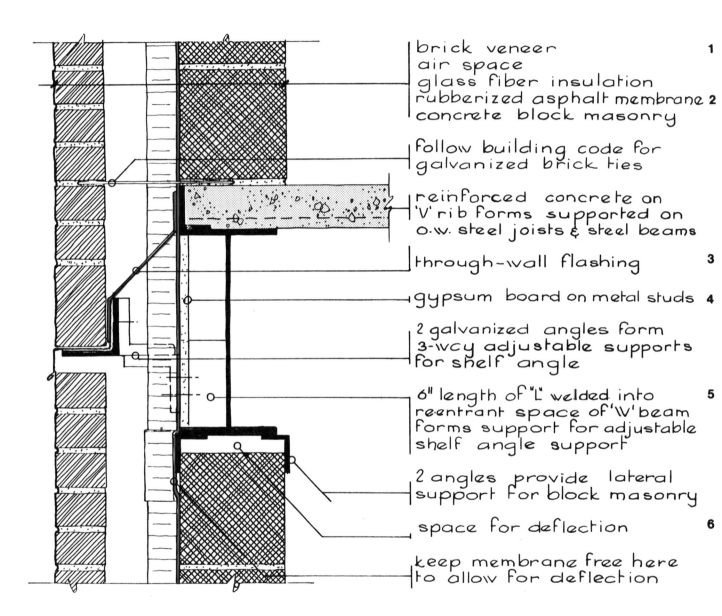

brick veneer   **1**
air space
glass fiber insulation
rubberized asphalt membrane   **2**
concrete block masonry

follow building code for
galvanized brick ties

reinforced concrete on
'V' rib forms supported on
o.w. steel joists & steel beams

through-wall flashing   **3**

gypsum board on metal studs **4**

2 galvanized angles form
3-way adjustable supports
for shelf angle

6" length of "L" welded into   **5**
reentrant space of 'V' beam
forms support for adjustable
shelf angle support

2 angles provide lateral
support for block masonry

space for deflection   **6**

keep membrane free here
to allow for deflection

1. With an air space as wide as this it will be possible to keep the cavity clean. A board is laid on one set of brick ties. Before placing the next ties, the board is drawn up bringing the excess mortar and droppings with it. A clear cavity is essential in reducing water transfer from the bricks to the backup wall. (3.2,   3.3.2)

2. A rubberized asphalt membrane, torched to the masonry, gypsum board and metal, forms the air/vapor barrier. It also provides a perfect water barrier behind the notoriously leaky brick veneer. (3.6.3)

3. Where through–wall flashing is required, use strips of rubberized asphalt adhered to the air/vapor barrier membrane. In this case it laps over the metal counterflashing that sits on the shelf angle. The metal counterflashing must be compatible with the galvanized shelf angle. Note that the metal is formed to cover the space for deflection. (3.6.4, 7.4.11)

4. Gypsum board on metal studs gives a flush face to carry the continuous rubberized asphalt membrane. Although the use of metal studs to support masonry is not recommended in this book. these short lengths will be stiff enough to provide adequate support here. (Prolegomenon)

5. One leg of the angle is welded into the beam. The other forms a strong face, flush with the gypsum board, to which the shelf angle supports can be bolted. (3.6.5)

6. Have your structural engineer design all structural elements as well as the space needed for deflection. Note that the steel members outside the air barrier membrane are galvaized and that they must have bolted connections, both for adjustment and to prevent the welding heat from burning off the zinc coating. Don't think you can patch the burned off galvanizing with paint. (3.6.5)

detail A5

CLADDING   BRICK

PANEL WALL   CONCRETE BLOCK

STRUCTURAL FRAME   STEEL

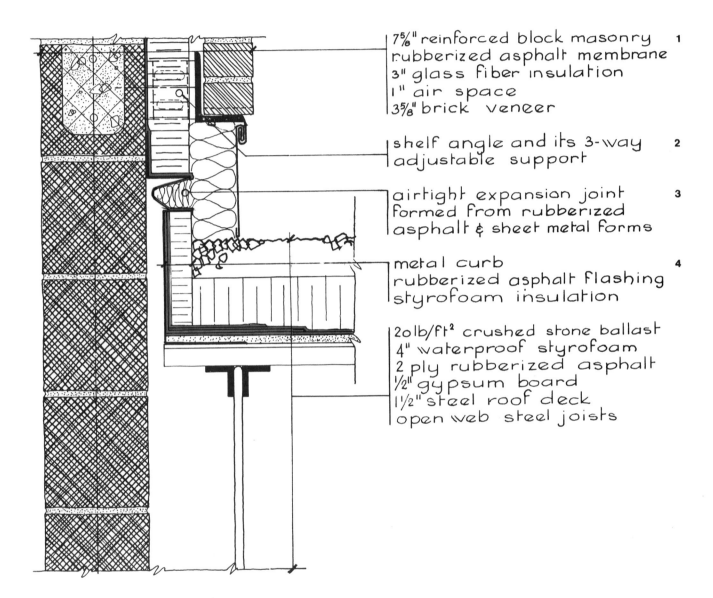

7⅝" reinforced block masonry   1
rubberized asphalt membrane
3" glass fiber insulation
1" air space
3⅝" brick veneer

shelf angle and its 3-way   2
adjustable support

airtight expansion joint   3
formed from rubberized
asphalt & sheet metal forms

metal curb   4
rubberized asphalt flashing
styrofoam insulation

20lb/ft² crushed stone ballast
4" waterproof styrofoam
2 ply rubberized asphalt
½" gypsum board
1½" steel roof deck
open web steel joists

This detail shows an insulated brick and block cavity wall rising above a roof as it might in an elevator penthouse or in a hospital, where a tower of nursing floors rises above a one or two-storey service pedestal. It would make a lot more sense if the roof structure could be built so that it would not deflect with respect to the wall. In some instances it may be possible to carry the edge of the metal deck on an angle supported by the wall. If the concrete blocks require a structural support at each floor, be sure the beams and columns are inserted in a way that allows the air barrier membrane and its insulation to run uninterrupted. See Detail A5.

1   Because the wythe of brick is cantilevered out from block wall, the block wall must be well reinforced to carry the load. This is a job for your structural engineer.

2   The galvanized three-way adjustable support for the brickwork is described in 3.6.6.

3   This junction is the most difficult of all to achieve. The rubberized asphalt air barrier membrane is extended from the roof membrane to join the air barrier in the wall. As well as being continuous and airtight it must be flexible at the roof/wall joint where deflection movements may be quite large. One and a half inches is common. It is relatively easy to insulate the air barrier where it is well adhered to the wall. It is much more difficult where movement occurs, especially if we are to keep the insulation tight to the rubberized asphalt membrane. One edge of a strip of rubberized asphalt is torched to the sheet metal curb. Enough slack is left to allow for deflection. (Get the amount from your engineer.) The top edge is continuously welded to the sheet metal angle that forms the top of the expansion joint where it is welded to the air barrier on the wall. This whole assembly is insulated with batt insulation and protected with a galvanized sheet metal two-piece cover supported from the shelf angle.

4   In this detail a bent sheet metal curb is fastened to the steel roof deck. It forms a curb to which the rubberized asphalt base flashings are torched.

CLADDING   BRICK

PANEL WALL   CONCRETE BLOCK

STRUCTURAL FRAME   STEEL

detail A6

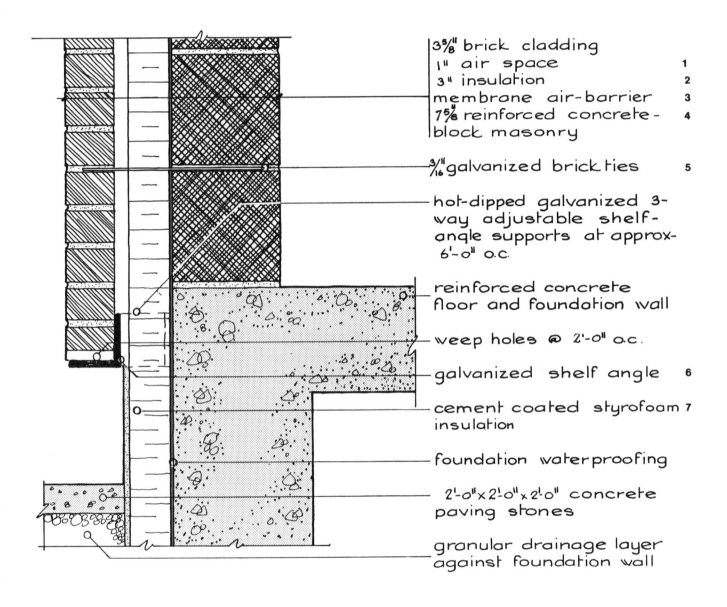

$3\frac{5}{8}$" brick cladding
1" air space   1
3" insulation   2
membrane air-barrier   3
$7\frac{5}{8}$" reinforced concrete- 4
block masonry

$\frac{3}{16}$"galvanized brick ties   5

hot-dipped galvanized 3-
way adjustable shelf-
angle supports at approx-
6'-0" o.c.

reinforced concrete
floor and foundation wall

weep holes @ 2'-0" o.c.

galvanized shelf angle   6

cement coated styrofoam   7
insulation

foundation waterproofing

2'-0"x 2'-0"x 2'-0" concrete
paving stones

granular drainage layer
against foundation wall

1 Air spaces as pressure equalizing devices are of uncertain value here. (Chapter 3)   They impede water transfer across the space and it is a good place to take up dimensional deviations. Such deviations are always present.(CBD 171)

2 Insulation thickness comes from the guidelines in NRCC 22432. Do not apply insulation with daubs of adhesive. Keep it tight to the masonry or you will get convection currents behind it that can reduce its value 40%.(1.2.3) (CBD 50)

3 The best air barrier is a torched-on rubberized asphalt membrane.(Chapters 3, 4) (CBD 72)   The membrane can be applied to the block masonry with the brick ties protruding, but it will be much easier if the ties can be applied after the membrane.

4 This is where the wind stops. Design the wall to transmit the wind force to the structure. Reinforce to take the earthquake load of its own mass plus the weight of the brick veneer.(N.B.C.(1980) 4.1.8, 4.1.9)

5 There are two important things about ties. First, they must be strong enough to act as "columns" against wind and earthquake loads. Second, they must be rust and corrosion proof. Hot dipped galvanized is the minimum requirement. See Grim, C.T., Journal, Struc. Div,. Am. Soc. Civ. Eng., April 1976. The National Building Code is not adequate here.

6 Do not rest the brick on the foundation or you will get a heat bridge, problems with foundation insulation and may aggravate problems arising from concrete creep in the structure above.(CBD 125)   A 3-way adjustable shelf angle that will accommodate building inaccuracies is suggested. It is described in Figure 9, Chapter 3 and 3.6.6. Do not forget weep holes. No flashing is needed here, but you may wish to place a screen to exclude bugs and birds.

7 There are two good solutions here. One solution is to use extruded cement-coated styrofoam where insulation is exposed above grade. High density glass fiber roof insulation without paper cover will withstand the pressures of backfilling and will keep water from accumulating against the foundation wall. (NRCC 16574)

CLADDING   **BRICK**

PANEL WALL   **CONCRETE BLOCK**

STRUCTURAL FRAME   **CONCRETE**

detail A**7**

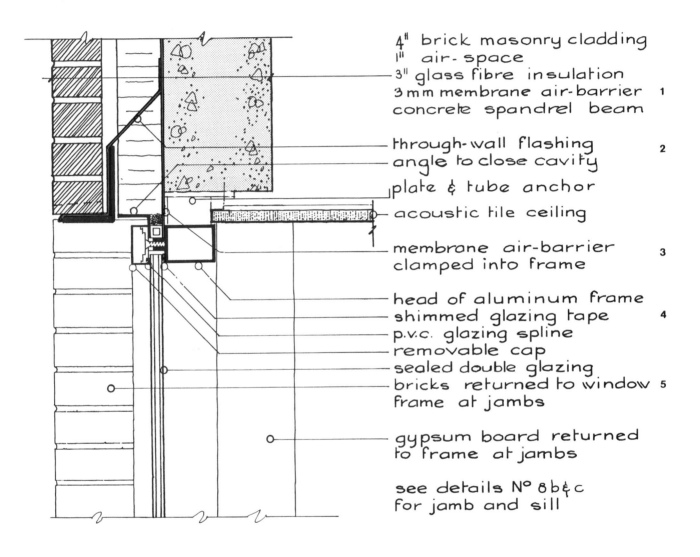

4" brick masonry cladding
1" air-space
3" glass fibre insulation
3mm membrane air-barrier   1
concrete spandrel beam

through-wall flashing
angle to close cavity   2

plate & tube anchor
acoustic tile ceiling

membrane air-barrier   3
clamped into frame

head of aluminum frame
shimmed glazing tape   4
p.v.c. glazing spline
removable cap
sealed double glazing
bricks returned to window   5
frame at jambs

gypsum board returned
to frame at jambs

see details N° 8 b & c
for jamb and sill

1 You must not let cold air get in behind the frame, so do not use an open window frame section and do not try to close off the wall cavity with the frame.(5.13.4) Keep the frame in the warm part of the wall. Caulking for airtightness is very difficult, so use the rubberized asphalt membrane as shown here. This self-adhering, reinforced, modified asphalt membrane is continuous all around the window frame. The membrane is put in place by the mason, who leaves a flap to be cut and fitted by the window installer.(5.3, 5.13.1)

2 This is one place in the wall where you really need through-wall flashing. Ensure that it can be installed easily and that it slopes down and out.

3 Now that you have a good air barrier, keep it warm. One inch (25mm) of one of the new asphalt impregnated compressible foams does not look like much insulation, but it is twice as much as the window itself.(5.2)

4 The window frame must incorporate two-stage waterproofing. The outer spline (or gasket) will stop most of the rain. Any that leaks through will drain out through small holes in the sill without reaching the air seal, where leakage into the building might occur. This seal must be complete all around the frame. Be sure that corners of the frame are sealed.(5.5) The frame is fastened to the spandrel beam by means of an aluminum tube and plate. The tube fits into the vertical box section of the window frame. The plate is bolted to the spandrel beam.

5 An alterative to returning the brick would be to use a piece of preformed aluminum, similar to that used at the head, to close off the cavity and conceal the insulation. The caulking shown here between the window frame and the brick is simply a rain deterrent. If it leaks (and it will) no harm is done, for we are assuming that the back of the brick is wet anyway.(3.6.2)

detail A8a

CLADDING BRICK

PANEL WALL CONCRETE BLOCK

STRUCTURAL FRAME STEEL

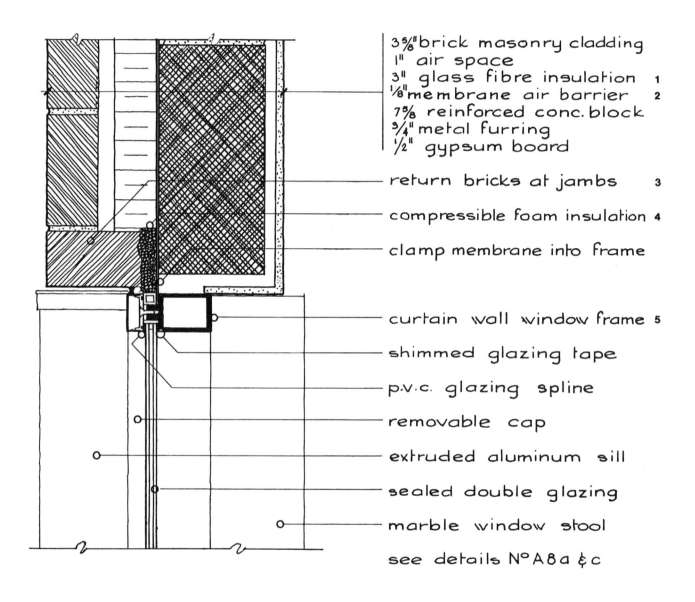

3⅝"brick masonry cladding
1" air space
3" glass fibre insulation   1
⅛"membrane air barrier   2
7⅝ reinforced conc. block
¾" metal furring
½" gypsum board

return bricks at jambs   3

compressible foam insulation 4

clamp membrane into frame

curtain wall window frame 5

shimmed glazing tape

p.v.c. glazing spline

removable cap

extruded aluminum sill

sealed double glazing

marble window stool

see details N° A8a & c

1 | With 3" (75mm) of glass fiber insulation, this wall assembly has a calculated thermal resistance of R 17 (Rsi 3). If the insulation thickness is increased to 4" (100mm), the resistance rises to R 21 (Rsi 3.71).

2 | This membrane is particularly important in masonry construction: first, because block masonry leaks air at an unbelievable rate (2.3.1); secondly, because rain leaks through the brick cladding at an unexpectedly high rate. (3.1)   Properly selected and applied, the membrane air barrier can stop both air and rain leakage.(4.6)

3 | In this detail the jamb is shown in brick. It would be equally valid to use a purpose-formed piece of aluminum to close the cavity. This would make it easier to follow the air barrier with insulation. Note that the brick jamb can be caulked to the window frame.

4 | It is necessary to keep the air barrier above the dewpoint of the inside air, otherwise there will be condensation and frost on the inside of the membrane. (1.5.1)   To do this the membrane is carefully insulated from the place where it leaves the wall insulation to the place where it is clamped into the window frame. Expanding asphalt-impregnated foam has been used successfully. The insulation must be held in close contact with the membrane.(1.5.2)

5 | The curtain wall window frame makes an almost ideal window.(5.13)   The configuration of the frame makes it possible to get a good air seal to the frame and to get it in the correct location. The frame employs two-stage waterproofing (Chapter 3) with a rain deflecting spline on the outside between the frame and the glass and a good non-extruding air seal on the inside.

detail A8b

CLADDING   BRICK

PANEL WALL   CONCRETE BLOCK

STRUCTURAL FRAME   STEEL

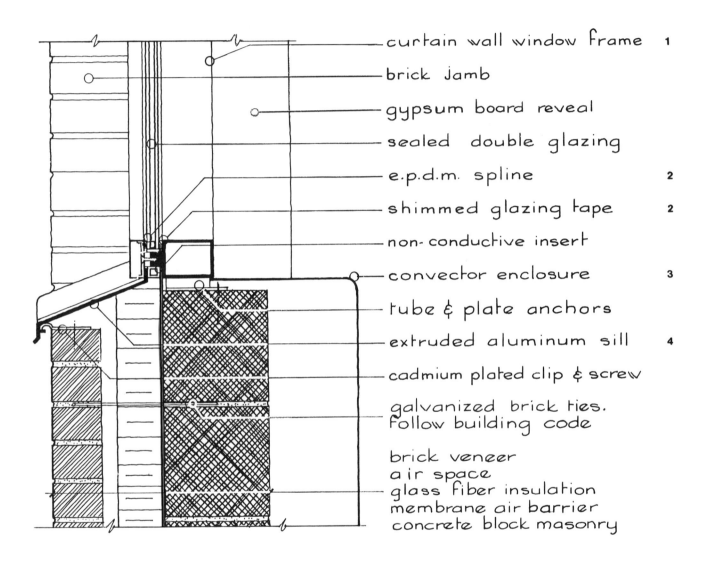

curtain wall window frame   1

brick jamb

gypsum board reveal

sealed double glazing

e.p.d.m. spline   2

shimmed glazing tape   2

non-conductive insert

convector enclosure   3

tube & plate anchors

extruded aluminum sill   4

cadmium plated clip & screw

galvanized brick ties.
follow building code

brick veneer
air space
glass fiber insulation
membrane air barrier
concrete block masonry

1. The subject of curtain wall frames is discussed in Chapter 5, where a larger scale section is shown. All of the curtain wall frames are similar in design but differ in some details. Look for one with the best thermal break between the inner and outer parts of the frame. The outer pressure plates should be designed to keep outside air from reaching the glazing rebate. Note that the glazing rebate and cap at the sill have been drilled to provide drainage holes.

2. As in other details this sill incorporates two-stage waterproofing.(Chapter 3 and 5.5) The outer spline is a water deflector. Some water may get past it. If this occurs, it is drained to the outside through small drain holes. The second stage, the line of airtightness, is at the back (inside) of the glass. It is self-adhering glazing tape and is raised up a few millimeters so that it is not in contact with any water that may lie in the sill glazing rebate. Constant buffeting by wind has been known to squeeze soft glazing tape out of the rebate. To prevent such extrusion, good tapes now include one or two small (about 2mm) rubber rods to act as shims and take the pressure off the tape.

3. In much contemporary construction, air handling (convector) enclosures fill the space, wall-to-wall, beneath the windows. When this is the case, no other finish need be applied to the blockwork. However, great care is needed to assure that this enclosure does not connect directly with adjacent rooms (including the room below). Quite often pipe chases and wiring conduits are wide open between rooms.

4. Bricks can be wetted or frozen thousands of times with no sign of deterioration. However, when snow can accumulate on a more or less horizontal surface and, in melting, dribble water into masonry slowly and over a fairly long period of time, the combination of saturated masonry and freezing soon damages the masonry, especially the mortar. When brick sills are used, they should slope very steeply, 60° or more from the horizontal, and have a sloping damp course underneath them. A horizontal damp course will simply retain moisture in the bricks. With this extruded sill, no such precautions are needed, except that water must be thrown clear of the face of the bricks and water from melting snow must not run off the two ends. Rain water, running down the jambs, will do no harm for it will soon dry.

CLADDING   BRICK

PANEL WALL   CONCRETE BLOCK

STRUCTURAL FRAME   STEEL

detail A8c

Series B: Stone Cladding, Concrete Block Panel Wall

The "B" series of details show how the arrangements of elements that were developed in the Prolegomenon can be used in stone clad buildings with concrete masonry backup. In this series, the walls are nonbearing and rest on steel or concrete structural frames.

As in the "A" series, the details show several ways of achieving the same ends. Details B4, B5, and B6 show a system of applying thin stone veneer to masonry backup. Creep and deflection must be reduced to a very small amount so that the clips holding the stone will not work like "can openers" and chip the edge of the stone. Other fasteners are available.

The other details show a more traditional way of anchoring stone, differing from conventional construction only in the strength of the anchors. Much of this work has been very poorly done.

Notice that Details A1, B1, C1, etc., are all wall-roof intersections; similarly A2, B2, C2, etc., are wall-floor intersections. This has made it possible to distribute some of the more general notes among several details. Thus it is suggested that one study several details that are similar to those that seem most appropriate.

As in Series A, the details in Series B have been arranged to allow the roof to be completed before the panel walls are built. Note that where there is a concrete roof slab the membrane air barrier on the walls is not always connected to that on the roof. This arrangement depends on the concrete slab for airtightness. This assumption of airtightness will require careful on-site inspection.

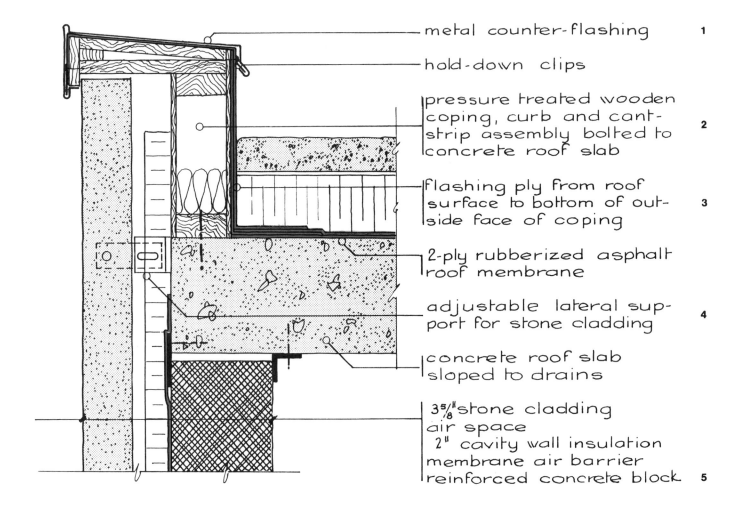

metal counter-flashing   1

hold-down clips

pressure treated wooden
coping, curb and cant-   2
strip assembly bolted to
concrete roof slab

flashing ply from roof
surface to bottom of out-   3
side face of coping

2-ply rubberized asphalt
roof membrane

adjustable lateral sup-   4
port for stone cladding

concrete roof slab
sloped to drains

3⅝" stone cladding
air space
 2" cavity wall insulation
membrane air barrier
reinforced concrete block   5

1 In Montreal or Ottawa, it is difficult to find a stone coping that has not been capped with metal. This additional protection is needed because snow accumulates on the coping. Melting slowly, it provides a trickle of water that saturates the masonry below it. The conventional damp-course or through-wall flashing help to retain the moisture in the coping. The combination of wet masonry and recurring freeze-thaw cycles cause frost damage to the components and may force them out of place. In this design, coping watertightness is provided by the membrane (rubberized asphalt). It is protected from sunlight and mechanical damage by the metal counterflashing. Be sure they both slope toward the roof.(7.4)

2 This curb and coping assembly has been built and tested. Well nailed and bolted to the slab, it was quite strong enough as a cantilever. Here it is suggested that an additional tie may be placed in the stone joints.

3 When rubberized asphalt roofing and flashing are used, it is recommended by the manufacturers that two plies of roofing be interleaved with two plies of flashing. One flashing ply is carried out and over the wood coping form. (7.4, Figures 7-9, 7-10)

4 Because it is the usual practice to support the stone with a shelf angle at each floor, the only support required here is against wind and earthquake loads. A surprising variety of bent rods is often trusted to hold these heavy stones in place. Use heavy $\frac{1}{4}$" x 2" (6 to 8mm x 50mm) anchors with 3/8" (10mm) cross rods that penetrate at least 3" (75mm) into holes in the stone. Observe the slotted angle that allows the adjustment required to set the stones perfectly plumb and true-to-line. All components must be hot-dipped galvanized.

5 The concrete block wall must be reinforced to withstand wind loads, as well as earthquake loads, on the total mass of the stone and concrete blockwork. (N.B.C.(1980), Sections 4.1.8, 4.1.9) These forces must be transmitted into the building structure, in this case the roof slab. Not only that, but it must be done in a way that places no vertical loads on the concrete block panel wall. Here it is suggested that two angles will provide horizontal restraint. Clearance for deflection and creep (CBD 125) is provided by the gap between the roof slab and the top course of concrete blocks.

CLADDING **STONE**

PANEL WALL **CONCRETE BLOCK**

STRUCTURAL FRAME **CONCRETE**

detail B1

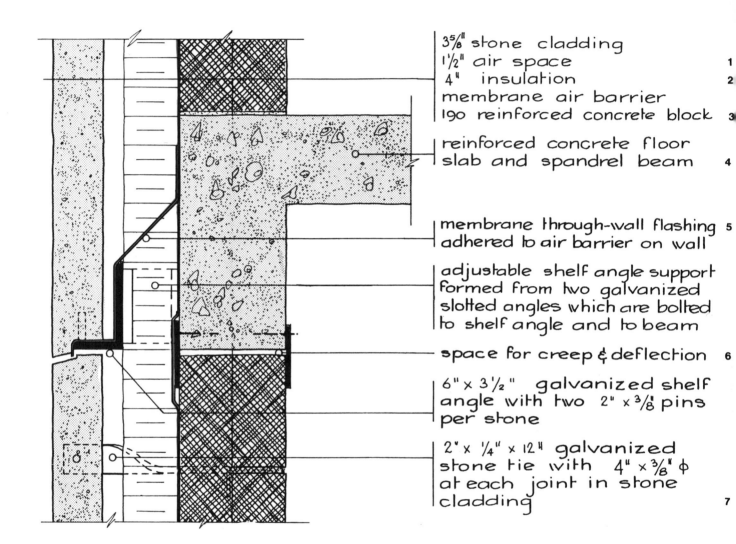

3⅝" stone cladding   1
1½" air space
4" insulation   2
membrane air barrier
190 reinforced concrete block   3

reinforced concrete floor
slab and spandrel beam   4

membrane through-wall flashing 5
adhered to air barrier on wall

adjustable shelf angle support
formed from two galvanized
slotted angles which are bolted
to shelf angle and to beam

space for creep & deflection   6

6" x 3½" galvanized shelf
angle with two 2" x ⅜ pins
per stone

2" x ¼" x 12" galvanized
stone tie with 4" x ⅜" φ
at each joint in stone
cladding   7

1 Joints in the stone cladding can be left open, since some water will penetrate into the cavity, whether or not the joints are caulked or pointed. This air space forms a path for the water down to the cavity flashing, where it is drained to the outside. It also provides some clearance for construction inaccuracies, particularly those in the concrete structural frame. (CBD 171)

2 The 4" (100mm) of insulation shown here, along with the other components in the wall, give a total thermal resistance of R 19.5 (Rsi 3.44), not counting any inside finish that may be added. (NRCC 22432)

3 Horizontal support for the stone comes from the reinforced concrete block panel wall. See N.B.C.(1980), Section 4.1.8 and 4.1.9 for the loads that must be accommodated. Note the slip joint comprised of two plates that transfer horizontal loads from the block wall to the spandrel beam.

4 This detail shows a spandrel beam as part of the reinforced concrete floor structure. When no spandrel beam is required, the shelf angle support will be raised to the edge of the floor slab.

5 Cavity flashings are very difficult to install properly. If, as often happens, they are threaded out through a horizontal joint in the insulation, the membrane is just as likely to slope inward as outward. It is suggested here that the membrane lap the shelf angle. (7.4.11)

6 Unless the spans are very long, creep and deflection will be small when a spandrel beam is provided. However, when flat slab construction is used, plastic creep in the concrete may cause a permanent deflection several times the expected elastic deflection. Note the space for deflection beneath the shelf angle. (CBD 125)

7 Some designers show a longitudinal groove in the bottom of the stone to receive a rod that is welded along the top of the outstanding leg of the angle. The rod and groove act as a tongue and groove to hold the stone on the angle. This is not good practice, for the rod holds water on the angle.

CLADDING STONE

PANEL WALL CONCRETE BLOCK

STRUCTURAL FRAME CONCRETE

detail B2

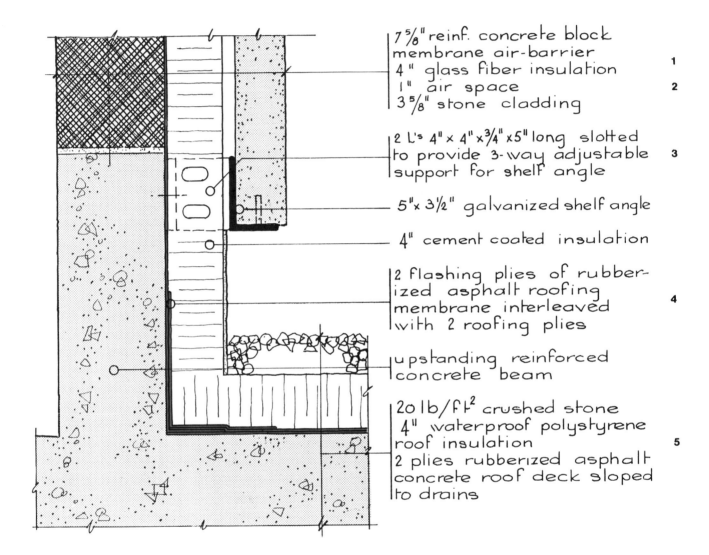

7 5/8" reinf. concrete block
membrane air-barrier
4" glass fiber insulation   **1**
1" air space
3 5/8" stone cladding   **2**

2 L's 4" x 4" x 3/4" x 5" long slotted
to provide 3-way adjustable   **3**
support for shelf angle

5" x 3 1/2" galvanized shelf angle

4" cement coated insulation

2 flashing plies of rubberized asphalt roofing
membrane interleaved   **4**
with 2 roofing plies

upstanding reinforced
concrete beam

20 lb/ft² crushed stone
4" waterproof polystyrene
roof insulation   **5**
2 plies rubberized asphalt
concrete roof deck sloped
to drains

1 | As mentioned in Detail B2, this assembly provides a thermal resistance of R19.5 (Rsi 3.44). Rubberized asphalt is the preferred material for the membrane. It is torched (welded) onto the blocks and concrete and will readily span any imperfections in the masonry. The mechanical fasteners for the insulation can also be welded directly to the membrane.

2 | The air space conducts any leaking water down the back of the stone. It will take up most construction inaccuracies (CBD 171) and so allow the stone to be set plumb and true-to-line.

3 | This shelf angle and its supporting angles are adjustable so that the shelf angle can be set perfectly true and level, no matter how irregular the upstanding beam may be. It is important that this adjustment is made with bolted connections. Otherwise, the brackets will be cut and welded on site, thus damaging the galvanizing. No amount of "touching-up" with zinc-rich paint can reach the concealed surfaces. (Figure 3-7 in Chapter 3)

4 | Soprema and other reputable manufacturers of polyester reinforced rubberized asphalt recommend two plies of roofing interleaved with two flashing plies. (7.4.8) One ply is sealed to the air barrier membrane, which is the same material. Thus the air barrier is airtight, vapourtight and watertight. This drawing shows that the air barrier is cut to clear the shelf angle support. When this is done at the block masonry, the air barrier should be caulked to the steel with a compatible caulking.

5 | The insulation shown in the wall is glass fiber. On the roof and down below the stone where it will frequently be wetted, extruded polystyrene foam is used. (Roofmate) The vertical section is shown with an integral cement coating. The horizontal insulation is the regular variety with about 20 lb/ft^2 of gravel ballast. This gravel ballast could have been replaced, if cement coated T & G Roofmate had been used over a parting sheet. (6.3.2)

detail B**3**

CLADDING
STONE

PANEL WALL
CONCRETE BLOCK

STRUCTURAL FRAME
CONCRETE

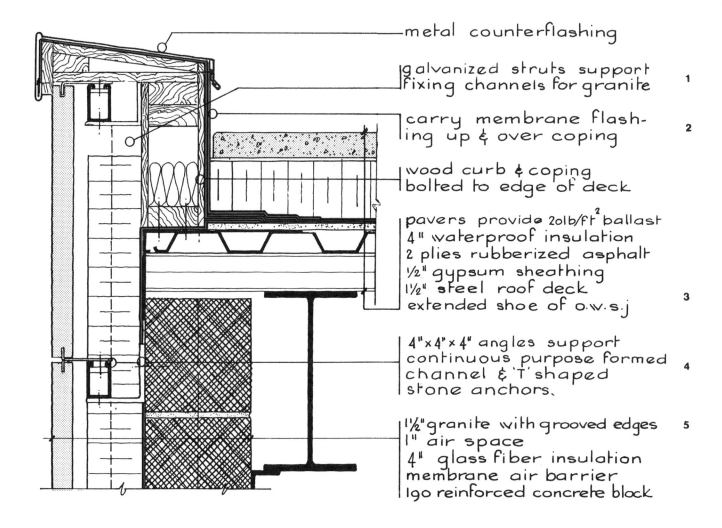

metal counterflashing

galvanized struts support
fixing channels for granite   1

carry membrane flash-
ing up & over coping   2

wood curb & coping
bolted to edge of deck

pavers provide 20lb/ft² ballast
4" waterproof insulation
2 plies rubberized asphalt
½" gypsum sheathing
1½" steel roof deck
extended shoe of o.w.s.j   3

4"×4"×4" angles support
continuous purpose formed
channel & 'T' shaped
stone anchors.   4

1½"granite with grooved edges   5
1" air space
4" glass fiber insulation
membrane air barrier
190 reinforced concrete block

1 This wooden parapet form, covered with a waterproof, rubberized asphalt membrane, is a simple effective construction. Since the problems of stone copings, discussed in the notes to Detail B1, do not apply to this open, mortar-free, well-ventilated stonework, a stone coping might be considered here.

2 There are two extensions of the roof membrane. The first provides an umbrella over the wall cavity. It extends out over the coping and is fastened to the outer face of the wooden form. The second extension is the air barrier. It is a ply of rubberized asphalt that runs from the bottom of the roof membrane, through the wooden parapet assembly and down the face of the metal roof deck to join the air barrier on the outer face of the concrete blocks. Its path is made smoother by a bent sheet metal roof edge (that tidies up the edge of the metal deck and the extended shoes of open-web steel joists) and by a continuous steel plate that acts as a retainer for the reinforced concrete block wall. The air barrier membrane should have a little surplus material where it leaves the steel plate. This will allow deflection of the plate.(Figure Proleg.-5)

3 To bring the roof deck out flush with the concrete block wall(Prolegomenon), the open web steel joists are designed with extended "shoes". The metal deck is carried out on these extensions. To provide strong fastening for the wooden parapet form, the edge of the deck is reinforced with 16 gauge sheet metal, bent as shown. As noted above, it also smooths the path of the air barrier.

4 These supports for the granite cladding are readily available. Bolts are set in concrete in the blockwork. The upstanding leg of the angle is slotted to allow vertical adjustment. The horizontal leg is also slotted so that the channel can be moved in and out. A purpose-formed fitting holds the "T" in place anywhere along the channel. The whole assembly, including the bolts, should be hot dipped galvanized.

5 This thin granite cladding is a relatively new construction material. It is available in any finish. The edges are grooved to receive the supporting "T" sections. The joints need not be filled or caulked.

CLADDING
STONE

PANEL WALL
CONCRETE BLOCK

STRUCTURAL FRAME
STEEL

detail B4

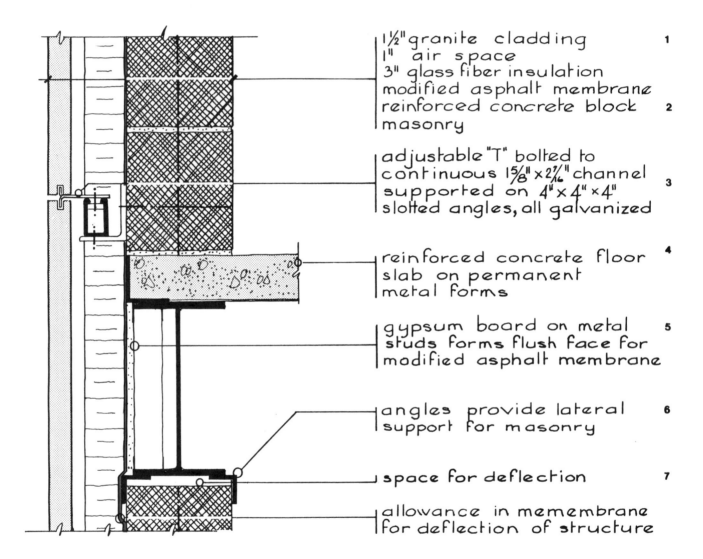

1½"granite cladding   **1**
1" air space
3" glass fiber insulation
modified asphalt membrane
reinforced concrete block   **2**
masonry

adjustable "T" bolted to
continuous 1⅝"x2⅞"channel
supported on 4"x4"x¼"   **3**
slotted angles, all galvanized

reinforced concrete floor   **4**
slab on permanent
metal forms

gypsum board on metal   **5**
studs forms flush face for
modified asphalt membrane

angles provide lateral   **6**
support for masonry

space for deflection   **7**

allowance in memembrane
for deflection of structure

1. In this construction, granite is sliced into sheets $1\frac{1}{2}''$ (38mm) thick. Commonly, slab heights do not exceed 4'6" (1372mm). The top and bottom edges are grooved to receive the "T" supports, usually two or three per slab. Joints can be left open and the slabs are free to expand or contract in their setting. There must be enough clearance in each joint so that the installation can absorb the expected deflection and thermal movement. Deflection must be minimized or the T supports will act like a can opener and break the edges of the stone.

2. Although 7 5/8" (140mm) thick concrete blocks are shown here, the block thickness and reinforcement must be engineered to take wind and earthquake loads as well as the cantilevered load of the granite. (N.B.C. 1980, Sections 4.1.8 and 4.1.9)

3. This detail shows reinforced block masonry supporting the granite and its accessories. However, another excellent system is available that uses a gridwork of steel struts to carry the cladding. Lighter backup walls can then be used. The same system can be used to reclad existing buildings. Information is available from the Georgia Marble Company, Nelson, Georgia 30151.

4. This floor slab is supported on steel beams and open web steel joists.

5. When steel frames are built into a masonry wall, the masonry is cut to pieces to accommodate steel beams, columns and cross bracing. Not only that but the steel members will have different widths, depths and profiles. To get a face flush with the masonry, use drywall or metal covers over the steel structural elements.

6. These angles provide horizontal restraint to the block masonry while allowing deflection to take place.

7. Panel walls, even in concrete masonry construction, are not designed to support loads from the floor system; thus, when dimensioning this space, it is important to get the engineer's estimate of the deflection which will tend to close the gap. Design for minimal deflection.

CLADDING STONE

PANEL WALL CONCRETE BLOCK

STRUCTURAL FRAME STEEL

detail B 5

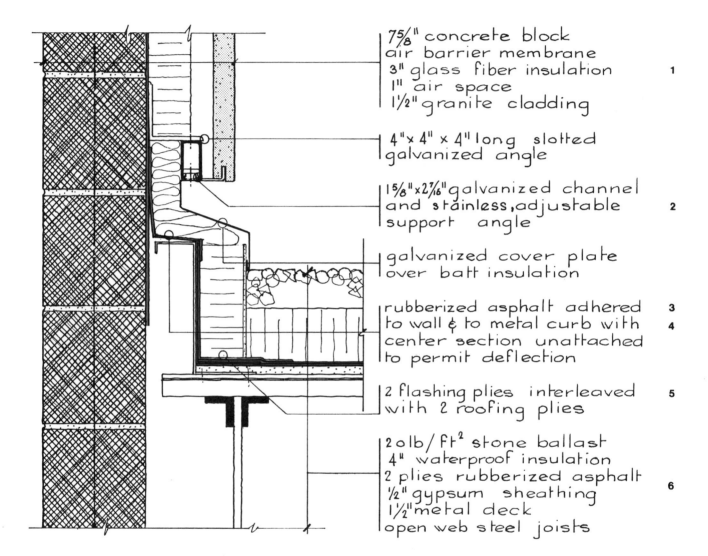

7⅝" concrete block
air barrier membrane
3" glass fiber insulation
1" air space
1½" granite cladding
1

4" x 4" x 4" long slotted
galvanized angle

1⅝"x2⅞"galvanized channel
and stainless,adjustable
support angle
2

galvanized cover plate
over batt insulation

rubberized asphalt adhered   3
to wall & to metal curb with   4
center section unattached
to permit deflection

2 flashing plies interleaved   5
with 2 roofing plies

20lb/ft² stone ballast
4" waterproof insulation
2 plies rubberized asphalt
½" gypsum sheathing   6
1½"metal deck
open web steel joists

1 This wall construction is relatively new but quite straightforward. The slotted angles are fastened to bolts set in the concrete block masonry. With 3" (75mm) of glass fiber insulation, the wall has a theoretical thermal resistance of R 15 (Rsi 2.7). In practice there will be little thermal resistance from the granite and the air space, because cold outside air has ready access to the air space.

2 The 1 5/8" x 2 7/16" (42mm x 64mm) channel is inverted to support the lower course of granite. The gap between the channel and the back of the granite should be screened to keep out birds and insects.

3 The differential movement that will occur between the metal roof deck and the wall requires a flexible connection between the air barrier on the wall and the roof membrane. This flexible membrane must be insulated to keep it warm. The air barrier is a sheet of rubberized asphalt.(4.6) The top 3" (75mm) is welded to the air barrier on the concrete block wall. The next 7" (180mm) retains its parting sheet so that it will not stick to the wall or to the metal curb. The lower 2" (50mm) is welded to the base flashing on the metal curb. The membrane is insulated with flexible glass fiber held in place by the galvanized cover plate, which also serves as a rainscreen.

4 The purpose-formed sheet metal curb must be quite stiff, since it is fastened only to the roof deck. 16 gauge (1.5mm) galvanized steel is recommended. It can be fastened to the metal deck with power driven screws so that the galvanizing is not burned off by welding. It and the base flashings are insulated with a strip of cement coated Roofmate.

5 The roofing and flashing systems are described in Chapter 7 and shown in Figures 7-1 to 7-11.

6 The protected membrane roofing system and the metal deck assembly are quite common. The weakest component is the water-sensitive gypsum board, so the roof membrane must be especially reliable. This is no place for built-up roofing if the work is done in anything but the best of weather. Ballast can be eliminated if cement-coated tongue and groove Roofmate is used for insulation. (6.3.2)

CLADDING **STONE**

PANEL WALL **CONCRETE BLOCK**

STRUCTURAL FRAME **STEEL**

detail **B 6**

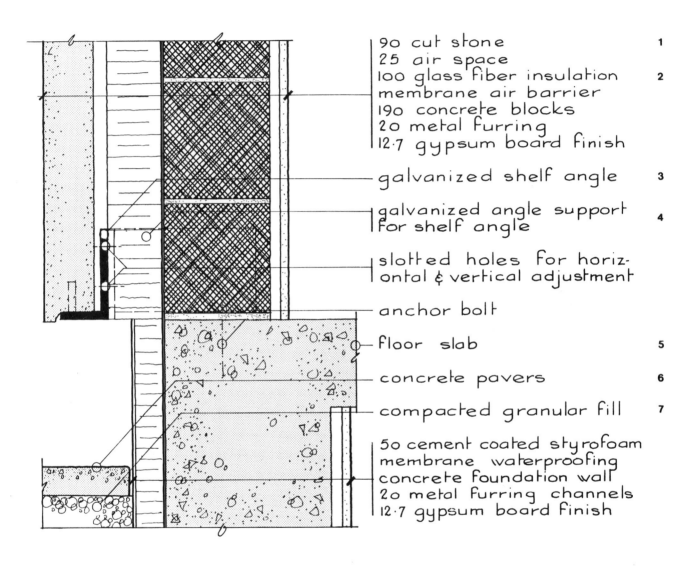

90 cut stone   1
25 air space
100 glass fiber insulation   2
membrane air barrier
190 concrete blocks
20 metal furring
12.7 gypsum board finish

galvanized shelf angle   3

galvanized angle support   4
for shelf angle

slotted holes for horiz-
ontal & vertical adjustment

anchor bolt

floor slab   5

concrete pavers   6

compacted granular fill   7

50 cement coated styrofoam
membrane waterproofing
concrete foundation wall
20 metal furring channels
12.7 gypsum board finish

1 | Although cutting the bottom of the stone to recess the lintel results in a better appearance, it does leave a rather vulnerable lip that will require careful handling. Skilled cutters and masons are quite capable of cutting and setting such delicate work. The real test will be the care with which maintenance workers handle lawnmowers and snow shovels.

2 | This wall, including the furring and drywall finish, has a thermal resistance of R 21 (Rsi 3.69). Reducing the insulation to 3" (75mm) lowers the resistance to R 17 (Rsi 2.99).

3 | The galvanized shelf angle includes pins to provide horizontal restraint to the bottom of the stones. There must be open joints or grooves in the stone to drain water that may accumulate on the angle. This angle has horizontal slotted holes for adjustment.

4 | Similarly, the supports for the shelf angle are galvanized and fabricated with slotted holes. The idea is to provide 3-way adjustment, so that the stone can be perfectly aligned and level.

5 | No matter whether the structural frame of the building is steel or concrete, it is suggested here that the floor slab and foundation walls be of concrete. This gives a firm base for any construction and makes it much easier to keep the foundation/floor/wall junction airtight and waterproof. Do not let column base plates project through the air barrier.

6 | Two disfiguring problems frequently arise at this juncture. First, the earth around the building is seldom well compacted, for the contractor is reluctant to cause high earth pressures against new walls. The result is settlement. These pavers can be removed while the grade is repaired. It is difficult to cut lawns neatly up against wall. Pavers against the foundation resolve this problem.

7 | Granular material should always be placed against foundations, so that water will drain down to the footing tiles. Clay will hold water against the wall, increasing the risk of leaking.

CLADDING STONE

PANEL WALL CONCRETE BLOCK

STRUCTURAL FRAME CONCRETE

detail B7

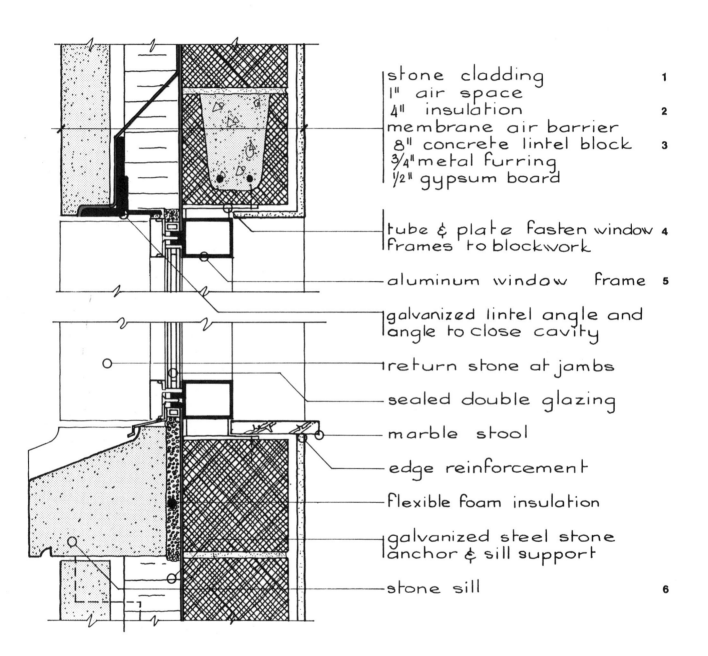

stone cladding   1
1" air space
4" insulation   2
membrane air barrier
 8" concrete lintel block   3
¾" metal furring
½" gypsum board

tube & plate fasten window 4
frames to blockwork

aluminum window   frame 5

galvanized lintel angle and
angle to close cavity

return stone at jambs

sealed double glazing

marble   stool

edge reinforcement

flexible foam insulation

galvanized steel stone
anchor & sill support

stone sill   6

1 | The bottom of the stone has been rebated to conceal the galvanized lintel angle. The lip is a little delicate, so it is a refinement that is not always observed. If the joints in the stone are closed and pointed, then weepholes must be cut to allow water to drain from the galvanized steel lintel.

2 | The 4" (100mm) of glass fiber insulation give the wall a thermal insulation of R 21 (Rsi 3.69). The insulation is held tightly to the air barrier with mechanical fasteners. If the air barrier has been heat-welded in place, the mechanical fasteners can be heat-welded directly to the membrane. The insulation is cut on the diagonal to allow the through-wall flashing to slope downward and outward to the top of the galvanized steel lintel. (7.4.11)

3 | The lintel block is reinforced to carry the concrete blocks above it; both the wall and the concrete block lintel are reinforced to provide lateral support for the stone cladding and for the window.

4 | Each tube has a plate welded to one end. The tubes fit into the hollow vertical mullions of the window frame to form a slip joint. The windows are placed in setting blocks (under the setting blocks for the glass). After they are levelled and plumbed, the plates are bolted to the masonry. Remember the buffeting that these windows will take from the wind. Do not use lead anchors.

5 | The window is built from so called curtain wall box sections. These sections fulfill the requirements for a good window.(Chapter 5, particularly 5.9) Note how the membrane air barrier is clamped into the back of the frame and how the flexible foam insulation follows along over it to keep it warm. Note that the glazing rebate at the sill is drained.

6 | This sill will work either with this traditional 4" (100mm) stone or with the thin slabs that are shown in details B4 and B5. In fact, something like these head and jamb stones will be required to close the cavity when thin slabs are used. The sill has a drip so that snow and dirt that accumulate on the sill are thrown clear of the wall. If another kind of sill is contemplated, it is a good idea to see how it has worked on another building. Look particularly for dirt streaks and for frost damage beneath the sill.

CLADDING **STONE**

PANEL WALL **CONCRETE BLOCK**

STRUCTURAL FRAME **CONCRETE**

detail B 8

Series C: Precast Concrete Cladding, Drywall Panel Wall

The "C" Series of details show how the arrangements of elements that were developed in the Prolegomenon can be used in buildings with precast concrete cladding. In this series the backup or panel wall is made from metal studs and gypsum board.

No details in this series are shown using concrete block as a backup for precast concrete (see Detail H5). In the past, openings have been left in the block masonry to allow access to the precast concrete fasteners. Attempts to patch these openings have been spectacularly unsuccessful. With care, however, the system shown in Detail C5 might be applied to block masonry. Note that an air barrier and insulation must be applied to the outside of the blocks.

Because it is so much safer and more economical to fasten the precast concrete from inside the building, Details C1, C2, and C3 show airtight "drywall" construction that can be erected after the precast is in place. The inner facing of gypsum board is the air barrier and a strip of rubberized asphalt is used to provide a flexible seal between the gypsum board and the other elements of the air barrier.

In Details C4 and C5, the drywall construction can be erected before the precast, for access holes have been left in it so that the precast can be fastened from inside the building. The idea was developed in Newfoundland where they know about wind and air leakage. These access openings are arranged so that they can be sealed from inside the building. The system is described in Detail C5. In this case the outer gypsum board forms the air barrier. Joints in the gypsum board are taped and joints between the gypsum board and other parts of the air barrier are sealed with rubberized asphalt tape. Insulation is then placed on the outside of this air barrier. Finally, the precast concrete panels are installed.

Some details show exterior gypsum board as the air barrier. Because this material should be exposed to a minimum of wetting, it should only be used with a superior rainscreen.

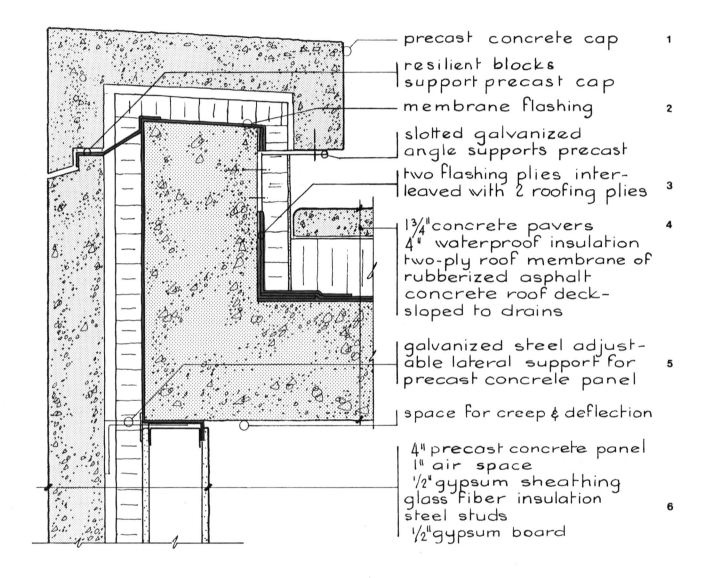

precast concrete cap   1

resilient blocks
support precast cap

membrane flashing   2

slotted galvanized
angle supports precast

two flashing plies inter-
leaved with 2 roofing plies   3

1¾" concrete pavers   4
4" waterproof insulation
two-ply roof membrane of
rubberized asphalt
concrete roof deck-
sloped to drains

galvanized steel adjust-
able lateral support for   5
precast concrete panel

space for creep & deflection

4" precast concrete panel
1" air space
½" gypsum sheathing
glass fiber insulation   6
steel studs
½" gypsum board

1 It is very difficult to fasten metal supports for precast concrete to a parapet without compromising the watertightness of the roof and the airtightness and watertightness of the air barrier. (Chapter 3) Cutting the membrane as shown for these supports provides the least vulnerable assembly.

2 Because the top of the parapet is covered with an unperforated, waterproof membrane and can be built with a substantial slope, there is really no need to be concerned if some water should get by the precast cap.

3 The base flashings are rubberized asphalt, "welded" to the concrete and to each other with propane torches. No matter how well described, this process sounds improbable but, in fact, it works remarkably well. The manufacturer recommends that the base flashings be interleaved with the two roofing plies as shown. (7.4.8) A third ply is carried across the top and down the outer face of the parapet. It is held between the first runner channel and the underside of the roof slab, then turned down to engage the inner face of the gypsum board. No caulking is needed.

4 Concrete pavers 2" (50mm) thick weigh a little more than 20 lb/ft^2 (108 Kg/m^2), which is the recommended ballast for 4" (100mm) of Roofmate insulation. The subject of protected membrane roofs and whether or not these pavers should sit directly on the insulation is discussed in 6.3.2.

5 To overcome the distortion caused by creep and deflection (CBD 125), the precast panels are best supported on their centerlines at the bottom of the panels. They are then stabilized, at their upper corners, against wind and earthquake loads. These horizontal supports will allow some vertical movement between the panel and its support. Because the supporting steel is galvanized, the connections are bolted.

6 After the precast panels are installed, the metal studs, gypsum sheathing and insulating sheathing are assembled on the floor, then raised into place. The membrane air barrier is carried forward to make contact with the gypsum board. The inner runner channel is free to move vertically. Note the space for creep and deflection between the two runner channels. Sometime later, the glass fiber insulation is carefully fitted in and between the metal studs. Then the gypsum board finish is pressed tightly against the flap of air barrier membrane and carefully taped, top to bottom, to achieve airtightness.

CLADDING **PRECAST**

PANEL WALL **DRYWALL**

STRUCTURAL FRAME **CONCRETE**

detail **C1**

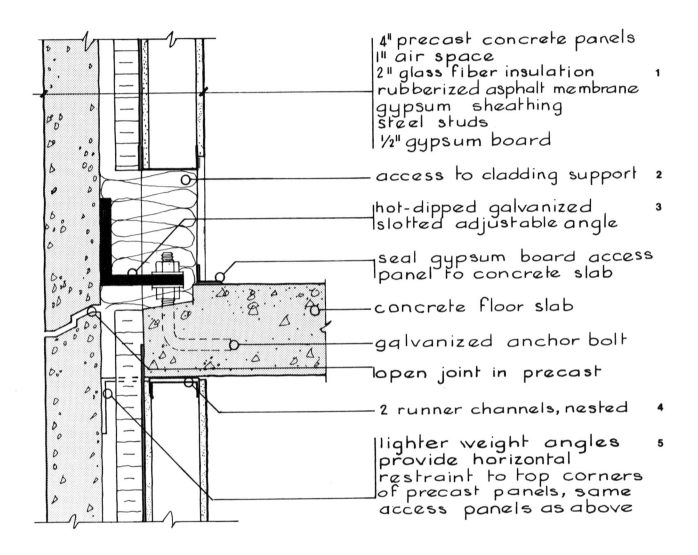

4" precast concrete panels
1" air space
2" glass fiber insulation   1
rubberized asphalt membrane
gypsum sheathing
steel studs
½" gypsum board

access to cladding support   2

hot-dipped galvanized   3
slotted adjustable angle

seal gypsum board access
panel to concrete slab

concrete floor slab

galvanized anchor bolt

open joint in precast

2 runner channels, nested   4

lighter weight angles   5
provide horizontal
restraint to top corners
of precast panels, same
access panels as above

1 You can add batt insulation in the stud space but its insulating value will be reduced to half by the heat bridges formed by the metal studs. In cold climates no more than a third of the insulation should be inside the air barrier. You will require a careful engineering analysis of the response of the metal stud assembly to the wind loads on it.

2 It is so much safer and less expensive to fasten the precast concrete from inside the building that it is worth going to some trouble to do so. Here, where the rubberized asphalt air barrier is cut, an airtight metal box brings the line of airtightness to the inner face of the metal studs, where it can be gasketed and sealed after the precast is installed. It will be rather messy trying to fit the metal box around the anchor bolt, so simply seal the lower edges of the box to the floor slab.

3 This single support will allow some plastic creep deflection to occur in the floor slab without twisting the precast panel. Be sure the panels are reinforced to resist the bending moment induced by this anchor. Note that the angle can provide three-way adjustment without on-site welding. Note also that water may run into the wall on the surface of the angle. The recess in the floor slab is designed to run it out again.

4 Have your engineer calculate the expected creep and deflection (CBD 125), then design the metal studs and gypsum board to accommodate the movement. Here it is achieved by nesting the runner channels, leaving the required space between them. The top channel is attached to the underside of the slab and the lower channel is fastened to the studs.

5 The weight of the precast panel is supported by a single angle at the bottom of the panel. Stabilizing angles are placed at each of the upper corners. They provide horizontal restraint against wind and earthquake loads while allowing a small amount of vertical movement to accommodate plastic creep and deflection in the floor slab. (CBD 125)

CLADDING PRECAST

PANEL WALL DRYWALL

STRUCTURAL FRAME CONCRETE

detail C2

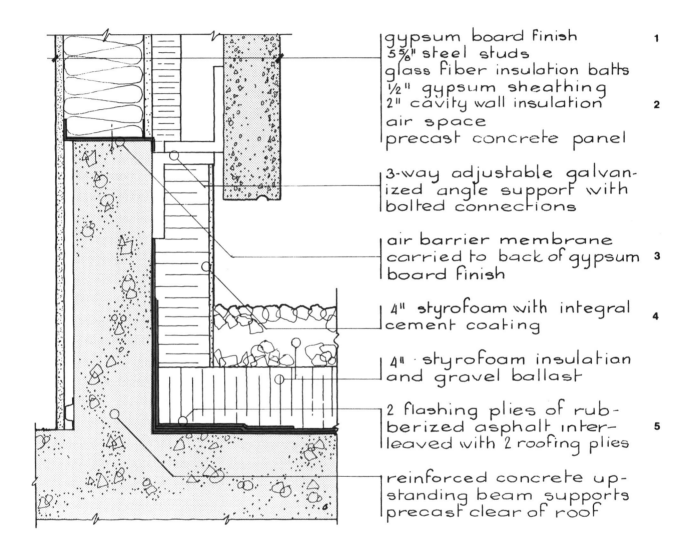

gypsum board finish   1
5⅝" steel studs
glass fiber insulation batts
½" gypsum sheathing
2" cavity wall insulation   2
air space
precast concrete panel

3-way adjustable galvan-
ized angle support with
bolted connections

air barrier membrane
carried to back of gypsum   3
board finish

4" styrofoam with integral
cement coating   4

4" styrofoam insulation
and gravel ballast

2 flashing plies of rub-
berized asphalt inter-   5
leaved with 2 roofing plies

reinforced concrete up-
standing beam supports
precast clear of roof

1 | This detail is intended for use at a penthouse or wherever a wall rises above a roof. Well-fastened gypsum board provides a good air barrier; if a vapour barrier is needed, use foil-backed gypsum board.(2.5.2) Polyethylene sheet material is not advised, for it will interfere with airtightness. Joints in the gypsum board must be taped. The interior gypsum board is both finish and air barrier.

2 | Metal studs cause heat bridges through the insulation and reduce its value by nearly 50%. The additional 2" (50mm) of insulating sheathing is needed to bring the wall up to a R 19 (Rsi 3.43).(1.5.3)

3 | The air barrier is sealed to the concrete structure with rubberized asphalt clamped between the gypsum board and the runner channel. The same system is used all around the panel wall.(2.5.4)

4 | In most installations of wall insulation, it has been emphasized that mechanical fasteners are essential. When the insulation includes a protective cement coating, as it does here, that kind of secure fastening is impossible. A good, compatible adhesive must be used here. It can be aided at the bottom by the ballast. At the top, small blocks of styrofoam can be placed between the cement-coated insulation and the back of the precast concrete panels. The roofing and flashing details show a protected membrane roof using heat-welded rubberized asphalt for membrane and base flashings.(6.4.3, 7.4.8)

5 | Holding the bottom of the precast concrete panels well away from the deck provides good drainage from the wall cavity and makes it relatively easy to install a continuous well-insulated air barrier from the roof to the inner gypsum board (which in this case is the air barrier). The material suggested is rubberized asphalt, either self-adhering or "torched-on".(7.4.3) There is no chance for independent movement between the deck and the wall, so there is no need for a flexible joint. The upstanding beam is not likely to be airtight for the same reason that the roof slab is not watertight. Satisfactory airtightness could be achieved if all construction joints, cracks and holes were sealed; then only a strip of rubberized asphalt would be needed between the concrete and gypsum board.

CLADDING **PRECAST**

PANEL WALL **DRYWALL**

STRUCTURAL FRAME **CONCRETE**

detail C3

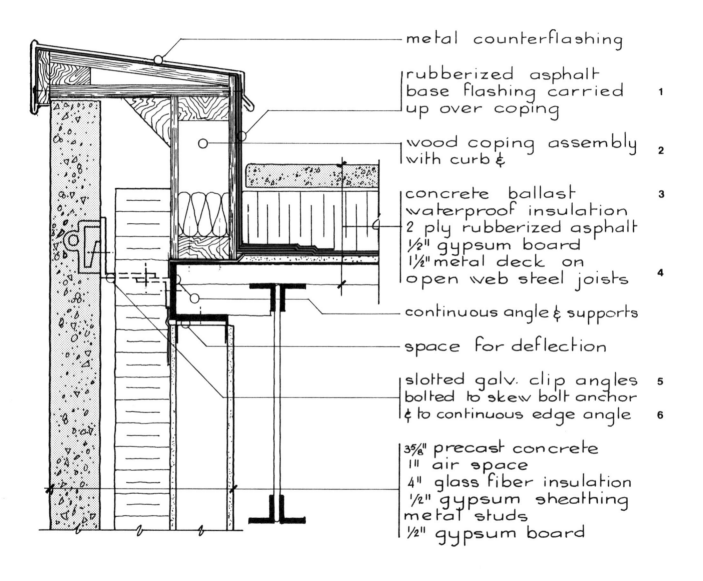

metal counterflashing

rubberized asphalt
base flashing carried   1
up over coping

wood coping assembly   2
with curb &

concrete ballast   3
waterproof insulation
2 ply rubberized asphalt
½" gypsum board
1½" metal deck on
open web steel joists   4

continuous angle & supports

space for deflection

slotted galv. clip angles 5
bolted to skew bolt anchor
& to continuous edge angle 6

3⅝" precast concrete
1" air space
4" glass fiber insulation
½" gypsum sheathing
metal studs
½" gypsum board

1 | Because the gypsum board is vulnerable to water, it is important to have a perfectly watertight coping assembly here. Although most architects would prefer a precast concrete coping in this location, such copings cannot be made reliably watertight. This coping is made watertight by the rubberized asphalt layer. The metal is simply a decorative sunscreen. Do not bother to caulk or solder it, and do not carry it down to the roof or someone will nail through it.(7.4.2)

2 | This wooden cantilever assembly allows the roof to be completed before the walls are erected, a great advantage in our climate. Well-nailed, it is quite adequate for wind and snow loads. The $1\frac{1}{2}$" (38mm) blocking that supports it can be fastened to the deck with power driven studs. A rubberized asphalt air barrier must join the roof membrane to the gypsum sheathing of the wall. The simplest location is the one shown here. If you wish, the coping can be fastened down at the vertical joints in the precast panels.

3 | There is some danger that the insulation will become saturated with water because of diffusion. A wet deck combined with a considerable temperature gradient across the insulation provides ideal conditions for vapour migration. Unless the bottoms of precast concrete pavers are heavily textured, they may inhibit the escape of this moisture. Holding the pavers $\frac{1}{4}$" (6mm) away from the insulation on some waterproof shims would help.(6.3.2) In winter when the roof is covered with snow, nothing helps very much.

4 | This a lightweight, inexpensive deck. It is also flexible and subject to rapid deterioration if water penetrates the roof membrane. It requires a dependable roof membrane(6.3.2) and well-designed flashings.(Chapter 7)

5 | Fortunately, the precast concrete cladding will need only lateral support along the roof edge. The support should be slightly flexible in the vertical direction to allow the roof to deflect under snow loads. Also it must be bolted, galvanized and adjustable.

6 | This edge angle must be supported from the adjacent joist or beam, for it is used to carry the supporting angles for the precast concrete. It stiffens the edge of the roof deck, provides a support for the steel stud runner channels and provides a smooth continuous surface to which the rubberized asphalt air barrier can be adhered.

CLADDING **PRECAST**

PANEL WALL **DRYWALL**

STRUCTURAL FRAME **STEEL**

detail C4

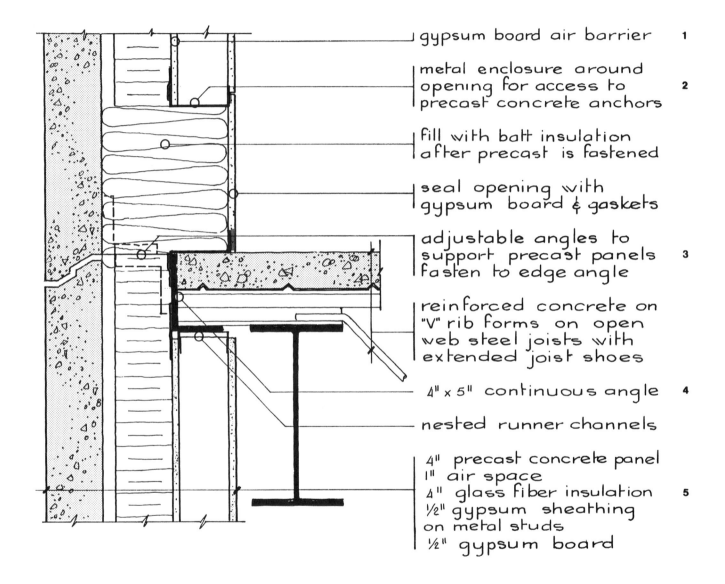

gypsum board air barrier   **1**

metal enclosure around opening for access to precast concrete anchors   **2**

fill with batt insulation after precast is fastened

seal opening with gypsum board & gaskets

adjustable angles to support precast panels fasten to edge angle   **3**

reinforced concrete on "V" rib forms on open web steel joists with extended joist shoes

4" x 5" continuous angle   **4**

nested runner channels

4" precast concrete panel
1" air space
4" glass fiber insulation   **5**
½" gypsum sheathing on metal studs
½" gypsum board

1   Because of the interference of the steel framing system, the inside gypsum board finish makes a very uncertain air barrier. The exterior gypsum sheathing will provide a much moredependable plane of airtightness. If high humidity conditions require a vapour barrier, foil-backed gypsum board can be used. The foil would be best on the inside. Joints in the gypsum board, including movement joints, can be taped with self-adhering rubberized asphalt.

2   To allow the precast to be fastened from within the building, access panels are built into the drywall system. The principle observed is that the air barrier(Chapter 2) is carried from the outside face of the studs to the inside face. This allows the air barrier to be completed on the room-side face of the wall, where it is most accessible. The airtight, sheet metal enclosure around the access opening is screwed to the studs and made airtight to the outer gypsum board with strips of self-adhering rubberized asphalt. Another strip at the inside will act as a gasket when the inside gypsum board is screwed into place. Note the nested runner channels to accommodate deflection.

3   Where precast panels are supported on a concrete floor structure, plastic creep in concrete makes it advisable to support the panels at one point, usually the centre of the bottom of the panel.(CBD 125) There is no appreciable creep in this steel structure, so the panels can be supported in two or more places. Three-way adjustment is necessary. Often this is achieved by welding. This is a most inadvisable technique, for the welding will burn any rustproofing off the angles. Use galvanized angles with slotted holes to allow three-way adjustment. These panel supports are placed at the panel corners, so that four of them can be reached through one access panel.

4   The $3\frac{1}{2}$" x 5" (89mm x 127mm) angle provides a form for the edge of the concrete; it allows the supporting angles for the precast concrete to be placed where they are needed and it provides a surface to which the runner channels for the metal studs can be attached.

5   This wall is designed so that the metal stud and gypsum board panel wall can be erected and insulated before the precast panels are placed. As in other details where metal studs are used, it is recommended that the insulation be placed outside the stud space, because the thermal conductivity of the metal studs reduces the resistance of the insulation between the studs to about half of its nominal value.(1.5.3)

CLADDING **PRECAST**

PANEL WALL **DRYWALL**

STRUCTURAL FRAME **CONCRETE**

detail C5

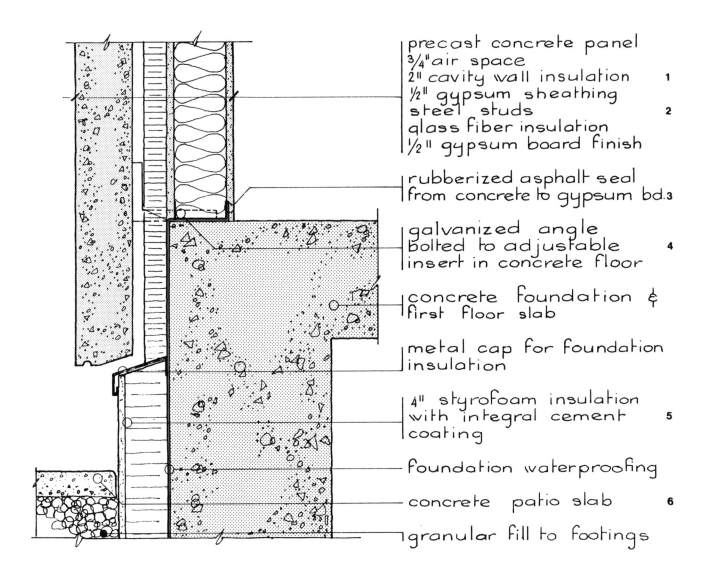

precast concrete panel
3/4" air space
2" cavity wall insulation   1
1/2" gypsum sheathing
steel studs   2
glass fiber insulation
1/2" gypsum board finish

rubberized asphalt seal
from concrete to gypsum bd. 3

galvanized angle
bolted to adjustable   4
insert in concrete floor

concrete foundation &
first floor slab

metal cap for foundation
insulation

4" styrofoam insulation
with integral cement   5
coating

foundation waterproofing

concrete patio slab   6

granular fill to footings

1 | Because the metal studs carry a large amount of heat through the insulation (1.5.3), the thermal resistance of that insulation is reduced to half of its nominal value. Adding 2" (50mm) of insulation cladding brings the thermal resistance of the whole wall to R 17 (Rsi 3). Note that structural members are insulated first.

2 | Economy and safety demand that the precast concrete panels be fastened from inside the building. However this makes it very difficult to maintain an effective air barrier. To overcome that difficulty, the metal studs, gypsum sheathing and cavity wall insulation can be pre-assembled on the floor and raised into place after the precast panels are fitted. The stud space insulation and gypsum board finish can then be applied. Use oil based paint to finish the gypsum board. Alternatively, the insulated metal stud walls can be built first and the precast concrete panels fastened to the structure through access openings, as described in Detail C2.

3 | Since the gypsum board finish is also the air barrier (Chapter 2), it is sealed to the foundation with the membrane, as shown. This seal must also extend along the tops and sides of each run of wall.

4 | As there will be no appreciable creep in the floor-foundation assembly, it is not necessary to support the panels on the single support that is recommended in other details. However there is nothing wrong with such supports and one is used here for the sake of consistency.

5 | This cement-coated polystyrene insulation is intended for roof application (6.3.2), but it is an ideal solution to the problem of protecting exposed foundation insulation. A 2'-0" (600mm) wide strip will usually be adequate, for the insulation requires no protection below grade.

6 | There is a continuing problem of soil settlement around all buildings with basements. It is caused by inadequate compaction of the back fill. The reasons for this inadequate compaction are easily understood when one recalls that it is done when the basement walls are relatively green and often unbraced by partitions, floors, etc. These small pavers are readily removed and replaced to allow the grade to be adjusted.

CLADDING **PRECAST**

PANEL WALL **DRYWALL**

STRUCTURAL FRAME **CONCRETE**

detail C7

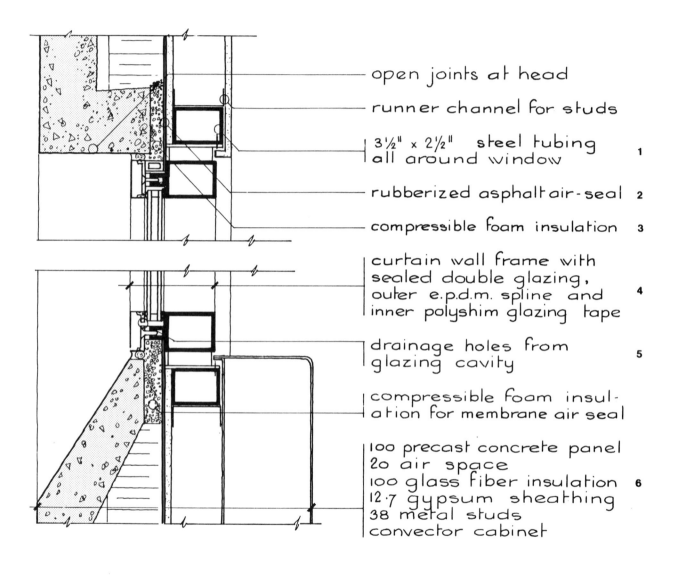

open joints at head

runner channel for studs

3½" x 2½" steel tubing
all around window   1

rubberized asphalt air-seal   2

compressible foam insulation   3

curtain wall frame with
sealed double glazing,
outer e.p.d.m. spline and   4
inner polyshim glazing tape

drainage holes from   5
glazing cavity

compressible foam insul-
ation for membrane air seal

100 precast concrete panel
20 air space
100 glass fiber insulation   6
12.7 gypsum sheathing
38 metal studs
convector cabinet

1 It would be ideal if a spandrel beam always reached down to the window head but frequently there will be a section of wall either above or below the window. Where the window openings are less than 10' (3m) wide they can be reinforced with metal tubing. Usually the tubing at the jambs runs from floor to floor. In designs where the window opening is continuous, or very wide, some support can be gained from the precast panels. A galvanized stud is threaded into a bolt insert in the precast. Two nuts on the stud provide fastening and adjustment for a 4" x 4" (100mm x 100mm) continuous angle, to which may be fastened the runner channels for the metal studs. See note 4 on Detail D8b.

2 In this detail, all of the insulation is on the outside of the metal stud wall. This makes it possible for the outer layer of gypsum board to support the air barrier.(2.5.4)   At the window it is only necessary to connect this air barrier to the window frame with a strip of rubberized asphalt.

3 It is important that all of the air barrier be kept warm with a layer of insulation. That becomes difficult in restricted spaces. This expanding asphalt-impregnated foam strip material has been used successfully for this purpose.

4 Here, as in other details, it is necessary to keep the bulk of the window frame in the warm part of the wall. This prohibits using the frame to close the wall cavity. Wooden frames can be used to bridge a wall cavity, but with metal frame it almost always leads to cold air circumventing the thermal break and chilling the frame.

5 If two-stage waterproofing is to work, not only is an outer rain deterrent and an inner air seal required but the space between must be drained to the outside. Many building scientists also believe that these holes equalize the air pressure in the glazing rebate with the wind pressure outside, thus reducing the pressure difference that might drive water through any holes in the glazing spline.(5.5)

6 The wall has a calculated thermal resistance of R 20 (Rsi 3.57) when 1mm thick studs are used. Adding insulation between the studs will raise the total resistance to R 25 (Rsi 4.44).(1.5.3)

CLADDING **PRECAST**

PANEL WALL **DRYWALL**

STRUCTURAL FRAME **CONCRETE**

detail C8

Series D: Precast Concrete Cladding, Metal Pan Panel Wall

This series shows how buildings with precast concrete cladding and metal panel walls can be detailed to achieve the insulated airtight arrangements developed in the Prolegomenon. As in Series C, these details allow the precast panels to be erected from inside the building. The metal panels are then insulated, erected and sealed to the structure, with the compressible asphalt-impregnated foam strip as described in note 5 to Detail D1.

Details D4 and D5 show structural tubing forming part of the air barrier. Great care must be taken to seal the joints between these tubular beams and their columns. It is a system that should be examined with a structural engineer, for usually beams will not all be the same size and often not in alignment. Alternatively, a wide flange beam can be used with a metal or gypsum board cover to provide a flat surface for a membrane. Remember that the re-entrant spaces of the columns must be covered too.

As noted in 5 on Detail D3, the wooden curb and cant strip are not strictly necessary, for there will be no movement to accommodate at the roof-wall junction and, as well, the rubberized asphalt roofing and flashing are often installed without a cant strip (see Chapter 7, section 7.4.8). However, it is well to think ahead to the extension of these details to other parts of the roof and then to choose a consistent system.

The best system for applying the air/vapor barrier would be to keep the beams and columns free of the wall on the inside of the building.

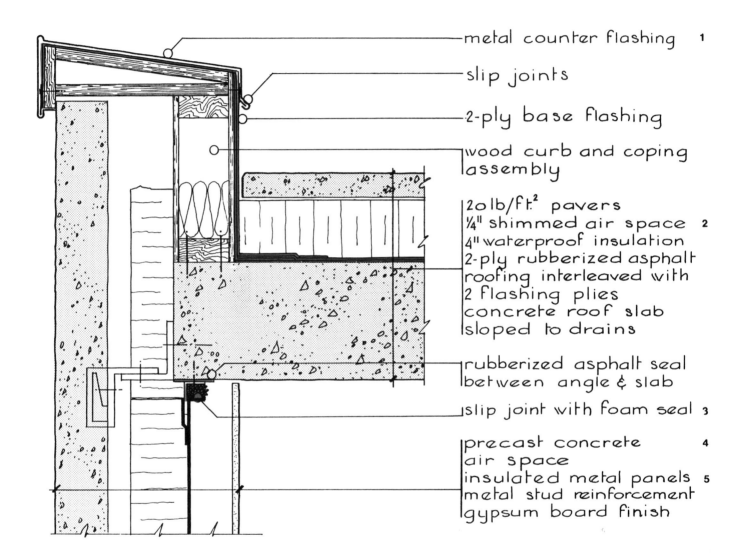

metal counter flashing   1

slip joints

2-ply base flashing

wood curb and coping
assembly

20 lb/ft.² pavers
¼" shimmed air space   2
4" waterproof insulation
2-ply rubberized asphalt
roofing interleaved with
2 flashing plies
concrete roof slab
sloped to drains

rubberized asphalt seal
between angle & slab

slip joint with foam seal   3

precast concrete   4
air space
insulated metal panels   5
metal stud reinforcement
gypsum board finish

1 Temperature swings normally encountered on a parapet will cause 10 ft (3m) lengths of aluminum to expand and contract about 3/8" (10mm). (7.3) Caulking and soldering cannot withstand such movement, except in specially designed expansion joints. Let the metal serve as a decorative sunscreen. Use single S lock for the cross joints and fasten the edges down with clips as shown.

2 The insulation will remain dryer if air can get at its top surface. Thus the pavers should have a very rough undersurface or be held a quarter inch or so (a few millimeters) away from the insulation on Roofmate shims. The manufacturers of Roofmate recommend 20 lb/ft^2 (1.5 Kg/m^2) of ballast. Concrete pavers, 1 3/4" to 2" (45mm to 50mm) thick, will provide this weight.

3 If the roof slab is to deflect (CBD 125) without buckling the metal panels, room must be left for deflection. Here it is achieved with a slip joint running continuously along the top of the panels. If the top of the panel is formed as shown, expanding asphalt-impregnated foam can be placed from the inside to assure a flexible airtight joint. The drawing shows the metal panel offset from the slab edge only to show the kind of on-site conditions that may be expected.(CBD 171)

4 2.3.2 discusses the permanent deflection of concrete beams and CBD 125 discusses the stresses and strains that this deflection causes in precast concrete panels. Support the panels with a single strong support at the center of the bottom of the panel, then stabilize the top corners with two adjustable anchors that will resist horizontal loads but will allow some slight vertical movement. Consult your engineer.

5 Use mechanical fasteners to hold the insulation tight to the metal panel. This wall has a theoretical resistance of R 20 (Rsi 3.6). Filling the space between the studs with insulation will add approximately R 5 (Rsi 0.88).(1.5.3) Install the precast concrete first, then install the metal panels with the insulation already mechanically fastened to them. Alternatively, the metal panels can be erected first and access gained to the precast fasteners through access panels cut in the metal panels. Because the main panels are so accessible, these access openings can be insulated by carefully placing batt insulation into the spaces, then sealing them with gasketed metal closers.

CLADDING **PRECAST**

PANEL WALL **METAL**

STRUCTURAL FRAME **CONCRETE**

detail **D1**

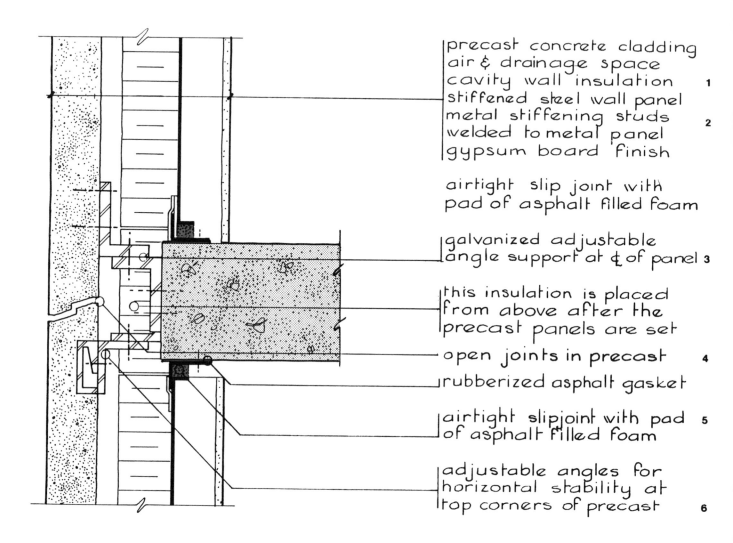

precast concrete cladding
air & drainage space
cavity wall insulation   1
stiffened steel wall panel
metal stiffening studs   2
welded to metal panel
gypsum board finish

airtight slip joint with
pad of asphalt filled foam

galvanized adjustable
angle support at ¢ of panel 3

this insulation is placed
from above after the
precast panels are set

open joints in precast   4

rubberized asphalt gasket

airtight slipjoint with pad 5
of asphalt filled foam

adjustable angles for
horizontal stability at
top corners of precast   6

1 The wall has a theoretical thermal resistance of R 20 (Rsi 3.58). Filling the stud spaces with R 14 (Rsi 2.55) insulation will add only another R 5 (Rsi 0.88) because the metal studs are such serious heat bridges.(1.5.3)

2 After the precast is in place, the stiffened sheet metal panels, with insulation in place on the outside, are raised into place. When plumb and true, the retaining angles are fastened to the concrete floor slab. They should be set on a gasket of rubberized asphalt.

3 It is recommended that the entire weight of the panel be supported at one location near the center bottom of the panel. Additional horizontal support and stabilization must be provided at both of the top corners. All of these supports must be adjustable, for the concrete floor slab is not likely to be accurately placed.(CBD 171) In most construction, these adjustments are made by cutting, shimming and welding on site. Such practices destroy the rustproofing on the supports. Calling for the rustproofing to be "touched-up" is really wishful thinking, for the most vital areas are concealed.

4 These open joints are formed in a way that will prevent water penetration in all but the heaviest wind and rain. Complete watertightness requires 4" (100mm) of rise in the joint and either caulking or a gasket at the inner face of the panel. Such measures are unnecessary with this construction. Note that the profiles do not have sharp acute angles that would be chipped easily. The vertical joints should include a rain deflector.(3.6.2 and Figure 3-6)

5 This joint is designed to maintain the air seal while allowing deflection in the floor slab. Also the joint will take up construction inaccuracies.(CBD 171) It can be sealed from inside and is consistent with the other panel joints.

6 The stresses on these fasteners are not too great to allow these convenient skew-bolt anchors to be used. They are anchored into the precast concrete by passing a reinforcing rod through a ring that is part of the forging. The anchors must be galvanized. The two angles should be strong enough to withstand horizontal wind and earthquake loads, but flexible enough to allow some vertical movement. Remember that while earthquake loads are horizontal, they can occur in any horizontal direction, not just at right angles to the panels.

CLADDING **PRECAST**

PANEL WALL **METAL**

STRUCTURAL FRAME **CONCRETE**

detail D**2**

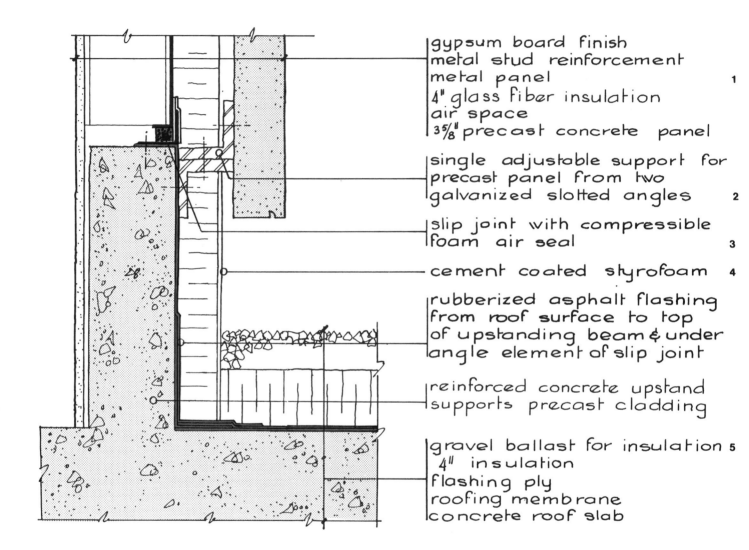

gypsum board finish
metal stud reinforcement
metal panel
4" glass fiber insulation
air space
3⅝" precast concrete panel   1

single adjustable support for
precast panel from two
galvanized slotted angles   2

slip joint with compressible
foam air seal   3

cement coated styrofoam   4

rubberized asphalt flashing
from roof surface to top
of upstanding beam & under
angle element of slip joint

reinforced concrete upstand
supports precast cladding

gravel ballast for insulation 5
4" insulation
flashing ply
roofing membrane
concrete roof slab

1 The real wall here is the sheet metal panel. In this case, metal studs are welded to it as stiffeners. These studs are also used to support the inside finish. The very wide metal studs shown here are to allow the gypsum board finish to run continuously. Some manufacturers stiffen the panels by roll-forming flutes in them, or otherwise bending them. Usually when this is done, it is impossible to hold the insulation in close contact with the panel, a condition that drastically reduces the value of the insulation.(1.5.2)

2 The required adjustment is commonly achieved by cutting and welding. However, welding destroys any rustproofing. The rustproofing cannot be "touched up" after welding, for the most susceptible areas are hidden. Use slotted galvanized angles fastened with galvanized bolts. The precast concrete can be installed before the insulated metal panel walls are put in place.

3 No differential movement is likely here, but the joint provides an airtight adjustable connection that can be made from inside. It takes up any construction inaccuracies in the top of the upstanding beam.(CBD 171)

4 The integral cement coating protects the polystyrene insulation from the rapid disintegration that sunlight causes. However, the coating makes it impossible to use pin-type mechanical fasteners. Although fasteners placed in joints should work quite well, for this small area it should be possible to depend on a good, compatible adhesive.

5 With a 8" (200mm) concrete slab this roof assembly has an R value of 22 (Rsi 3.92). The insulation contributes R 20 (Rsi 3.5). The recommended weight of ballast is 21 lb/ft^2 (105 Kg/m^2) for 4" (100mm) of insulation. A layer of gravel 2$\frac{1}{2}$" (64mm) thick weighs 21 lb/ft^2 (105 Kg/m^2).

detail D3

CLADDING **PRECAST**

PANEL WALL **METAL**

STRUCTURAL FRAME **CONCRETE**

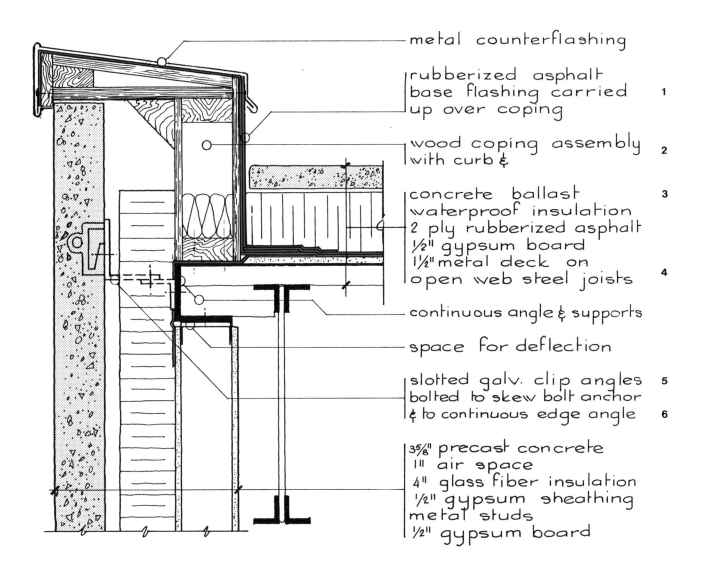

metal counterflashing

rubberized asphalt
base flashing carried   1
up over coping

wood coping assembly   2
with curb &

concrete ballast   3
waterproof insulation
2 ply rubberized asphalt
½" gypsum board
1½" metal deck on
open web steel joists   4

continuous angle & supports

space for deflection

slotted galv. clip angles 5
bolted to skew bolt anchor
& to continuous edge angle 6

3⅝" precast concrete
1" air space
4" glass fiber insulation
½" gypsum sheathing
metal studs
½" gypsum board

1 | The wood should be pressure-treated. Bolt the bottom plate to the reinforced metal edge of the deck with power driven studs. Adequately nail the curb and coping assembly.

2 | This roof assembly has a thermal resistance of R 21 (Rsi 3.72). Shims, $\frac{1}{4}$" (6mm) thick, are shown under the paving stones to aid evaporation of moisture diffusing through the Roofmate. They can be cut from the edge of an insulation board.(6.3.2)

3 | The recommended roofing is 2-ply rubberized asphalt. It is interleaved with two flashing plies. The exposed flashing membrane has a metal or mineral surface to protect the membrane from ultra-violet rays.(7.4.8)

4 | This sheet metal edge and rectangular beam give the edge of this steel roof assembly a profile that is nearly as regular and manageable as concrete.(Prolegomenon)

5 | Note the strip of membrane that is welded to the bottom of the first roofing ply. (Prolegomenon Fig.P-1b) It runs under the curb assembly, then down to join the hollow structural steel beam. The gypsum board cannot be left, even for a few hours, without the protection of a roof membrane. This path presupposes that the curb assembly will be built first and that the gypsum board and roofing will follow at a later date.

6 | Because of the regular profile of the beam, it is used here as part of the continuous air barrier. This must be done with great care, for the beams and columns may be of different thicknesses and there may be a wide joint between the two, to say nothing of the connections. All these joints must be taped.

7 | The weight of the precast panel is supported from the bottom, so only horizontal support is required here. The assembly is adjustable to allow the panels to be aligned. It is also flexible in respect to vertical movement.

8 | This airtight slip-joint allows the insulated metal panels to be erected after the precast concrete is erected. It will take up deflection and building inaccuracies. Note the rubberized asphalt gasket under the angle.

CLADDING **PRECAST**

PANEL WALL **METAL**

STRUCTURAL FRAME **STEEL**

detail **D 4**

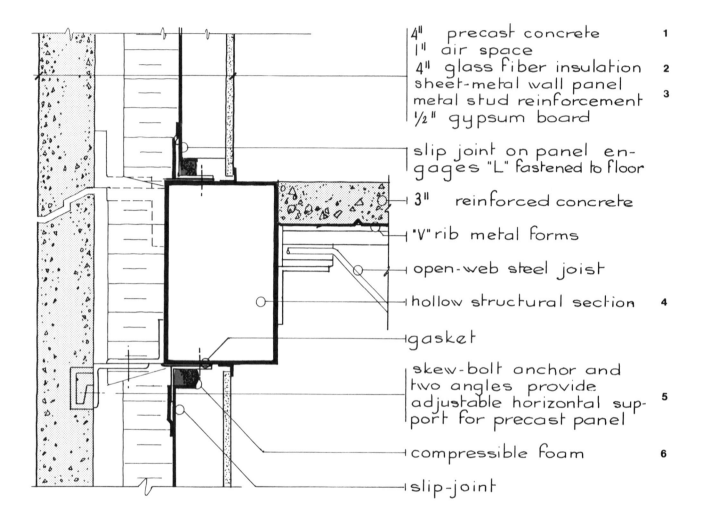

4" precast concrete   1
1" air space
4" glass fiber insulation   2
sheet-metal wall panel
metal stud reinforcement   3
½" gypsum board

slip joint on panel en-
gages "L" fastened to floor

3" reinforced concrete

"V" rib metal forms

open-web steel joist

hollow structural section   4

gasket

skew-bolt anchor and
two angles provide
adjustable horizontal sup-   5
port for precast panel

compressible foam   6

slip-joint

1 Each precast concrete panel is supported by an adjustable galvanized angle at center bottom, so that deflection of the floor will not distort the panels. (CBD 125) The angles are oversized, because the slotted holes in the angles require friction connections.

2 The insulation is fastened tightly to the metal panel wall with mechanical fasteners before the panel is erected.(1.5.2) This allows the precast concrete panels to be fastened from inside the building, a much safer and more economical procedure than dropping them down between a swing stage and the building.

3 Usually, specifications call for the panels to be built from dimensions taken on the job. This is always a desirable procedure, but the completion schedule seldom permits it to be done. The contractor fits and caulks on site to overcome any discrepancies. Caulked joints are seldom properly designed and, as a result of construction inaccuracies and poor caulking, the joints seldom remain airtight. The joints shown in these details are designed to remain airtight, even when the floor is neither level nor true-to-line.(CBD 171) The joints will also absorb the deflection.

4 If the width of these hollow sections is not constant, the outside face must remain in the same plane. Recall too that there is usually a gap of 3/8" (10mm) or so between column and beam. All these joints must be airtight. Theoretically, the air barrier membrane shown here will be needed only at such joints. See notes to D4.

5 Because all the weight of the precast concrete panels is taken at the bottom, the top connections need only provide horizontal restraint against wind, earthquake loads and twisting. They are purposely thinner than the main supports, so that they can absorb any differential vertical movement.

6 There are several asphalt-impregnated, precompressed foams that should work well in these connections. Note that the angle is made airtight to the floor, preferably with a strip of rubberized asphalt, glazing tape or even a bed of caulking. Similar joints are used at the columns.

CLADDING **PRECAST**

PANEL WALL **METAL**

STRUCTURAL FRAME **STEEL**

detail **D5**

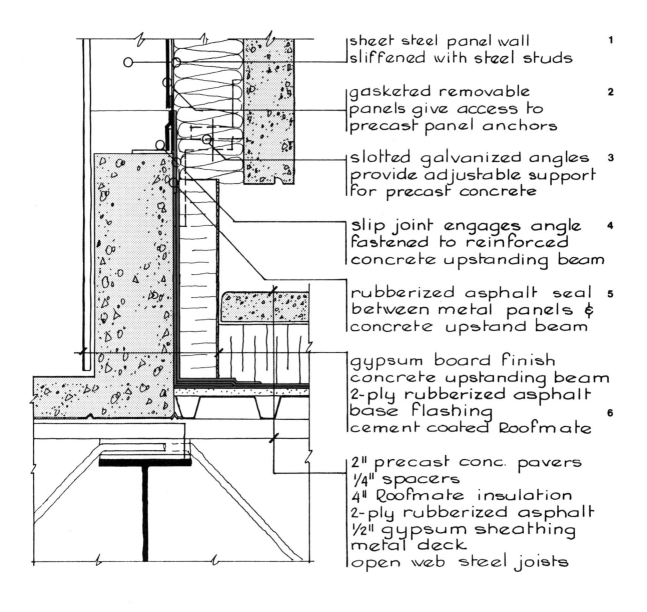

1 sheet steel panel wall stiffened with steel studs

2 gasketed removable panels give access to precast panel anchors

3 slotted galvanized angles provide adjustable support for precast concrete

4 slip joint engages angle fastened to reinforced concrete upstanding beam

5 rubberized asphalt seal between metal panels & concrete upstand beam

6 gypsum board finish
concrete upstanding beam
2-ply rubberized asphalt
base flashing
cement coated Roofmate

2" precast conc. pavers
¼" spacers
4" Roofmate insulation
2-ply rubberized asphalt
½" gypsum sheathing
metal deck
open web steel joists

This detail shows a wall rising above a roof, as might occur where the multi-story tower of a hospital rises above a wider 2-story pedestal. This junction does not allow for differential movement between the roof deck and the wall. Examine the structure carefully to see that this is true on all sides. Note that the beam must be examined and reinforced for torque.

1 | In this sheet steel panel wall, stiffness comes from the metal studs that are welded to it. In some buildings that use this construction, the stiffness comes from the shape of the metal. It must be possible for the insulation to follow the metal shape, leaving no gaps between wall and insulation.(1.5.2) This would not be possible with fluted metal.

2 | Other details in this section have been designed to allow the metal panel walls to be insulated, then erected after the precast concrete has been erected from inside the building. Here access panels are suggested. This will allow the metal walls to be erected, made airtight and insulated from the outside. The precast panels are then lifted into place and the connections made from inside through the access panels.

3 | These slotted galvanized angles allow 3-way adjustment.(3.6.6, Figure 3-7) Because they are galvanized, they must be bolted rather than welded. The slotted holes require a friction connection; thus the oversized angles and bolts.

4 | There will be little, if any, movement between the upstanding concrete beam and the metal wall panel. However, this joint will allow considerable irregularity in the dimension between the panel and beam. The resilient, airtight material is asphalt-impregnated plastic foam.

5 | Metal panels are sealed to the concrete and to each other with torched on strips of rubberized asphalt.

6 | The two-ply rubberized asphalt base flashing is interleaved with the two-ply roofing.(7.4.8) Note that it is insulated with 4" (100mm) of waterproof polystyrene foam insulation. The insulation is protected from sunlight by an integral cement coating. The insulation must be held tightly to the base flashing.

CLADDING PRECAST

STRUCTURAL FRAME PANEL WALL
STEEL METAL

detail D6

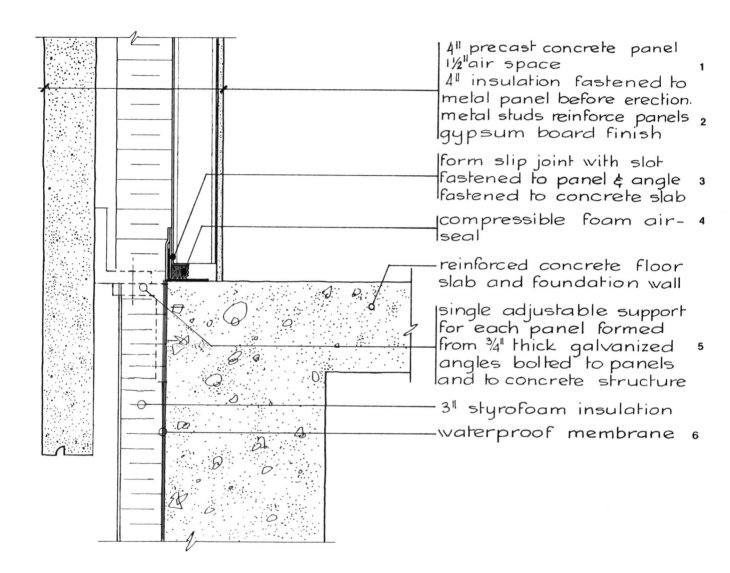

4″ precast concrete panel
1½″ air space   1
4″ insulation fastened to
metal panel before erection.
metal studs reinforce panels 2
gypsum board finish

form slip joint with slot
fastened to panel & angle   3
fastened to concrete slab

compressible foam air-   4
seal

reinforced concrete floor
slab and foundation wall

single adjustable support
for each panel formed
from ¾″ thick galvanized   5
angles bolted to panels
and to concrete structure

3″ styrofoam insulation

waterproof membrane   6

1 | The space between the precast concrete and the insulation allows water to run down the back of the precast panels. In this case it simply runs out the bottom, and no other drains or through-wall flashings are needed. The air space also provides a place for construction inaccuracies to be taken up. In CBD 171, Latta writes that these inaccuracies are usually in the order of plus or minus 1" (25mm), but often may reach plus or minus 2" (50mm).

2 | It is safer and more economical to fasten the precast concrete panels from within the building. When that is completed, these insulated metal panel walls are raised into place and fastened. Alternatively, the metal panels may be erected, made airtight and insulated from outside. With this system, gasketed access hatches are left in the metal panel walls so that when the precast is raised into place it can be fastened from inside. See Detail D6.

3 | These slip joints take up vertical and horizontal inaccuracies between the floor and the metal panel walls. As has been noted in other details, such joints will also absorb plastic creep and deflection.(CBD 125)

4 | This airtight, watertight material is installed in a compressed form, which then expands to fill the space. It allows the seal to be placed from inside the wall. This also has the advantage of access for repair. The retaining angle must be made airtight to the floor either in a bed of caulking or, preferably, on a gasket of rubberized asphalt.

5 | The need for rustproof, 3-way adjustable supports for the precast panels has been emphasized throughout this series of details. The 3-way adjustment is necessary to overcome construction inaccuracies. Commonly, the adjustment is made by cutting, shimming and welding on site; processes that destroy any rustproofing. (Chapter 3, Figure 3-7)

6 | There are several satisfactory waterproof membranes that work well on foundation walls. Two plies of glass fiber fabric and three or four coats of asphalt emulsion have been used successfully for many years. More recently, self-adhering rubberized asphalt has been used successfully. Two plies of reinforced rubberized asphalt fused to the foundation wall with propane torches provide the strongest and most dependable waterproofing.

CLADDING **PRECAST**

PANEL WALL **METAL**

STRUCTURAL FRAME **CONCRETE**

detail D7

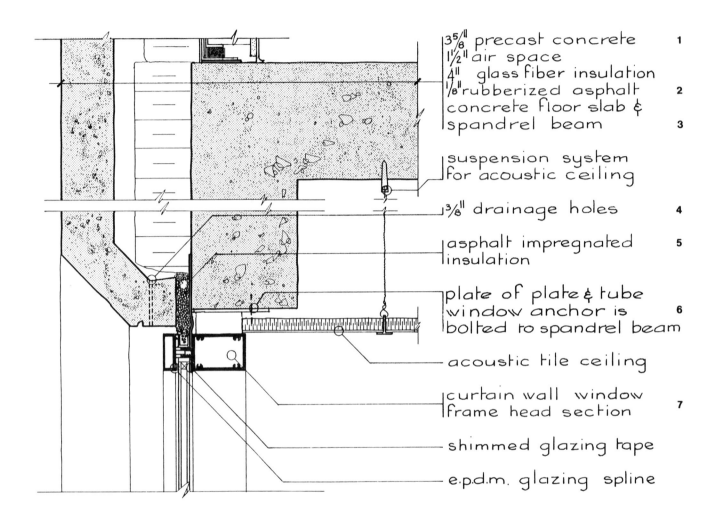

3⅝" precast concrete   1
1½" air space
4" glass fiber insulation
⅛" rubberized asphalt   2
concrete floor slab &
spandrel beam   3

suspension system
for acoustic ceiling

1⅜" drainage holes   4

asphalt impregnated   5
insulation

plate of plate & tube
window anchor is   6
bolted to spandrel beam

acoustic tile ceiling

curtain wall window
frame head section   7

shimmed glazing tape

e.p.d.m. glazing spline

1 Precast concrete panels with strong channel profile sections may be extended from column to column. Connections can be made to the columns for the full height of each panel.

2 In this detail the air barrier is transferred from the steel panel wall to the concrete structure by means of a bed of caulking under the retaining angle, or by bedding the angle on a strip of rubberized asphalt. Thence it is transferred to the window frame by means of a flap of membrane that is clamped into the window frame. If the membrane is not continuous over the concrete, then construction joints and other discontinuities must be sealed.

3 This spandrel beam makes detailing quite straighforward. Where there is no beam, a short section of wall can fill the space between window head and underside of beam. The top of such sections of wall can be supported by the floor slab. The bottom can be supported from the precast spandrel panel.

4 Some water, either from rain penetration or from condensation, may be present on the back of the panels. Open joints will drain it clear of the window head. The drip in front of these holes will prevent water reaching the window head from the face of the spandrel panel.

5 Where building envelopes must function in cold weather, one of the principal requirements is to keep the air barrier warm, at least above the dew point of the inside air.(1.5.1)   This 1" (25mm) strip of expanding asphalt–impregnated foam insulation can be placed after the precast concrete is in place. It is not much insulation but enough to serve this vital function.

6 The tubes are a snug sliding fit into the hollow vertical frame sections. The plates, which are welded to one end of the tubes, are bolted to the structure. This arrangement holds the window in place while allowing for creep and deflection.

7 That part of the frame that can be drawn up to clamp the glass in the frame is called the pressure plate. In this frame, there is a decorative cover clipped over the pressure plate once it is tightened into place.(5.5, Figure 5–6)

CLADDING **PRECAST**

PANEL WALL **METAL**

STRUCTURAL FRAME **CONCRETE**

detail **D8a**

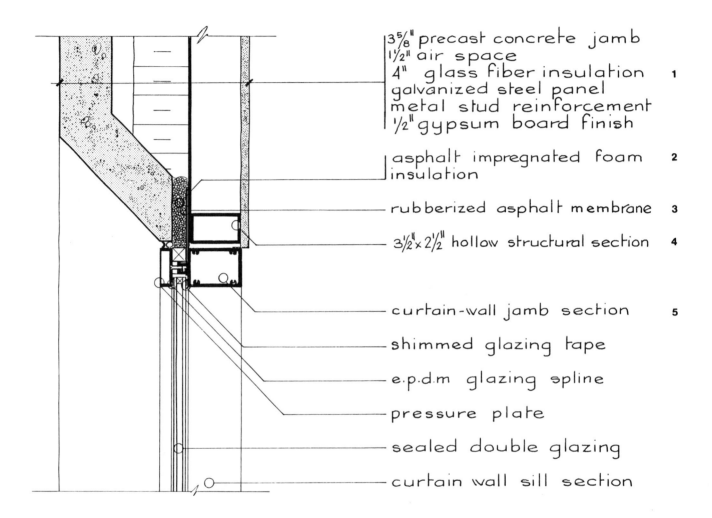

3⅝" precast concrete jamb
1½" air space
4" glass fiber insulation   1
galvanized steel panel
metal stud reinforcement
½" gypsum board finish

asphalt impregnated foam   2
insulation

rubberized asphalt membrane   3

3½"x 2½" hollow structural section   4

curtain-wall jamb section   5

shimmed glazing tape

e.p.d.m glazing spline

pressure plate

sealed double glazing

curtain wall sill section

1   This jamb detail will serve equally well at the sill if the glazing cavity is drained to the outside.(5.5)

2   The thermal resistance provided by this assembly is R 20 (Rsi 3.6), enough for any building in an area with 9000 or fewer °F degree days (5000 or fewer °C degree days).(1.7)   No insulation should be placed in the stud space for it may chill the metal panel down below the dew point.

3   It is important to insulate the air barrier all the way to the window frame. This material is waterproof and expands in place to fill the space.(1.5.2)

4   The strip of rubberized asphalt membrane carries the line of airtightness from the metal panel wall into the window frame.(5.3)   It is self-sealed to the metal panel and held in place by the expanding foam insulation. It is clamped into the frame by using a pressure block of some non-conducting material (a plastic tube for instance).

5   There are a number of ways of stiffening the panel around the window opening. Double metal studs are adequate for small openings. Also the metal panel may be formed to reinforce this edge. The tubular section shown has been used successfully on a number of buildings. The tubes at the jambs can be extended from floor to underside of beam or slab. When this is done, some provision usually must be made to take up creep and deflection in the slab. A strap of $\frac{1}{4}$" thick metal shaped like a leaf spring has been used and works quite well. The strap is welded to the end of the tubing and is retained in the runner channel.

6   The window opening is formed in the field. It is subject to all of the inaccuracies of on-site construction.(CBD 171)   The frame, on the other hand, is made to very close tolerances. These differences in precision make it necessary to leave a clearance of 3/8" (10mm) all around the frame. Once the frame is in place and accurately aligned and plumbed, it is usually held in place with tubes inserted into the vertical tubular sections. These tubes have a plate welded to one end. The plates are bolted to the walls at head and sill. These frames are designed with the maximum area exposed to the warm interior of the room and a minimum area exposed to cold outside air.

CLADDING **PRECAST**

PANEL WALL **METAL**

STRUCTURAL FRAME **CONCRETE**

detail D**8b**

Series E: Metal Cladding, Concrete Block Panel Wall

E1 and E4 Wall-Roof Detail
E2 and E5 Wall-Floor Detail
E3 and E6 Wall-Penthouse Detail

E7 Wall-Foundation Detail
E8 Wall-Window Detail

Series "E" shows how the principles developed in the Prolegomenon can be applied to buildings with metal cladding over reinforced concrete block panel walls. As in other series, the details attempt to show several ways of achieving the same ends.

All of the window details show a "curtain wall" section. However, each manufacturer may extrude the sections with slightly different profiles. Several different configurations are shown throughout the details, all achieving the same ends.

Similarly, the window details show a variety of ways of handling heads, jambs, and sills. Only the principles are intended to be consistent from detail to detail.

There have been instances in high wind areas, when the metal panels have been torn from the building. These would be lethal projectiles. Be sure that the panels and their fasteners are strong, well fastened, and corrosion proof. The supplier will not likely do it on his/her own for this is a very competitive world and safety outside his/her lifetime will not be a major concern.

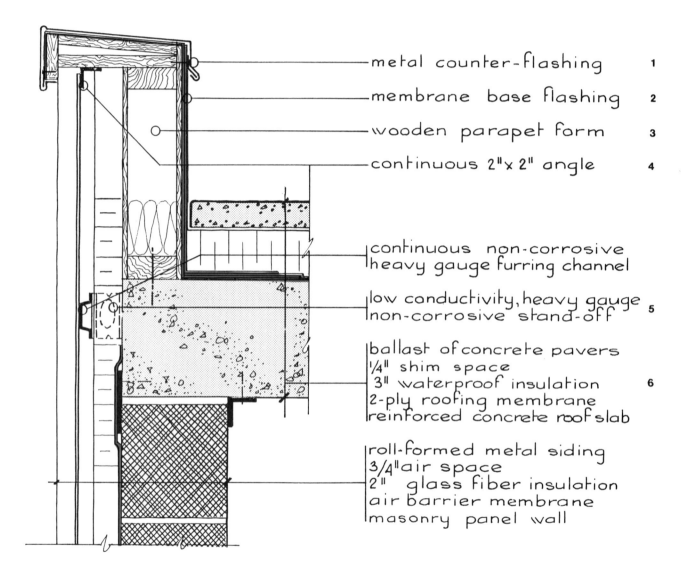

1   metal counter-flashing

2   membrane base flashing

3   wooden parapet form

4   continuous 2" x 2" angle

continuous non-corrosive
heavy gauge furring channel

low conductivity, heavy gauge   5
non-corrosive stand-off

ballast of concrete pavers
¼" shim space
3" waterproof insulation   6
2-ply roofing membrane
reinforced concrete roof slab

roll-formed metal siding
¾" air space
2" glass fiber insulation
air barrier membrane
masonry panel wall

1 │ When the face of the metal cladding is not exactly true-to-line, it will not be quite so obvious if the counterflashing projects 3/4" to 1" (20mm to 25mm) beyond it, as it does here. (7.4.1)

2 │ The top of the wall is waterproofed by an uninterrupted rubberized asphalt membrane that runs from the roof to the outer face of the coping. The metal couterflashing provides a sunscreen and some protection from mechanical damage. Its most useful function is decorative, for membranes are readily available with integral sunscreens. With high quality rubberized asphalt roofing systems, there will be two flashing plies interleaved with the two roofing plies where they intersect. (7.4.8)

3 │ When built-up roofing is used, this curb should be replaced with a curb and cant strip to ease the bend in the membrane.

4 │ As the coping deflects (with the roof slab), it will move with respect to the cladding. This movement is accommodated by fastening the cladding through slotted holes in the 2" x 2" (50mm x 50mm) angle. The amount of movement to be accommodated must be calculated by the structural engineer. (CBD 125)

5 │ The short stand-off sections provide a small path for heat, particularly if the cross sectional area is reduced as shown here. Continuous "Z" bar supports for the metal cladding would form serious heat bridges through the insulation. (1.5.3) These details show supports for the metal cladding only at the floor and roof slabs. This is not because the block wall cannot support the metal cladding but because the cladding and its supports must be heavy gauge to withstand corrosion over 50 to 100 years. Such heavy gauge components can easily span from floor to floor. Connections should be bolted.

6 │ This assembly provides a thermal resistance of R 22 (Rsi 3.81). Concrete pavers, 2" (50mm) thick, will provide the 20 lb/ft² (105 Kg/m²) ballast recommended for this thickness of insulation.

CLADDING **METAL**

PANEL WALL **CONCRETE BLOCK**

STRUCTURAL FRAME **CONCRETE**

detail E1

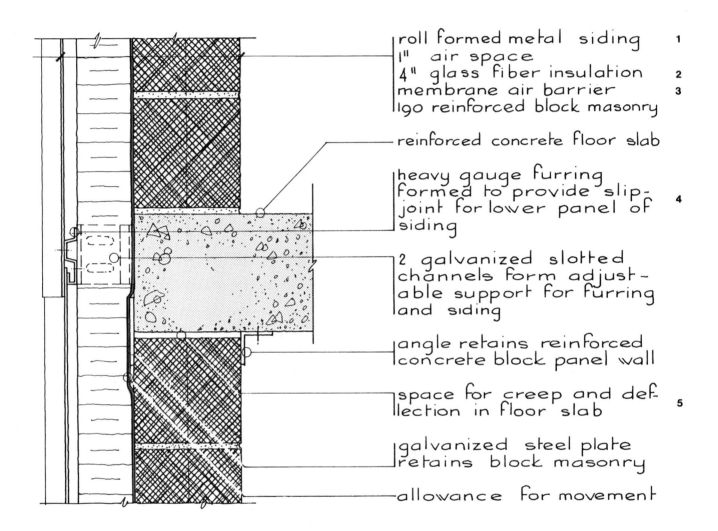

roll formed metal siding   1
1" air space
4" glass fiber insulation   2
membrane air barrier   3
190 reinforced block masonry

reinforced concrete floor slab

heavy gauge furring
formed to provide slip-
joint for lower panel of   4
siding

2 galvanized slotted
channels form adjust-
able support for furring
and siding

angle retains reinforced
concrete block panel wall

space for creep and def-
lection in floor slab   5

galvanized steel plate
retains block masonry

allowance for movement

Metal siding over concrete block panel walls is usually encountered in building envelopes where part of the cladding is brick, which needs concrete blocks for support.

1 The metal siding is of very heavy gauge and fastened with rustproof bolts rather than sheet metal screws. Although this is done primarily for corrosion resistance, it makes it possible in most installations to support the panels only at the floor levels.

2 This assembly, with 4" (100mm) of glass fiber cavity wall insulation, provides a thermal resistance of R 19 (Rsi 3.38). Adding furring and gypsum board finish on the inside will raise the resistance to R 21 (Rsi 3.64). (1.7)

3 The most important element in the wall is this membrane air barrier.(Chapter 2) It is of polyester reinforced rubberized asphalt, "welded" to the concrete masonry with propane torches. In some buildings, a self-adhering material has been used. In one case it was not well-adhered. The poor adhesion was attributed to concrete block masonry that was still damp. If there are no substantial cracks to bridge, it should be possible to use a spray-on formulation of rubberized asphalt with strips of the welded material used to seal joints where movement may occur. Note the allowance in the membrane below the floor slab for creep and deflection in the slab.

4 With concrete structural frames, particularly those with long spans, your engineer must calculate the amount of plastic creep and elastic deflection to be accommodated. (CBD 125) You must provide accommodation for the movement. Because of this split responsibility, it is a part of the design that is frequently overlooked, sometimes with disastrous results. Here creep and deflection of the floor slab are accommodated by providing a slip joint in the siding installation. This joint will also allow the large sheets of metal siding to expand and contract without damage.

5 Creep in the concrete slab must also be accommodated in the concrete block panel walls without compromising the reinforcing that transmits wind and earthquake loads to the building structure. Here a stong slip joint is provided by holding the blockwork between a plate and angle; one of which is installed after the blockwork is erected.

CLADDING **METAL**

PANEL WALL **CONCRETE BLOCK**

STRUCTURAL FRAME **CONCRETE**

detail E2

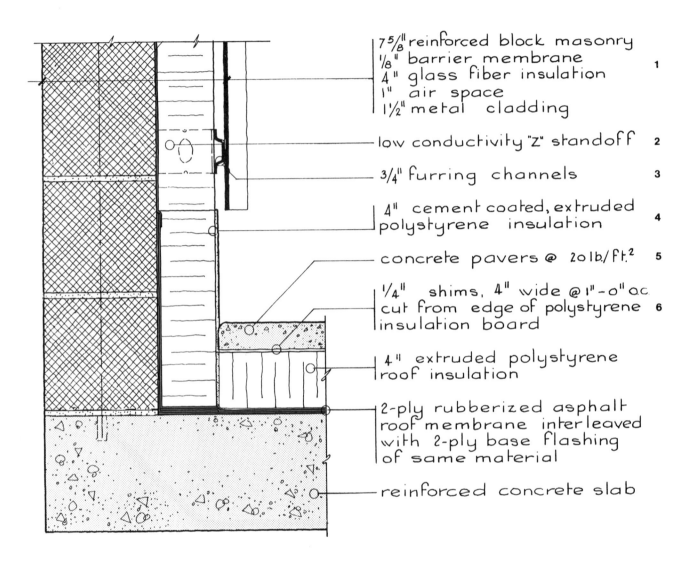

7⅝" reinforced block masonry
⅛" barrier membrane
4" glass fiber insulation
1" air space
1½" metal cladding   1

low conductivity "z" standoff   2

¾" furring channels   3

4" cement coated, extruded
polystyrene insulation   4

concrete pavers @ 20 lb/ft.²   5

¼" shims, 4" wide @ 1"-0" o.c.
cut from edge of polystyrene   6
insulation board

4" extruded polystyrene
roof insulation

2-ply rubberized asphalt
roof membrane interleaved
with 2-ply base flashing
of same material

reinforced concrete slab

1. This simple wall is completely airtight (Chapter 2) and has a thermal resistance of R 19 (Rsi 3.38). This is enough for a building with low internal heat gains in areas where there are 9000 F° (5000 C°) degree days.

2. If continuous steel Z bar furring at 40" (1000mm) o.c. had been used, it would have reduced the value of the insulation by 50%.(1.5.3) By contrast there will be hardly any heat loss through the low conductivity stand-offs shown in this drawing.

3. Steel stand-offs, furring channels and cladding must all be heavy gauge and hot-dipped galvanized, if rusting is to be avoided for the life of the building and if the assembly is to withstand wind buffeting for a long time, perhaps 100 years.

4. This cement-coated polystyrene insulation is produced by Dow for use on non-ballasted protected membrane roofs.(6.3.2) Here it is used because the cement coating protects the otherwise exposed wall insulation against sunlight and mechanical damage.

5. Polystyrene insulation floats. Chapter 6 describes several methods of dealing with that situation. This detail shows concrete pavers or patio stones used to weigh down the insulation.

6. When the bottoms of the insulation boards are wet and there is a sizable difference in temperature across the boards (winter conditions), a fairly large quantity of water vapour is forced through the insulation.(6.3.2, 6.4.3) It is quite possible for this vapour to condense in the boards. This will be particularly true if the moisture cannot escape from the top of the insulation. To allow moisture to escape, the paving stones are held $\frac{1}{4}$" or so (4mm or 5mm) away from the insulation on shims made from strips sawn from insulation boards. The material has a compressive strength of 30 psi (210 KPa), so you will need only a small area of shim.

All of the wind and earthquake forces must be sustained by this wall. The reinforcing should be carefully engineered to transmit these forces into the building structure.

CLADDING
METAL

PANEL WALL
CONCRETE BLOCK

STRUCTURAL FRAME
CONCRETE

detail E3

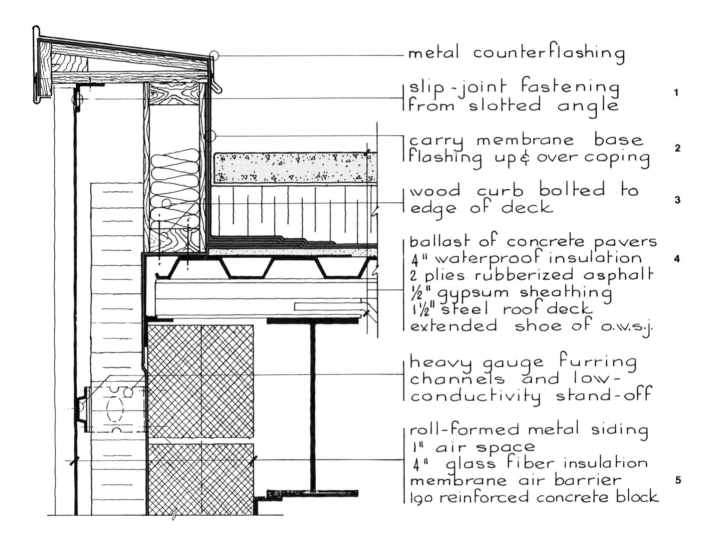

— metal counterflashing

slip-joint fastening
from slotted angle   **1**

carry membrane base
flashing up & over coping   **2**

wood curb bolted to
edge of deck   **3**

ballast of concrete pavers
4" waterproof insulation   **4**
2 plies rubberized asphalt
½" gypsum sheathing
1½" steel roof deck
extended shoe of o.w.s.j.

heavy gauge furring
channels and low-
conductivity stand-off

roll-formed metal siding
1" air space
4" glass fiber insulation
membrane air barrier   **5**
190 reinforced concrete block

1 | Because the parapet assembly is supported by the roof deck, live load deflections of the roof will cause the parapet to move up and down. The metal siding, on the other hand, is fastened to the concrete block panel wall which is supported by the floor below. It may deflect too, but not at the same time nor in the same amount as the roof. This slip joint must be designed to accommodate these differential movements.

2 | This roof wall assembly has been designed to allow the base flashing to be installed correctly. The usual manufacturer's requirement is satisfied by interleaving two plies of rubberized asphalt flashing with the two ply roof membrane. These two plies are then carried to the top of the curb. In this drawing one of these plies is carried to the outer edge of the coping, where it is turned down. This takes care of the leaking that inevitably accompanies copings that depend on metal for waterproofing.(7.4.1)

3 | Design to allow the roof and flashings to be installed at an early stage of construction, so that the building can be enclosed temporarily beneath its shelter, a great advantage in harsh climates. Obviously, the curb-coping assembly must be strong enough as a cantilever to withstand snow and wind loads. Note the insulation in the stud space of the curb. This is to keep the air barrier warm (Prolegomenon, Rule 4) where it passes beneath the curb.

4 | With 4" (100mm) of Roofmate, a waterproof extruded polystyrene foam roof insulation, this assembly has a thermal resistance of R 20 (Rsi 3.64). Note the space between the insulation and the concrete pavers. This is achieved with $\frac{1}{4}$" (4mm or 5mm) thick shims of Roofmate. Its purpose is to allow the evaporation of moisture from the insulation.(6.3.2) Roofmate has a compressive strength of 30 psi (210 KPa), so the area of the shims need not be large.

5 | A vital element, the unbroken air barrier of rubberized asphalt extends from the roof surface down to the concrete block panel wall.(Chapter 2) To provide a smooth surface for this transition, a sheet metal angle edges the roof deck and the ends of the extended joist shoes. Two angles support the blocks against horizontal forces without hindering vertical deflection of the roof.

CLADDING **METAL**

PANEL WALL **CONCRETE BLOCK**

STRUCTURAL FRAME **STEEL**

detail E**4**

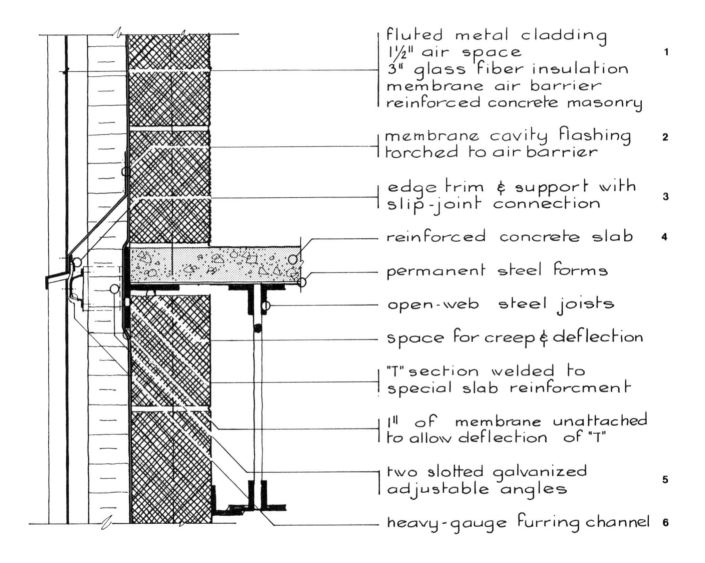

fluted metal cladding
1½" air space
3" glass fiber insulation
membrane air barrier
reinforced concrete masonry   **1**

membrane cavity flashing
torched to air barrier   **2**

edge trim & support with
slip-joint connection   **3**

reinforced concrete slab   **4**

permanent steel forms

open-web steel joists

space for creep & deflection

"T" section welded to
special slab reinforcment

1" of membrane unattached
to allow deflection of "T"

two slotted galvanized
adjustable angles   **5**

heavy-gauge furring channel   **6**

1 | The air space in this and many other wall assemblies is a compromise between the workable minimum and the need to keep the wall to a reasonable thickness. The air space is intended to let water run unimpeded down the back of the metal to a place where it can be drained out of the wall. It is a place where building inaccuracies (CBD 171) can be taken up without reducing the thickness of the insulation. Some authors believe it provides a space for pressure equalization to reduce water penetration.(3.4.2)

2 | Cavity flashing is so difficult to install properly that it should be eliminated except where it is absolutely necessary.(7.4.11) The intention here is to make it of rubberized asphalt with one edge torched to the air barrier, the other clipped into the edge piece.

3 | There may be considerable movement at this joint, both from deflection in the structure and from thermal movement in the metal siding. Thermal movement may reach $\frac{1}{4}$" (6mm) in 10' (3m).(CBD 26, CBD 56) Expected deflection should be calculated by the structural designer. The design of the joint is more complicated when drainage is required.

4 | The section of concrete slab that projects beyond the last joist is reinforced to carry the weight of one floor of the whole wall assembly. Note that the weight of the cladding is transferred directly to the "T" that edges the slab. For that reason reinforcing bars of adequate capacity should be welded to the T.

5 | With some metal siding the fluting may conceal construction inaccuracies. When this is so, non-adjustable, low conductivity stand-offs may be used. Where the surface must be true to line, the two adjustable angles shown here can be used. The angles and bolts must be galvanized.

6 | A piece of metal siding that has come loose is a very lethal projectile. Use heavy gauge non-corrosive metal or heavily hot-dipped galvanized steel to assure structural strength and freedom from dangerous corrosion. Such siding and fasteners will easily span from floor to floor. This will not preclude the use of intermediate fasteners. All sections and fastenings must be carefully engineered. Sheet metal screws are not advised.

CLADDING **METAL**

PANEL WALL **CONCRETE BLOCK**

STRUCTURAL FRAME **STEEL**

detail E5

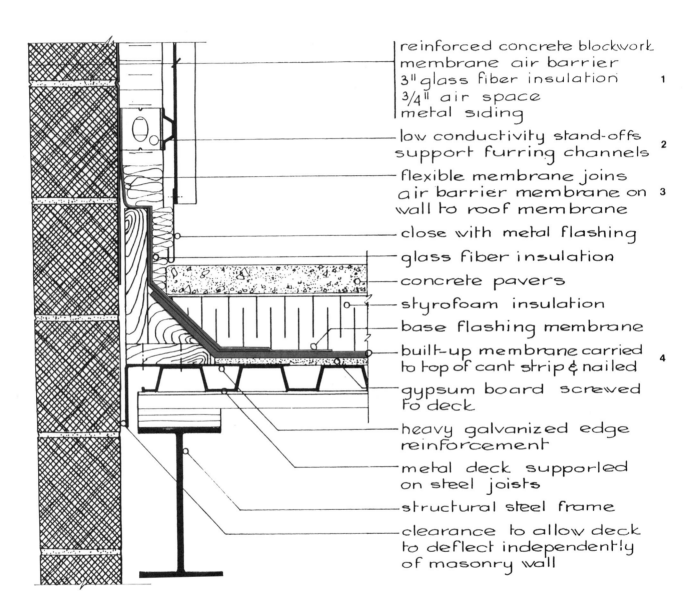

reinforced concrete blockwork
membrane air barrier
3" glass fiber insulation   1
3/4" air space
metal siding

low conductivity stand-offs   2
support furring channels

flexible membrane joins
air barrier membrane on   3
wall to roof membrane

close with metal flashing

glass fiber insulation

concrete pavers

styrofoam insulation

base flashing membrane

built-up membrane carried   4
to top of cant strip & nailed

gypsum board screwed
to deck

heavy galvanized edge
reinforcement

metal deck supported
on steel joists

structural steel frame

clearance to allow deck
to deflect independently
of masonry wall

This is one of the most difficult junctions in building design and construction. A waterproof, correctly placed and continuously insulated air barrier is esssential (Chapter 2), in spite of the movement that can take place between the roof and the wall. Where possible this movement should be eliminated by fastening the roof construction to the concrete block masonry. Do not do this without consulting the structural engineer. Frequently, because of where sections are drawn, the two will seem to be attached. However, closer examination will show areas that are not.

1   This wall, with 3" (75mm) of glass fiber insulation and no inside finish other than painted concrete block, has a thermal resistance of R 15 (Rsi 2.68), enough to satisfy the requirements of NRCC's "Measures for Energy Conservation in New Buildings" for a building with a high energy requirement in an area where there are 6300 F° (3500 C°), or fewer, degree days.(1.6) Four inches (100mm) of insulation will raise the thermal resistance to R 19 (Rsi 3.38).

2   Again in this detail it is emphasized that the sheet metal and its supports must be strong and stiff. Only the longest lasting rustproofing (e.g. heavy hot-dipped galvanizing) is good enough. All connections should be bolted. The stand-offs shown do not contribute significantly to heat loss. Any sort of continuous Z bar furring that bridges the insulation will likely reduce insulation value by half.(1.5.3)

3   This flexible seal is achieved by sealing 2" or 3" (50mm or 75mm) of rubberized asphalt to the roof flashing. The same amount is sealed to the air barrier on the wall. The intervening 4" (100mm) is not sealed and is free to straighten out as the roof deflects.(Prolegomenon, Rule 3)

4   This built-up membrane is very difficult to install properly in the Canadian climate.(Chapter 6) First, the gypsum board must be securely fastened to the metal deck with mechanical fasteners, for it is vital to have a strong substrate. Next, the membrane must be securely mopped to the gypsum board. Finally, the materials must be dry and correctly applied.(6.4.1)

CLADDING   METAL

PANEL WALL   CONCRETE BLOCK

STRUCTURAL FRAME   STEEL

detail E6

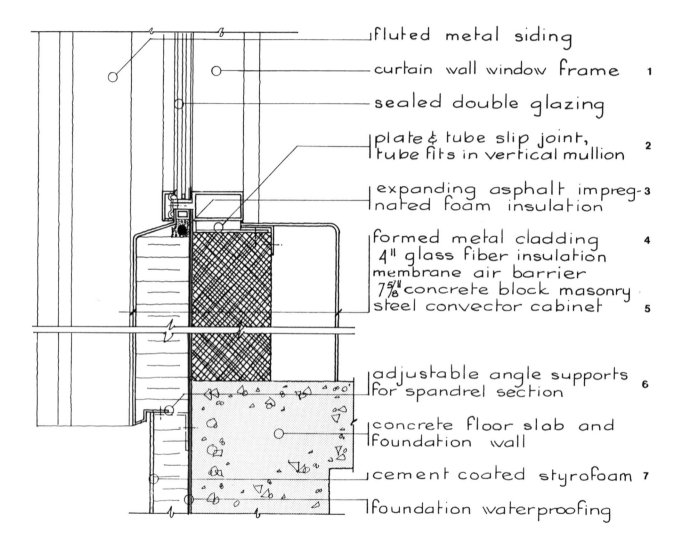

fluted metal siding

curtain wall window frame   1

sealed double glazing

plate & tube slip joint,   2
tube fits in vertical mullion

expanding asphalt impreg-3
nated foam insulation

formed metal cladding   4
  4" glass fiber insulation
membrane air barrier
7⅝" concrete block masonry
steel convector cabinet   5

adjustable angle supports   6
for spandrel section

concrete floor slab and
foundation wall

cement coated styrofoam 7

foundation waterproofing

1 The advantages of "curtain wall" frames are described at length in Chapter 5. Here, the larger part of the frame is placed inside the air barrier and insulation, where it can act as a heat sink to prevent excessive chilling of the sealed edges of the double glazing.

2 The tube provides a snug sliding fit into the vertical mullions. The plate is anchored to the masonry. The windows will be subject to many years of wind buffeting, so only the best masonry anchors should be used. Lead anchors, which creep under stress, should never be used.

3 The membrane air barrier is clamped into the window frame as shown in the drawing. To keep it warm, it is necessary to insulate it continuously where it leaves the masonry wall and continues into the window frame. (Prolegomenon Rule 4, 1.5.1) Carefully fitted, compressed glass fiber insulation would also provide enough insulation.

4 The metal cladding at the spandrel has been held back from the face of the building only to show the versatility of the assembly. Drainage holes are provided at the bottom of this metal panel.

5 In most installations, convector cabinets are carried the full width of the room. Some care must be exercised, for if the cabinet is pressurized, the pressurized air will have access to all of the cavities in the concrete block masonry. In this detail, such leakage is not a matter of concern for it occurs inside the air barrier and insulation; in other words, within the heated part of the room. In many installations, this pressurized air will also get into the four adjacent rooms through chases for piping, wiring and ductwork.

6 The panels are held at the bottom and at each top corner with slotted angles so that they may be adjusted to be plumb and true-to-line. The angles must be rust-proof and compatible with the cladding.

7 The integral cement coating on this waterproof styrofoam insulation will protect it from sunlight and mechanical damage.

CLADDING METAL

PANEL WALL CONCRETE BLOCK

STRUCTURAL FRAME STEEL

detail E7

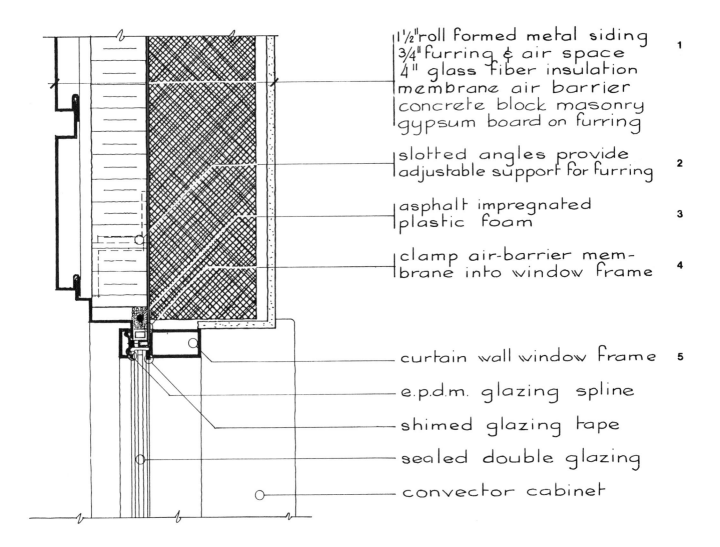

1½" roll formed metal siding
¾" furring & air space
4" glass fiber insulation
membrane air barrier
concrete block masonry
gypsum board on furring   **1**

slotted angles provide
adjustable support for furring   **2**

asphalt impregnated
plastic foam   **3**

clamp air-barrier mem-
brane into window frame   **4**

curtain wall window frame   **5**

e.p.d.m. glazing spline

shimed glazing tape

sealed double glazing

convector cabinet

1 Again in this detail it is recommended that the roll formed metal siding be heavy enough to span from floor to floor. This will assure that the siding, fasteners, furring channels and their adjustable supporting angles are all heavy enough to withstand the corrosion and wind forces imposed on them. If the siding is steel, then the supports and fasteners should be heavily hot-dipped galvanized. If it is aluminum, then the supports can be aluminum of adequate cross section or steel with a heavy rustproof coating compatible with the aluminum. Cadmium is frequently used.

2 Since the structural frame of the building is never adequately plumb, level or true-to-line (CBD 171), the supports for the metal siding should be adjustable. Here this is achieved by using a pair of slotted angles which will give 3-way adjustment.

3 One of the most difficult parts of the air barrier to insulate is this short width that leaves the protection of the wall insulation on its way to the window frame. To ensure that insulation completely covers the membrane, an expanding asphalt-impregnated foam strip is used.(1.5.1)

4 To assure airtightness all around the window frame (Chapter 2), a width of the wall membrane is clamped into the back of the frame, head, jambs and sill. A hollow plastic low-conductivity spacer is employed to fill the remainder of the glazing rebate.

5 Note that the greater part of the frame is on the warm side of the thermal break. This is to aid in keeping the sealed edge of the glass warm.(5.13.5, 5.13.6) On no account should the window frame be used to close the wall cavity, for that will allow cold outside air to circumvent the thermal break.

detail E8

CLADDING   METAL

PANEL WALL   CONCRETE BLOCK

STRUCTURAL FRAME   STEEL

Series F: Metal Cladding, Metal Backup

In Series "F" the air barrier is provided by the interior metal liner on the panels. Where this skin extends beyond the heated part of the building, for instance at the parapet, this metal liner becomes a serious heat bridge and may chill the metal that is exposed to the interior enough to cause condensation or frost. To reduce this possibility, both sides of the metal liner are insulated where it projects above the roof.

Note that the line of airtightness provided by the panels must be joined to windows, to the roofing, and to the foundation waterproofing with a flexible connection. Considerable care must be taken at the horizontal joints if these joints are to be flexible, airtight, insulated, and drained to the exterior. One joint suggested here is somewhat more elaborate than those proposed by manufacturers but does provide the required qualities.

As mentioned in some of the notes, it will be difficult to predict the length of time that baked enamel will maintain a presentable appearance. Look at the automobiles in any area.

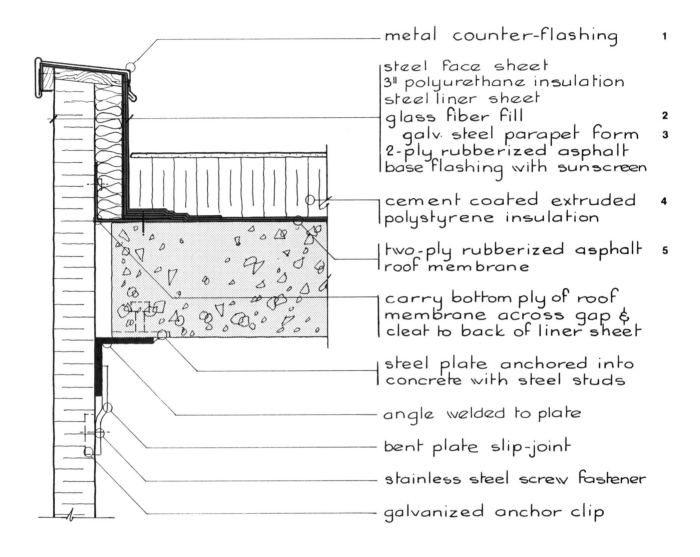

metal counter-flashing   1

steel face sheet
3" polyurethane insulation
steel liner sheet
glass fiber fill   2
 galv. steel parapet form   3
2-ply rubberized asphalt
base flashing with sunscreen

cement coated extruded   4
polystyrene insulation

two-ply rubberized asphalt   5
roof membrane

carry bottom ply of roof
membrane across gap &
cleat to back of liner sheet

steel plate anchored into
concrete with steel studs

angle welded to plate

bent plate slip-joint

stainless steel screw fastener

galvanized anchor clip

1 This metal counterflashing (7.4.2) can be of the same prefinished material as the face sheet, or it can be monel or stainless steel. Copper may stain a light-coloured building. It is held front and back with clips. Make sure there is a good slope towards the roof.

2 The base flashing is two plies of rubberized asphalt, the top ply includes a sunscreen. Note that one ply is carried over the top of the coping. Throughout most of the building the liner sheet is exposed to the inside air which may be quite humid. This causes no problems because the liner sheet is warm. Here, however, it is outside the heated part of the building where it may become cold enough to cause condensation. Two steps are taken to prevent this. First is an air barrier membrane to keep warm inside air away from the coldest part of the liner sheet. Second is the glass fiber insulation that reduces the area of the liner sheet that is exposed to the cold.

3 The galvanized steel parapet form is fastened to the concrete deck through the air barrier membrane mentioned above.

4 Because polystyrene foam insulation floats so readily, it is normal practice to hold it in place with gravel ballast, paving stones or earth. Dow Chemical Company, the holders of the patent on these IRMA roofs and the manufacturers of Roofmate which is shown in all of these roof details, offer this cement-coated insulation with tongue and groove edges. The insulation may float if the roof floods, but the tongue and groove joint is intended to hold it in place. The cement coating protects it from sunlight and mechanical damage. (6.3.2)

5 The preferred roofing, two-ply rubberized asphalt, is interleaved with two flashing plies. The outer ply must have a metallic or mineral surface to protect the counterflashing from sunlight. Do not carry the metal counterflashing down to protect the base flashing; the fastenings will puncture the membranes. (7.4.8)

detail F**1**

CLADDING **METAL**

PANEL WALL **METAL**

STRUCTURAL FRAME **CONCRETE**

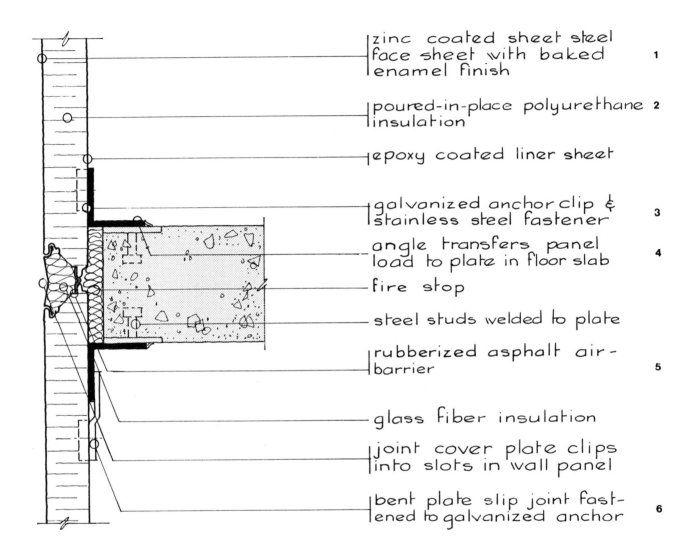

zinc coated sheet steel
face sheet with baked   1
enamel finish

poured-in-place polyurethane   2
insulation

epoxy coated liner sheet

galvanized anchor clip &
stainless steel fastener   3

angle transfers panel
load to plate in floor slab   4

fire stop

steel studs welded to plate

rubberized asphalt air-
barrier   5

glass fiber insulation

joint cover plate clips
into slots in wall panel

bent plate slip joint fastened to galvanized anchor   6

1 Most of the construction detailed in this book is designed to have a very long life, perhaps 100 years. The painted finish on this metal is not likely to last over 20 years. Theoretically it could be repainted, perhaps with a coating not yet invented. To date, field painting has neither the fine appearance nor lasting qualities of factory application and baking.

2 Three inches (75mm) of partly aged polyurethane has a thermal resistance of approximately R 19 (Rsi 3.33). However in many applications, polyurethane has displayed a fairly rapid loss of this high resistance. Where the insulation is protected on two sides with metal sheets, as it is here, any deterioration will be extremely slow. At the worst, the 3" fully aged urethane insulation will have a resistance of R 12 (Rsi 2.1). (CBD 149)

3 The panels are held in place by power driven stainless steel screw fasteners driven through a special galvanized steel anchor clip set in the inner tongue of the side joints. (See manufacturers' catalogues.)

4 Since these angles are within the building and relatively free from corrosive forces, they can be carefully aligned, then welded in position to plates anchored into the concrete floor slab. The anchors for the plates shown here are the steel studs used in composite construction. The advantage of using these studs is that their holding capacity is well known.

5 This joint is not manufactured. It is shown here to show the potential of this system. As drawn, it shows one manufacturer's (Robertson) edge detail with one edge reversed so that it is possible to have a flexible repairable air barrier between the panels. The air barrier is insulated and protected by a rainscreen.

6 The panels are supported from the bottom, so they need only horizontal support at the top. This slip joint provides that support and allows the panel to expand and contract in length.

detail F**2**

CLADDING **METAL**

PANEL WALL **METAL**

STRUCTURAL FRAME **CONCRETE**

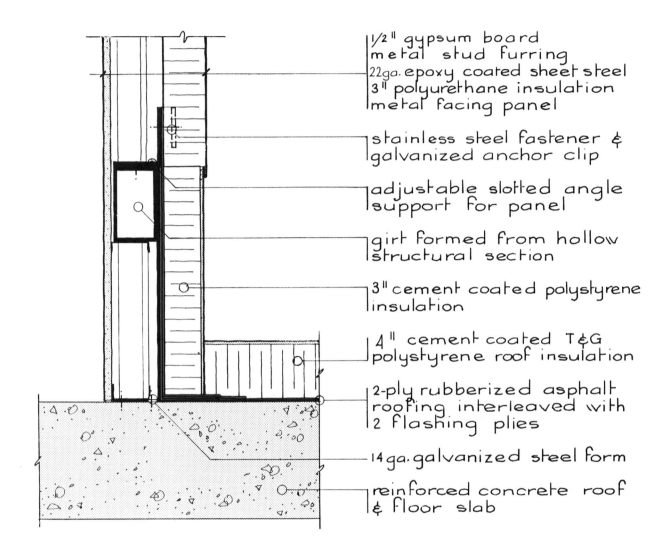

1/2" gypsum board
metal stud furring
22ga. epoxy coated sheet steel
3" polyurethane insulation
metal facing panel

stainless steel fastener &
galvanized anchor clip

adjustable slotted angle
support for panel

girt formed from hollow
structural section

3" cement coated polystyrene
insulation

4" cement coated T&G
polystyrene roof insulation

2-ply rubberized asphalt
roofing interleaved with
2 flashing plies

14ga. galvanized steel form

reinforced concrete roof
& floor slab

This detail shows a wall rising above a roof, as it might in a hospital where the first few floors have a larger area than the nursing tower. It also occurs in many manufacturing buildings where the plant is higher than the office area. The detail for steel construction will be identical except for the floor and roof deck support. See Detail D6.

1 This detail shows a gypsum board finish on metal stud furring. This finish may not be necessary. Other widths of stud may be used, depending on the unsupported height of the studs.

2 This power driven stainless steel screw and the galvanized clip that fits into the double tongue and groove vertical joint are the fittings used in Robertson Building Systems. Other manufacturers may use a slightly different system.

3 It will be painfully obvious if the precisely manufactured wall panels are not installed true-to-line. This angle is adjustable so that the panels can be supported flush and true-to-line in spite of building inaccuracies.(CBD 171)

Don't take the prefabricated wall down to the roof deck where it may be immersed in water. This girt supports the joint between the upper prefabricated metal wall and a curb arrangement.(7.4.8, 7.4.3) The support adds to the thickness of the wall, so it should be kept to a minimum.

4 This insulation keeps the air barrier warm to avoid condensation. It also reduces heat flow.(1.5.1, 1.7) Cement coating provides a suitable finish and protects the insulation against mechanical damage and sunlight.

5 Since no ballast is provided, this roof insulation depends on tongue and groove joints to hold it in place should roof flooding cause the insulation to float. (6.3.2)

6 This heavy-gauge galvanized sheet metal curb supports the base flashing. The bottom is fastened to the concrete slab, the top to the hollow structural girt. (7.4.8)

CLADDING
METAL

PANEL WALL
METAL

STRUCTURAL FRAME
STRUCTURAL STEEL,
CONCRETE

detail F3

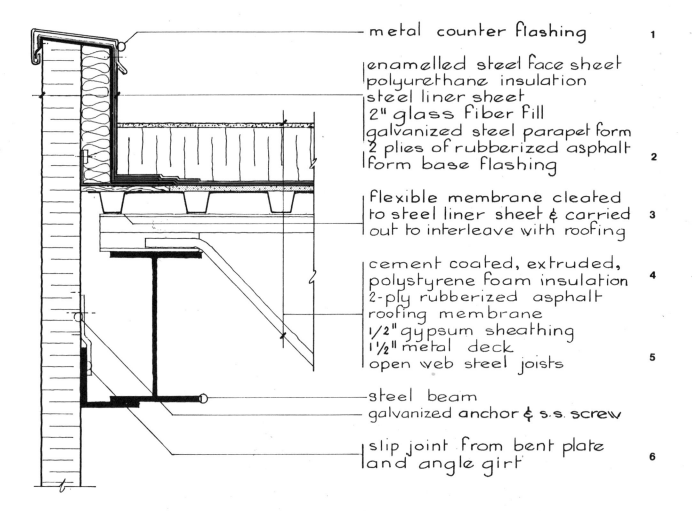

metal counter flashing   1

enamelled steel face sheet
polyurethane insulation
steel liner sheet
2" glass fiber fill
galvanized steel parapet form
2 plies of rubberized asphalt
form base flashing   2

flexible membrane cleated
to steel liner sheet & carried   3
out to interleave with roofing

cement coated, extruded,
polystyrene foam insulation   4
2-ply rubberized asphalt
roofing membrane
1/2" gypsum sheathing
1 1/2" metal deck
open web steel joists   5

steel beam
galvanized anchor & s.s. screw

slip joint from bent plate   6
and angle girt

1 Note that the waterproof part of this coping assembly (7.4.1) is the layer of rubberized asphalt that runs from the roof membrane up the steel parapet form, out over the coping, to turn down the outside face. The metal counterflashing is a decorative sunscreen for the membrane. It also provides protection from mechanical damage that may be caused by ladders, etc. It can be any non-corrosive metal except copper, which may stain the face of the building. Another way of capping this little parapet is shown in Detail F1.

2 Two base flashing plies are shown here interleaved with the two plies of the roofing membrane. This is in accordance with the recommendations of Soprema S.A., one of the principal manufacturers of polyester reinforced modified asphalt membranes. (7.4.8)

3 If it weren't for this membrane, warm moist air from inside the building could reach the cooler parapet area where it would condense and freeze.

4 The waterproof polystyrene roof insulation is shown here without a ballast to hold it down against roof flooding. The cement-coated insulation boards shown here are manufactured with tightly fitting tongue and groove edges. Should the boards float, the tongues and grooves hold the assembly together, so that it can settle back into place when the water drains away. The cement coating protects the plastic insulation from sunlight and from mechanical damage.

5 This light steel roof assembly is widely used. Its flexibility under load and the camber built into the open web steel joists cause irregularities in the plane of the roof where water may pond, sometimes to a dangerous extent. For that reason, a good slope to drains, 1:50 or more, must be built into the roof structure. (CBD 151)

6 Because the panels are supported at their lower edge, they require only horizontal support here. This is provided by the slip joint fashioned from a bent plate and angle. The slip joint will tolerate construction inaccuracies, as well as deflection in the steel deck.

CLADDING
METAL

PANEL WALL
METAL

STRUCTURAL FRAME
STRUCTURAL STEEL

detail F**4**

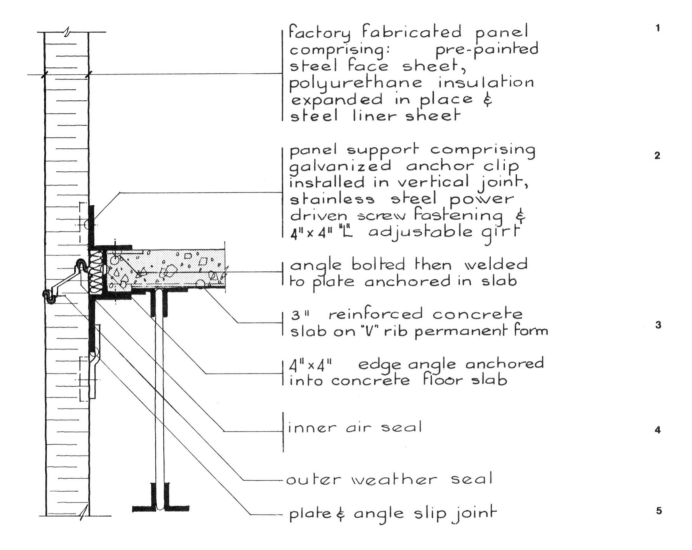

1   factory fabricated panel comprising: pre-painted steel face sheet, polyurethane insulation expanded in place & steel liner sheet

2   panel support comprising galvanized anchor clip installed in vertical joint, stainless steel power driven screw fastening & 4"x 4" "L" adjustable girt

angle bolted then welded to plate anchored in slab

3   3" reinforced concrete slab on "V" rib permanent form

4"x4"   edge angle anchored into concrete floor slab

4   inner air seal

outer weather seal

5   plate & angle slip joint

1 | This panel is faced with zinc-coated steel and finished with baked enamel. There is no reason, except first cost, why the face sheet cannot be formed from a non-corrosive metal such as bronze or stainless steel. Partly aged 3" (75mm) polyurethane insulation has a thermal resistance of R 19 (Rsi 3.29). (1.4.2) When the resistance of the inside and outside still air layers are added, the thermal resistance of the wall is R 20 (Rsi 3.46). The resistance remains high because there is no metal to metal contact between the face and liner panels.

2 | The weight of the panel is transferred to the floor structure by this assembly. The slip joint at the top of the panel holds the panels in place against horizontal wind and earthquake loads.

3 | This light-weight floor construction imposes a relatively light load on the foundations, a significant advantage in multi-storey buildings, particularly where the bearing value of the soil is low. The steel joists are usually built with excessive camber and the whole assembly is quite springy and subject to sizable deflections. These deflections must not exceed the movement capacity of the panel system and its seals. Usually, in multi-storey buildings, the steel structure will require fireproofing.

4 | This is one manufacturer's horizontal jointing system. The only problem is repairing the inner air seal if it develops leaks due to aging or deflection, or if it is not installed perfectly to begin with. A design (not manufactured) that would allow repair is suggested in Detail F1.

5 | The panel fastenings can be adjusted to accommodate construction inaccuracies. The gap between the panels and the slip joint at the lower angle allows the floor assembly to deflect without loading the bottom panel.

Note the fire stop between the edge of the slab and the back of the panels.

CLADDING
METAL

PANEL WALL
METAL

STRUCTURAL FRAME
STRUCTURAL STEEL

detail F5

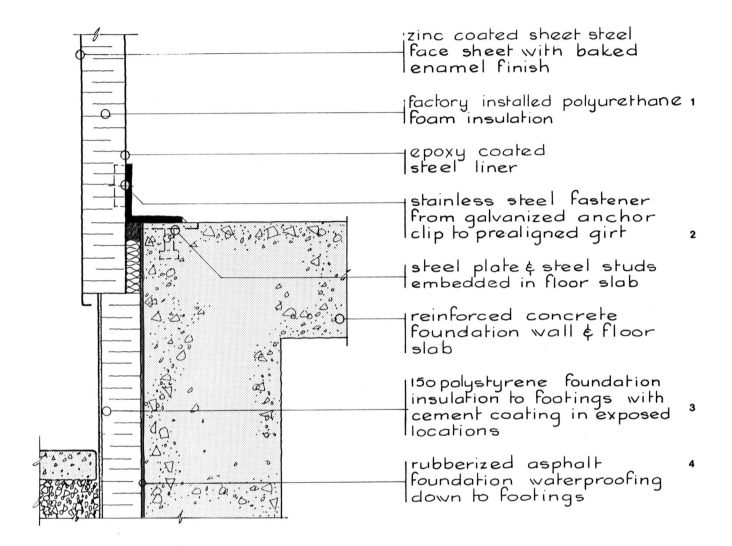

zinc coated sheet steel
face sheet with baked
enamel finish

factory installed polyurethane 1
foam insulation

epoxy coated
steel liner

stainless steel fastener
from galvanized anchor
clip to prealigned girt   2

steel plate & steel studs
embedded in floor slab

reinforced concrete
foundation wall & floor
slab

150 polystyrene foundation
insulation to footings with
cement coating in exposed   3
locations

rubberized asphalt   4
foundation waterproofing
down to footings

1 Although polyurethane has a lower co-efficient of expansion than most plastics, it is 3½ times that of steel. One might be concerned that differential expansion and contraction might shear the expanded polyurethane insulation away from the metal face panels. However, the bond seems to test very well.

2 The 4" (101.6mm) angle can be adjusted before fastening to overcome inaccuracies in the linearity of the edge of the foundation wall.(CBD 171) Similarly, the panel and its anchor clip can be adjusted for height before the stainless steel screw is driven into the angle. The manufacturer's assistance should be sought in the design of the supports and connections, which must be designed by a professional engineer.

3 Cement-coated polystyrene insulation is intended for unballasted roofs.(6.3.2) Here it should provide the necessary protection from sunlight, children, snow shovels and lawn mowers. Lawn mowing close to the building is made easier by a perimeter row of concrete pavers. In its most exposed location between grade and the wall panels, this insulation will give the foundation wall a thermal resistance of R 18 (Rsi 3.2).(NRCC 22432) Below grade, the resistance of the earth can be added.

4 This foundation waterproofing is part of a line of airtightness and watertightness that surrounds the building. Note that this line is transferred to the steel liner sheet by a strip of asphalt impregnated foam. Pay special attention to the joints in the panels.

detail F7

CLADDING
METAL

PANEL WALL
METAL

STRUCTURAL FRAME
CONCRETE
OR STEEL

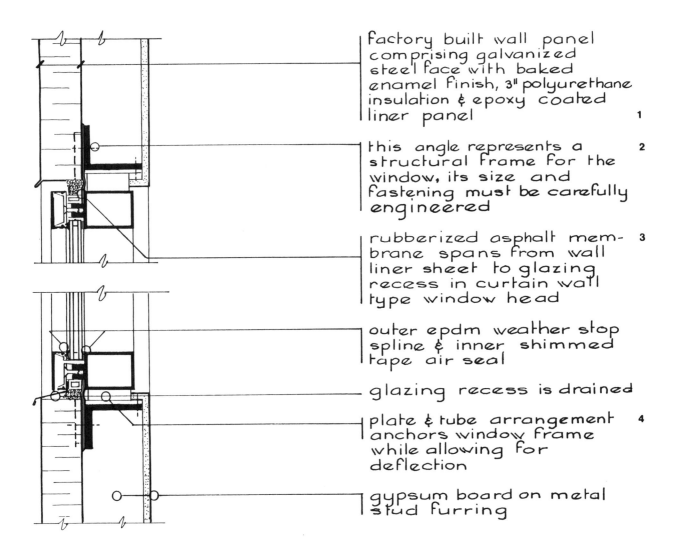

factory built wall panel
comprising galvanized
steel face with baked
enamel finish, 3" polyurethane
insulation & epoxy coated
liner panel   1

this angle represents a   2
structural frame for the
window, its size and
fastening must be carefully
engineered

rubberized asphalt mem-   3
brane spans from wall
liner sheet to glazing
recess in curtain wall
type window head

outer epdm weather stop
spline & inner shimmed
tape air seal

glazing recess is drained

plate & tube arrangement   4
anchors window frame
while allowing for
deflection

gypsum board on metal
stud furring

1 | The backs of these factory-built wall panels are quite smooth and true-to-line but, because of the fastenings, are seldom left exposed. It would be quite possible to cover the area beneath the window sill with a continuous convector cabinet as has been done in details E7 and H7. In this detail, the inside finish is $\frac{1}{2}$" (12.7mm) gypsum board on metal studs. The space behind the gypsum board can be used as a wiring chase or even for water piping, since both the air barrier (Chapter 2) and the insulation are outboard of this space.

2 | Manufacturers provide stainless steel screws fastening into galvanized screw anchors that fit in the vertical panel joints.

3 | It is important to make an airtight connection between the liner sheet, which forms the air barrier in the panel, and the line of airtightness in the window frame.(Chapter 2)   When the window is aligned as it is here, this is remarkably simple. One edge of a strip of rubberized asphalt is adhered to the liner sheet, the other edge is clamped into the frame behind non-conductive blocking. (5.3)   Note that insulation is continuous over this extension of the air barrier.

4 | To allow for deflection, the anchors shown here are comprised of plates welded to the end of aluminum tubes. The tubes are a sliding fit into the tops and bottoms of the vertical mullions. In this case, the plates are bolted to the angle frame around the window opening. Where there is no danger of deflection, there is little reason why the window cannot be shimmed and fastened directly to the frame around the opening.

No jamb detail is shown, as it will be nearly identical to the head, except that the little drip will not be needed.

detail F8

CLADDING
METAL

PANEL WALL
METAL

STRUCTURAL FRAME
CONCRETE OR STEEL

Series G: Glass and Metal Curtain Wall

Series "G" shows how curtain wall construction can be detailed following the "rules" developed in the Prolegomenon. Since the components have been designed and manufactured to observe these same rules, the manufacturers' brochures usually show satisfactory arrangements. Several window profiles are shown to illustrate how various manufacturers resolve design and manufacturing requirements. Note particularly the sections used in glass roofs.

Most problems arise where the curtain wall joins other construction. In such locations the "rules" developed in the Prolegomenon must be scrupulously observed. Workable solutions to such intersections are shown in these details.

In the details shown, the air barrier can be carried quite readily from the window frames to the adjacent roof or wall. However at head and sill, the nosing of the extrusions must be trimmed to allow the rubberized asphalt to run continuously. An isometric of this condition is shown in Detail H3.

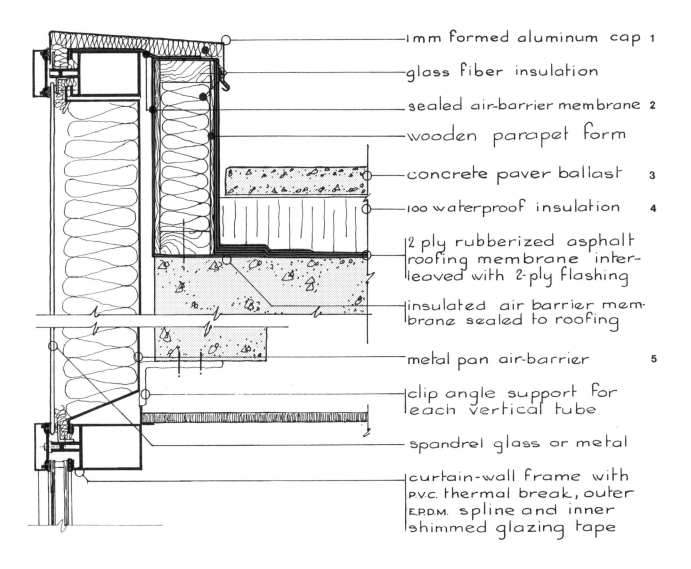

1mm formed aluminum cap 1

glass fiber insulation

sealed air-barrier membrane 2

wooden parapet form

concrete paver ballast 3

100 waterproof insulation 4

2 ply rubberized asphalt roofing membrane inter-leaved with 2-ply flashing

insulated air barrier mem-brane sealed to roofing

metal pan air-barrier 5

clip angle support for each vertical tube

spandrel glass or metal

curtain-wall frame with p.v.c. thermal break, outer E.P.D.M. spline and inner shimmed glazing tape

This unusual junction demands some preliminary explanation. If the junction of wall and roof is to fulfill the requirements laid down in the Prolegomenon, an insulated air barrier must run continuously from wall to roof. What is more, it must be flexible at junctions where movement may occur, and the appearance of the wall must be consistent throughout.

1 This aluminum cap serves as a rainscreen(Chapter 3) for the parapet. It serves the same purpose as the spandrel glass or metal on the face panels.

2 This sealed membrane joins the rubberized asphalt base flashing to the uppermost horizontal curtain wall frame section. The flexible membrane air barrier (Chapter 2) is kept above the dew point by the layer of glass fiber insulation that follows it beneath the metal cap and within the wooden parapet form.(1.5.1) Metal pans form the air barrier down the face of the building.

3 This is a fairly straightforward protected membrane assembly. The ballast in this case is provided by concrete pavers which must weigh 20 lb/ft^2 (108 Kg/m^2). There is some validity to the view that there should be a ventilation space between the insulation and the pavers.(6.3.2) If the bottoms of the pavers are deeply textured, this purpose will be served. Alternatively a ventilation space can be provided by raising the pavers off the insulation on $\frac{1}{4}$" (6mm) shims cut from insulation boards. Since the material has a compressive strength of 30 lb/in^2 (210 KPa), several strips per paver will be adequate.

4 With a 4" (200mm) concrete slab, the roof asembly has a thermal resistance of R 22 or Rsi 3.81 (1.7.1), not counting the ceiling assembly.

5 The insulated wall assembly is comprised of the metal pans, which provide the air barrier. They are sealed into the curtain wall frames with shimmed glazing tape. These metal pan air barriers are insulated with glass fiber insulation fitted tightly to the metal pans.(NRCC B.P.N.37) With 4" (100mm) of insulation this wall will have a thermal resistance of approximately R 18 (Rsi 3.18). The actual thermal resistance will be affected by the frame spacing. The exposed surface panels are usually coloured glass or anodized aluminum, although stainless steel or bronze are used in more expensive installations.

CLADDING
GLASS and METAL
CURTAIN WALL

STRUCTURAL FRAME
CONCRETE

detail G1

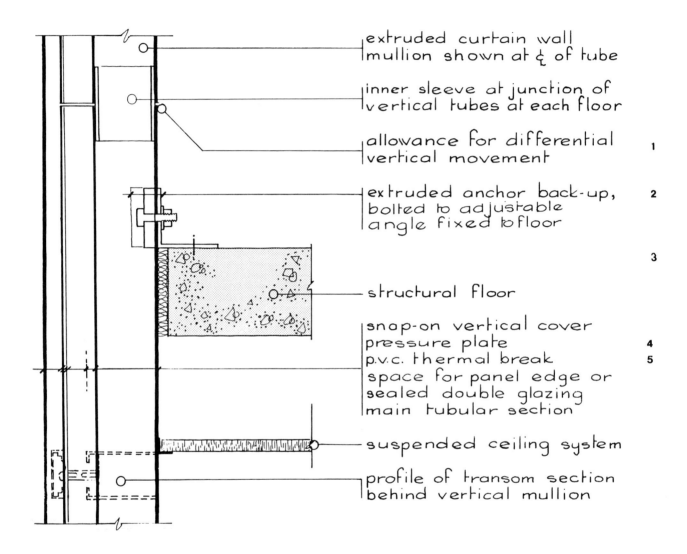

extruded curtain wall
mullion shown at ₵ of tube

inner sleeve at junction of
vertical tubes at each floor

allowance for differential   1
vertical movement

extruded anchor back-up,   2
bolted to adjustable
angle fixed to floor

                                  3

structural floor

snap-on vertical cover
pressure plate   4
p.v.c. thermal break   5
space for panel edge or
sealed double glazing
main tubular section

suspended ceiling system

profile of transom section
behind vertical mullion

This drawing shows a section at the center line of a vertical mullion in an extruded aluminum so-called curtain wall section. This makes the interior of the slip joint visible, as well as the extruded anchor backup.

1 | The vertical curtain wall sections run from floor to floor. If both ends were fastened directly to the floor slabs, undue stress would be placed on the curtain wall sections when the floor slabs deflect, particularly when the deflection is large and permanent, as it is when plastic creep occurs.(CBD 125) By fastening only the top end of the tube to the floor and then arranging this slip joint to retain the lower end of the tube above, independent movement at each floor can be accommodated. This arrangement also accommodates expansion and contraction of the tubular sections caused by temperature change.

2 | Wind forces on a considerable area of the building face are brought to the vertical tubular section and then transferred to the building structure through this bolted connection. These fittings distribute this large and fluctuating load over a safe area of the tubular section.

3 | Because the concrete floor slab is seldom where it should be(CBD 171), the curtain wall frame support must be adjustable. Drilling the frame as needed will accommodate vertical inaccuracies. Horizontal adjustment is readily achieved by the placement of the bolt anchor in the concrete floor slab.

4 | For good performance, it is essential that the pressure plate, which is also shown in Figure 5-7 (5.5), be drawn up tightly with a screw adjustment. In poor frames, pressure is applied simply by forcing a gasket between the stop and the glass.

5 | Tests have shown that these otherwise excellent frames often suffer from poor thermal breaks. As a result, the inner parts of the frame are colder than one would wish. This is a serious disadvantage when high humidities are carried within the building. Frames for critical conditions should be tested.(Chapter 5)

CLADDING
GLASS and METAL
CURTAIN WALL

STRUCTURAL FRAME
CONCRETE

detail G2

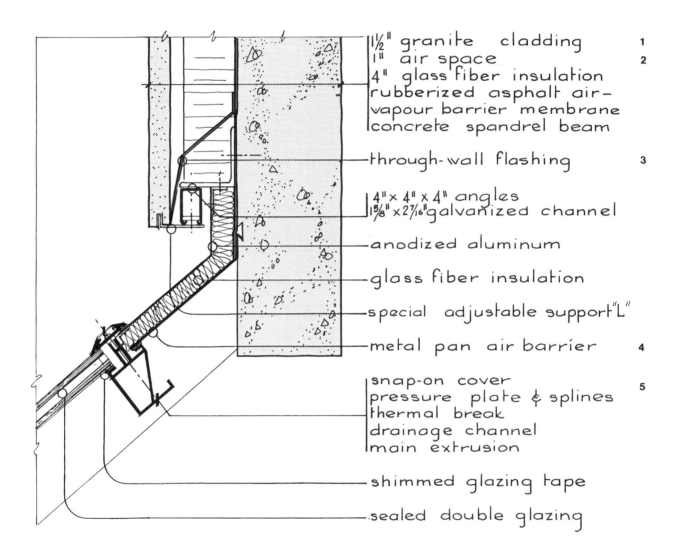

1½" granite   cladding   1
1" air space   2
4" glass fiber insulation
rubberized asphalt air-
vapour barrier membrane
concrete spandrel beam

through-wall flashing   3

4" x 4" x 4" angles
1⅝" x 2⁷⁄₁₆" galvanized channel

anodized aluminum

glass fiber insulation

special adjustable support "L"

metal pan air barrier   4

snap-on cover   5
pressure plate & splines
thermal break
drainage channel
main extrusion

shimmed glazing tape

sealed double glazing

1 | This drawing details the junction of a sloping glass roof and a vertical insulated wall. The key to success is continuity of the air barrier, which is achieved here by lapping and sealing the membrane air barrier over the edge of the pan.

2 | The top and bottom edges of the granite cladding are grooved to receive supporting angles at this bottom edge and "T"s at other joints. In some installations the joints between the stones are caulked. There is no benefit to such caulking.(3.4.1) These supports should be engineered carefully for, with only a little deflection, the angles or T's will act like a can opener and break off the lips on the stone.

3 | The 1" (25mm) air space should be considered a minimum. It is quite adequate to provide a path for water until it is led out of the wall, but in some buildings inaccuracies in construction(CBD 171) have closed that space and have even required the insulation to be trimmed so that the granite cladding could be installed.

4 | In many cases through-wall flashing is not required at the bottom of a wall such as this.(7.4.11) Here however the curtain wall panel is open at the top and must be protected against water descending in the wall cavity.

5 | Insulated metal pans are a standard method of achieving an insulated air barrier in the opaque parts of a curtain wall installation.(NRCC B.P.N.37) Here they have been specially formed to fit this junction and to allow the first horizontal frame member to sit clear of the granite wall. Note that a similar arrangement is required at the jambs.

6 | Here the horizontal member is fitted with a pressure plate and a snap-on cover. A system of drainage paths provide drainage in and through these special sections. Manufacturers have several methods of doing this.(Figure 5-7, 5.5)

CLADDING
GLASS and METAL
CURTAIN WALL

STRUCTURAL FRAME
CONCRETE

detail G3

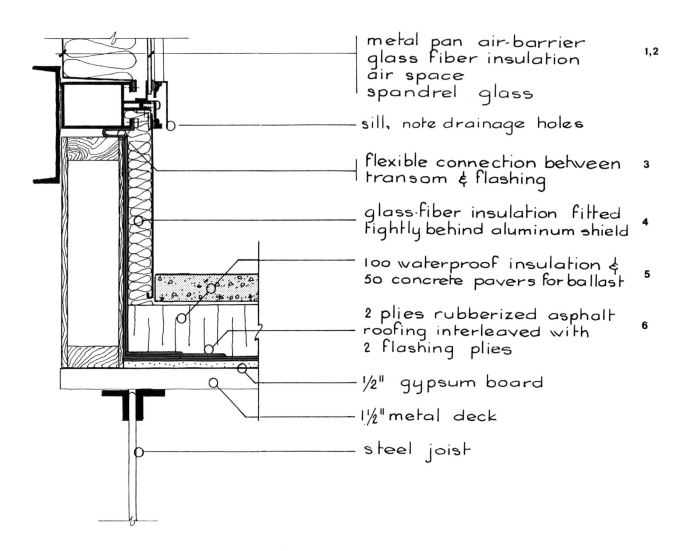

metal pan air-barrier
glass fiber insulation
air space
spandrel glass   1,2

sill, note drainage holes

flexible connection between   3
transom & flashing

glass-fiber insulation fitted   4
tightly behind aluminum shield

100 waterproof insulation &   5
50 concrete pavers for ballast

2 plies rubberized asphalt
roofing interleaved with   6
2 flashing plies

½" gypsum board

1½" metal deck

steel joist

1 In some installations this opaque insulated wall panel is replaced by a window. (Figure 5-6, Chapter 5) In such cases, the supporting channel would be moved to a less conspicuous position.

2 This drawing details a roof/wall connection where the wall, rising above the roof, is supported by the channel independently of the roof structure. As a result, the wall and roof can move indepently(Prolegomenon), requiring a flexible section of insulated air barrier membrane between the two. This junction can be quite deceptive, for frequently the wall and roof will share the same structural system. However, independent movement will occur at mid span of the roof joists when snow loads are imposed. Such deflections can be quite large; 3/4" (20mm) is not uncommon.

3 The flexible connection is made from reinforced rubberized asphalt clamped into the curtain wall frame at the top and welded to the base flashing at the top of the curb.(4.6)

4 If condensation is to be avoided, the flexible air barrier must be kept warm.(1.1)   That is achieved with a layer of flexible insulation in close contact with its outside face. Glass fiber cavity wall insulation has the resilience to expand and contract as the roof rises and falls.

5 This is a straightforward protected membrane roof, except that, in this detail, the ballast for the insulation is provided by concrete pavers rather than crushed stone or gravel. Note the ventilation space between the insulation and the pavers. Shims of insulation board, $\frac{1}{4}$" (6mm) thick, are used.(6.3.2)   This flashing is supported by a pressure-treated wood curb. Power-driven studs can be used to secure the blocking piece to the metal deck.

6 With rubberized asphalt roofing, the cant strip is not required to ease the turn in the membranes. A heavy gauge, galvanized bent plate could replace this wooden assembly.(7.4.3)

CLADDING **GLASS and METAL CURTAIN WALL**

STRUCTURAL FRAME **STEEL**

detail G4

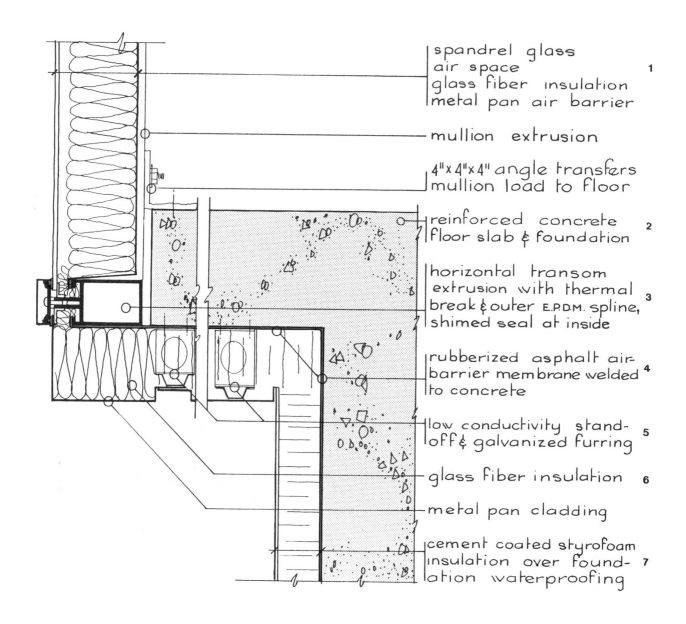

spandrel glass
air space
glass fiber insulation
metal pan air barrier   1

mullion extrusion

4"x 4"x 4" angle transfers
mullion load to floor

reinforced concrete
floor slab & foundation   2

horizontal transom
extrusion with thermal
break & outer E.P.D.M. spline,   3
shimed seal at inside

rubberized asphalt air-
barrier membrane welded   4
to concrete

low conductivity stand-
off & galvanized furring   5

glass fiber insulation   6

metal pan cladding

cement coated styrofoam
insulation over found-   7
ation waterproofing

1 The arrangement of these extruded.aluminum frames is governed by the designer's preference and by the bay size of the structure. In opaque parts of the wall, this grid is filled with the wall panels as detailed here. Metal pans of the required depth are formed to fit into the glazing rebates. They are insulated, usually with glass fiber insulation. (NRCC B.P.N.37)

2 In this detail the floor slab and the wall that it supports are cantilevered beyond the face of the foundation wall. The cantilever is not essential and is included only to show a solution for such common but difficult intersections. It must follow the rules laid down in the Prolegomenon.

3 Because the pans serve as the air barrier, they are carefully sealed into the framing members. A rainscreen is provided by the face panel, in this case a special glass made for the purpose. It is sealed to the frame with a glazing spline usually made of E.P.D.M. Because some water may penetrate the outer spline, the glazing rebate is drained to the outside.(Figure 5-6, Chapter 5)

4 The most important factor in the continuity of the wall is the air barrier. (Chapter 2) Here one end of it is clamped to the sill; the other is welded to the foundation waterproofing. Note that the membrane is flexible where movement may occur. (Prolegomenon Rule 3)

5 Over the insulation, the soffit is clad with aluminum panels bolted to furring channels, which are supported at intervals by these short Z section stand-offs. The stand-offs are perforated as shown to reduce the area of metal conducting heat through the insulation.(1.5.3)

6 As has been mentioned many times in other details, insulate the air barrier to keep it above the dew point of the air inside the building.(1.5.2) The insulation also reduces heat flow through the building envelope.

7 The cement coat in this extruded polystyrene insulation will protect it from sunlight and mechanical damage.(6.3.2)

CLADDING
GLASS and METAL CURTAIN WALL

STRUCTURAL FRAME
CONCRETE OR STEEL

detail **G5**

Series H: Miscellaneous Assemblies

These miscellaneous details are included to clarify a number of issues. Detail H1 shows an adjustable precast concrete cap over an insulated cast-in-place concrete parapet. Much of the membrane is probably superfluous, but it does show the line of airtightness that must be maintained. This design increases the area that is losing heat by a factor of 4 or 5. In some cases it will be many times that figure.

Detail H2 suggests that strong, well connected precast concrete panels over long strips of window may be used to support parts of the wall.

Detail H3 shows how parts of curtain wall window frames must be coped to allow the air barrier to be connected without interruption.

Detail H4 enlarges the proposed connection between metal panels and structure that may not be true-to-line or may deflect or creep. Caulking will not provide adequate airtightness.

H5 shows how a single lift of precast may be fastened.

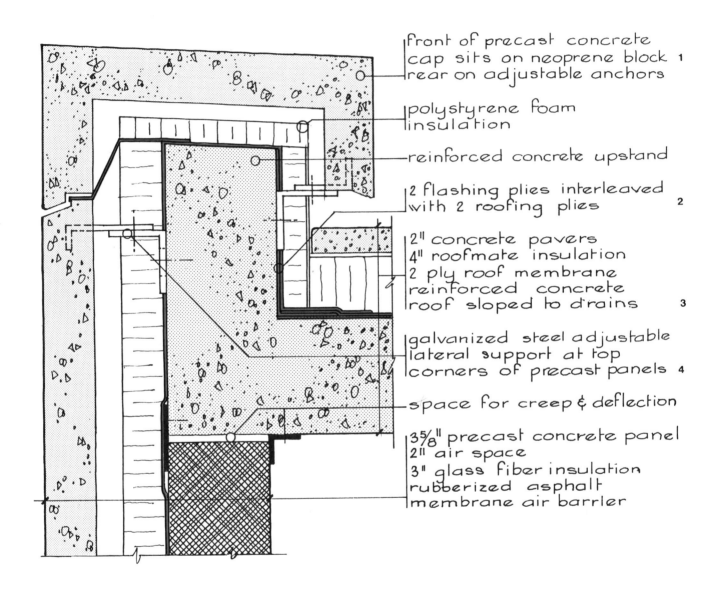

front of precast concrete
cap sits on neoprene block 1
rear on adjustable anchors

polystyrene foam
insulation

reinforced concrete upstand

2 flashing plies interleaved
with 2 roofing plies   2

2" concrete pavers
4" roofmate insulation
2 ply roof membrane
reinforced concrete
roof sloped to drains   3

galvanized steel adjustable
lateral support at top
corners of precast panels 4

space for creep & deflection

3⅝" precast concrete panel
2" air space
3" glass fiber insulation
rubberized asphalt
membrane air barrier

1 Although water is unwanted in any wall, it is not so damaging to the precast concrete in this wall as it would be to brick masonry cladding. This tolerance for water makes it possible to have a coping that may not be completely watertight. Rather than caulking the cross joints, the rain deflector shown in Fig.3-6. Chapter 3 should be used. Here, the precast concrete coping is positioned by the adjustable galvanized anchors on the roof side. The other side is supported by neoprene blocks in the joint.

2 Roofing manufacturers, such as Soprema and Bakelite, recommend this interleaved flashing system with no cant strip. The material is welded to the concrete with propane torches. See manufacturers' manuals. Other roofing and flashing systems are described in Chapters 6 and 7. Concrete is such a good air barrier that it should be necessary to seal only the cracks and joints. However, under field conditions it may be more practical to join roof and wall with a continuous membrane, as shown here.

3 The roof slab is sloped 1:50 to the roof drains. The top of the slab should be sloped, since low-strength light-weight toppings have not performed well in some locations. The protected membrane system is described in Chapter 6, in Dow brochures, in Sweets Catalogue and in CBD 150.

4 The precast panels are supported at the centre of their lower edges. These top brackets resist horizontal wind loads and earthquake loads from any horizontal direction. To preserve the galvanizing, they must not be welded in the field. They must be positioned high enough to be bolted with the panel in place.

detail H1

CLADDING PRECAST

PANEL WALL CONCRETE BLOCK

STRUCTURAL FRAME CONCRETE

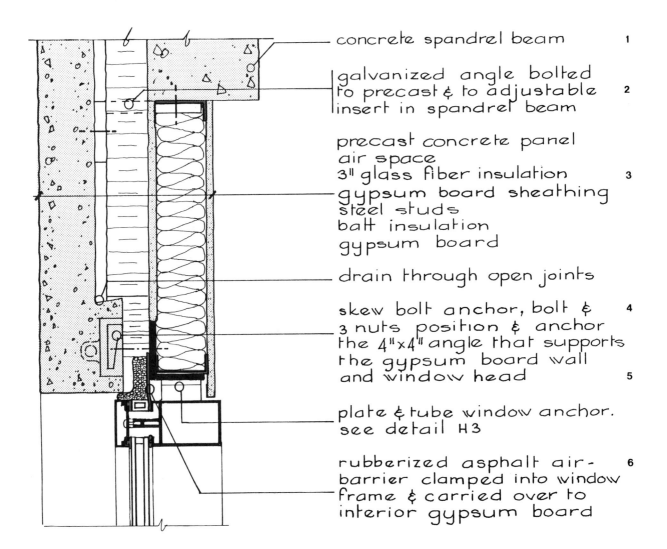

concrete spandrel beam   1

galvanized angle bolted
to precast & to adjustable   2
insert in spandrel beam

precast concrete panel
air space
3" glass fiber insulation   3
gypsum board sheathing
steel studs
batt insulation
gypsum board

drain through open joints

skew bolt anchor, bolt &   4
3 nuts position & anchor
the 4"x4" angle that supports
the gypsum board wall
and window head   5

plate & tube window anchor.
see detail H3

rubberized asphalt air-   6
barrier clamped into window
frame & carried over to
interior gypsum board

1. Where windows run for long distances horizontally, it would be ideal if a spandrel beam extended down to the window head. However, some buildings may require this infill of metal studs and gypsum board. A similar system may also be used beneath the windows.

2. The precast concrete spandrel panel will be supporting its own weight as well as some of the weight of the metal stud and gypsum board wall. It will also be required to resist the wind load on the building. These fastenings must be designed to resist these loads. They must also resist corrosion in what may be a very damp environment. Use bolted connections, because the hot dipped galvanizing cannot be adequately "touched-up" with zinc-rich paint after welding.

3. This glass fiber insulation is necessary because the metal studs form serious heat bridges through insulation that is placed between them (1.5.3), reducing the thermal resistance of the metal stud assembly to only R 7.6 (Rsi 1.35). Adding the insulating sheathing, 3/4" (20mm) air space and the precast concrete brings the resistance up to R 17.6 (Rsi 3.1). (1.6.1)

4. These skew bolt inserts are anchored into the precast concrete panels at approximately 6 foot (2m) intervals. A galvanized skew bolt supports the angle, described in 5 below, from the precast panel. Two nuts are used to adjust the distance from the panel and to tighten it in place. Another nut secures the bolt to the skew bolt anchor. Have your structural engineer calculate the bolt size and spacing for your building.

5. This slotted angle runs continuously to support the lower runner channel of the metal stud system.

6. This vital link in the air barrier begins where it is clamped into the window frame and runs to the back of the 4" x 4" (100mm x 100mm) angle. It reappears on the other side of the angle where it is carried to the back of the gypsum board. There it is compressed between the gypsum board and the runner channel. Tape joints in the gypsum board panels with self adhering rubberized asphalt membrane. (Chapter 2) Ensure that joints and gaps are sealed in the 4" x 4" angle.

CLADDING **PRECAST**

PANEL WALL **DRYWALL**

STRUCTURAL FRAME **CONCRETE**

detail H2

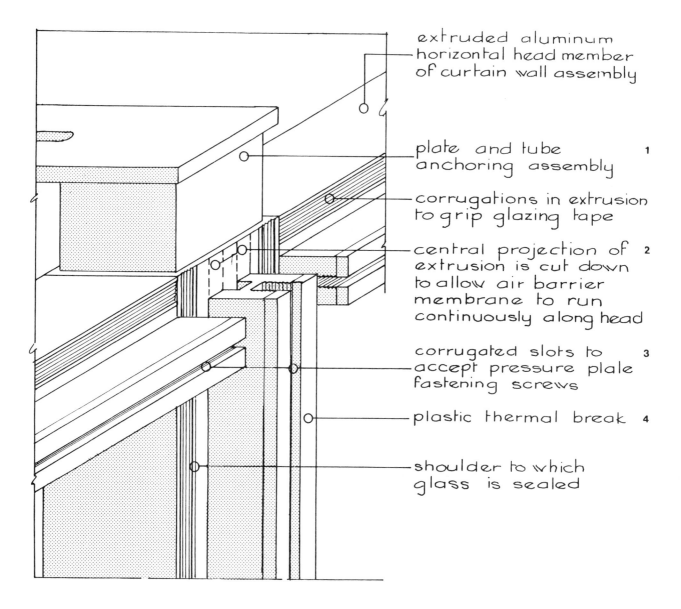

extruded aluminum
horizontal head member
of curtain wall assembly

plate and tube   1
anchoring assembly

corrugations in extrusion
to grip glazing tape

central projection of   2
extrusion is cut down
to allow air barrier
membrane to run
continuously along head

corrugated slots to   3
accept pressure plate
fastening screws

plastic thermal break   4

shoulder to which
glass is sealed

1 | This anchoring assembly is comprised of a tube that fits snugly into the extrusions used for jambs and vertical mullions. The sliding fit allows for deflection and other differential movements. The plate, to which the tube is welded, is bolted to a supporting member at the head or sill of the window. Here, of course, it is bolted at the head.

2 | Many of the window details show a strip of rubberized asphalt running form the window head to the air barrier in the wall above the window. Unless the central projection of the mullion extrusions is cut down as shown here, it will interfere with the continuity of the air barrier membrane. The same method is used at the top and bottom of all jambs and vertical mullions.

3 | These slots in the extrusions will accept a pressure plate screw anywhere along their length.

4 | In some windows these plastic strips are eliminated and an air space breaks the heat bridge between the inside and outside of the frame. Both of these systems allow an undesirable amount of cold outside air to reach the warm part of the frame.

detail H3

ISOMETRIC OF WINDOW FRAME
USED IN CURTAIN WALLS &
RECOMMENDED THROUGHOUT THIS BOOK

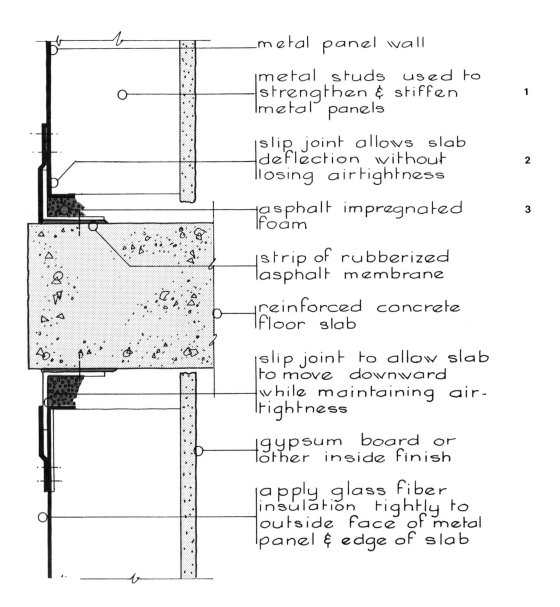

metal panel wall

metal studs used to
strengthen & stiffen   **1**
metal panels

slip joint allows slab
deflection without   **2**
losing airtightness

asphalt impregnated   **3**
foam

strip of rubberized
asphalt membrane

reinforced concrete
floor slab

slip joint to allow slab
to move downward
while maintaining air-
tightness

gypsum board or
other inside finish

apply glass fiber
insulation tightly to
outside face of metal
panel & edge of slab

1 Many important buildings have used metal panel walls caulked, top and bottom, to the structural concrete floor slabs. Thermographic examination invariably shows air leakage at these caulked joints. The leakage is due to plastic creep in the floor slabs.(CBD 125) Such deflections can be several times live load deflections. Irregularities and inaccuracies in construction(CBD 171) also cause signigicant loss of airtightness because it is impossible to design and install adequate surface caulking to seal these Irregularities.(Chapter 4) These slip joints are suggested to overcome these unfortunate failures.

2 Sometimes these metal panels are strengthened and stiffened by bending them in much the same way as fluted metal deck or siding is bent. If the folds are too small, it will be impossible for the insulation to remain in intimate contact with the entire surface of the metal, a very serious defect.(1.5.2.) In this example, metal studs are tack welded to the back of the metal panel walls to provide strength, stiffness and a place to apply the inside finish..

3 The slip joints are made airtight first by sealing the angle to the floor with a gasket. The gasket can be made of glazing tape or a strip of rubberized asphalt. The joint between this angle and the turned in lip of the bottom of the panel is filled with an expanding, asphalt impregnated, foam strip. Once you know the amount of deflection to expect, the foam manufacturer's advice should be sought in selecting the width of the joint.

This detail has been enlarged from those in Series D to show these slip joints more clearly. Floor and roof structures will display elastic deflection, and concrete will deform permanently due to plastic creep. The extent of these deflections must be calculated by a competent engineer, who must then design the thickness, overlap and fastenings of the slip joint elements. The deflections and forces in many instances will be much larger than you think.

STEEL PANEL
JOINT
ENLARGED

detail H4

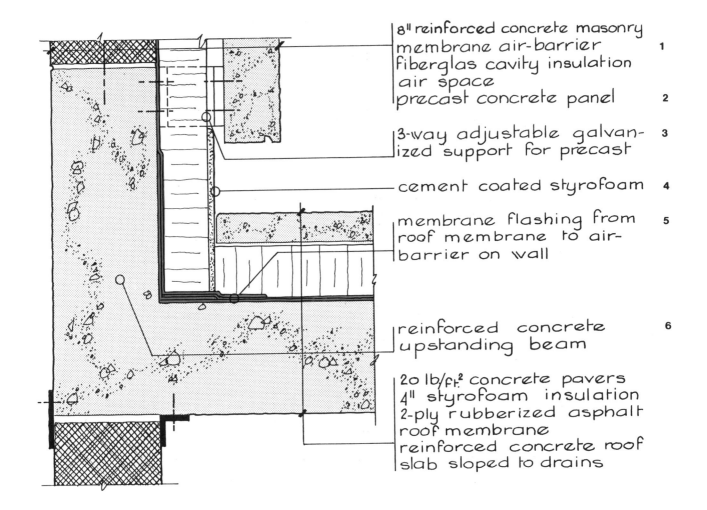

8" reinforced concrete masonry
membrane air-barrier   1
fiberglas cavity insulation
air space
precast concrete panel   2

3-way adjustable galvan-   3
ized support for precast

cement coated styrofoam   4

membrane flashing from   5
roof membrane to air-
barrier on wall

reinforced concrete   6
upstanding beam

20 lb/ft² concrete pavers
4" styrofoam insulation
2-ply rubberized asphalt
roof membrane
reinforced concrete roof
slab sloped to drains

1 | If the concrete block masonry is to have a dependable insulated air barrier, (Chapter 2) it must be applied before the precast concrete cladding is installed. Such a procedure is not very practical on multi-storey buildings where the panels would have to be lowered into place between the swing scaffold and the wall. Not only that, but the fasteners would be concealed by the panels. However in single storey buildings and in this penthouse application, fastening can be achieved from above and below the panels and no scaffolding is necessary.

2 | As in details of other walls that rise above the roof, the cladding is held well clear of the roof, so that the base flashings and air barrier can be properly installed and continuously insulated.

3 | Galvanized angles, approximately 4" x 4" x 4" x 3/4" (100mm x 100mm x 100mm x 20mm) thick, are slotted to allow the adjustment necessary to get the panels flush and plumb.(CBD 171) The 3/4" (20mm) thickness and 3/4" (20mm) bolts are needed because slotted holes in the angles result in a connection that depends on friction rather than the bearing capacity of the bolts.

4 | This strip of insulation requires protection from ultra-violet light and mechanical damage. Cement-coated Roofmate insulation is now available. It is intended for use in non-ballasted protected membrane roofs(6.3.2), but it will work equally well here.

5 | In this detail the roofing membrane and base flashing are shown schematically as a single ply. If the recommended two-ply rubberized asphalt roofing and flashing are used, then two flashing plies are interleaved with two roofing plies. This procedure is described in detail in 7.4.8.

6 | If the precast cladding is to be held clear of the roof deck, then there must be adequate support for the precast panels approximately 16" (400mm) above the roof deck. This upstanding beam is one solution. Another method would be to adequately reinforce the concrete block masonry.

CLADDING **PRECAST**

PANEL WALL **CONCRETE BLOCK**

STRUCTURAL FRAME **CONCRETE**

detail H5

Part 2

The Science
Behind the Details

1

Heat Flow and Insulation

1.1 INTRODUCTION

There are three principal uses for insulation. First, it controls heat flow in and out of the building. The temperature difference across building envelopes is much greater in cold parts of the country so more insulation is needed there. The details in Part 1 show how to get a lot of insulation in the building envelope. In warmer parts of the United States and Canada, some of it can be left out. Section 1.7 will help one decide how much is needed.

Also, insulation is used to keep the air barrier warm enough to prevent condensation, i.e., above the dew point. Although this is of little consequence in areas where the mean daily temperature seldom drops below freezing, it is very important in Canada and in parts of the United States where the winters are cold. The details in Part 1 are designed to make sure the air barrier is warm.

A third use is to improve comfort by keeping the inside wall surfaces moderately warm in winter and moderately cool in summer.

To choose the right kind of insulation and the most effective thickness, a designer should know the following:

- how heat flows and how insulations affect that flow,
- how much difference insulation makes,
- currently available insulations,
- how and where to install them, and
- how much insulation is needed.

1.2 HOW HEAT FLOWS AND HOW INSULATIONS AFFECT THAT FLOW

1.2.1 Conductivity

Temperature is actually a measure of molecular activity in a material; the busier the molecules, the hotter the temperature. If one end of an iron rod is hotter than the other, the more vigorous molecules at the hot end will collide with less vigorous (cooler) molecules and transfer some energy to them. This conduction of heat from

TABLE 1-1. Conductivity and resistance of some common building materials.

| Imperial | | | | SI (Systeme International) | |
Resistance R = 1/k	Conductivity K = BTU/hr/ ft²/°F/in.	Material	Resistance R = 1/C	Conductivity C = W/m²/°C/ 25.4mm	Resistance Rsi = m.k/W
0.0004	2700.0	Copper	0.00007	14000.0	0.003
0.003	314.0	Steel	0.0005	2000.0	0.02
0.08	12.0	Concrete	0.014	71.0	0.55
0.14	7.1	Glass	0.02	50.0	0.97
0.18	6.5	Limestone	0.03	33.0	1.2
0.2	4.8	Brick	0.035	29.0	1.38
0.48-0.72	2.1-1.4	Plastics	0.08-0.13	12.5-7.7	3.3-5.0
1.2	0.8	Softwood	0.21	4.8	8.32
3.3	0.3	Glass fiber batts	0.58	1.7	23.0
1.2	0.28	Beadboard	0.63	1.6	24.8
4.0	0.25	Glass fiber board	0.7	1.4	27.7
5.0	0.2	Roofmate	0.88	1.1	34.7
5.5	0.18	Air	1.0	1.0	38.0

Note: The last column shows the correct thermal resistance in SI terms. It is measured from face to face across a one meter cube. The other two columns show thermal resistance and conductivity per square meter one inch thick, a hybrid but commonly used measure.

one place to another would happen faster if the iron rod were copper, for copper has a higher conductivity. Conduction would happen more slowly if the rod were plastic, for plastics have a low conductivity.

Table 1-1 shows the thermal conductivity and resistance of some materials of interest in the design of buildings. Thermal resistance (1/k) is the reciprocal of the conductivity (k). The first five columns show the resistance and conductivity for a 1″ (25.4 mm) thickness of the named materials. In this table, conductivity in Imperial terms is measured in BTU per hour per square foot per degree Fahrenheit. Conductivity in Celsius terms is measured in Watts per square meter per degree Celsius. The last column shows a more acceptable method of measuring thermal resistance in SI units. It shows the resistance to heat energy transfer from one face to the opposite face of a one meter cube (m·k/W).

The process of conductivity, just described, is the only way that heat can move through opaque solid materials. Where there are few molecules to collide, as there are in outer space or within the evacuated part of a thermos bottle, little heat is conducted.

A material that is a good conductor is a poor thermal insulator. Thermal resistance noted in Table 1-1 is simply the reciprocal of the conductance. Putting insulation in a wall will reduce the heat flow through it.

I.2.2 Radiation

The heat that one can feel from the sun is transferred by radiation. Sunlight is only a part of a wide spectrum of electromagnetic radiation that includes light, radio waves, and x-rays. Unlike conductive heat flow, all of this radiation travels readily through air or through a vacuum. The interesting thing here is that light is simply a fairly narrow band of radiation to which our eyes are sensitive. Warm objects also radiate heat. There are several interesting differences between the radiation from hot sources and warm sources.

First, although some of the radiation can be seen that comes from the sun (a hot source), the radiation that comes from warm objects (infrared radiation) cannot be seen. However it can usually be felt.

Second, objects of different color react differently to the two kinds of radiation. Dark colors absorb more sunlight than light colors. Anyone who has had a convertible car with black upholstery will be painfully aware of this. Different colors are quite selective in the amounts of sunlight that they absorb or reflect and, of course, that is how they are identified. By contrast, colors are not very selective in the amount of infrared radiation that they absorb.

Third, glass is transparent to most of the radiation that comes from the sun, but it is opaque to the radiation that comes from objects that are not blazing hot, for instance from another person or from a radiator (Figure 1–1). This explains why a greenhouse is heated. The glass lets the sunlight in to warm the soil, plants, people, etc. The heat radiated from these warm objects cannot get back out through the glass since glass is opaque to this kind of radiation. Greenhouses and rooms with windows exposed to the sun accumulate heat this way. This is just fine when we need the heat but in many buildings it is just another cooling load.

Finally, both visible light and infrared radiation are reflected by shiny surfaces. A thermos bottle uses a vacuum space between two bottles to stop conduction. This vacuum does not stop radiation at all, so the bottles have a shiny surface which does reflect radiation.

To summarize, heat waves that can be seen (light waves) are absorbed by dark colors and reflected by light colors. With lower frequency (infrared) radiation, color does not make much difference; shininess does.

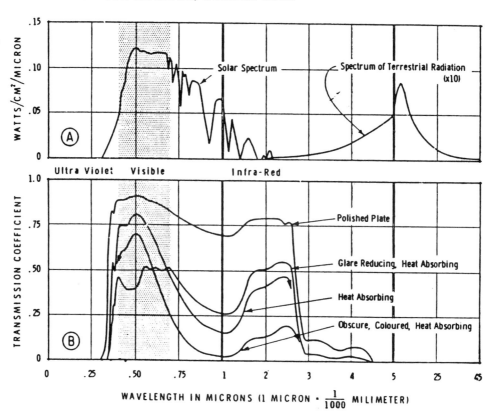

FIGURE I-I. Radiation from sun and from terrestrial body with transmission curves for several glasses. (Garden, G.K. 1968. Characteristics of window glass. *CBD 60*, DBR NRCC, Fig.1.)

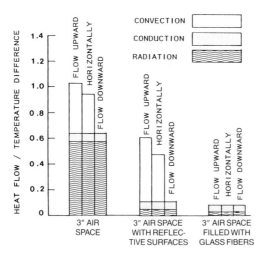

FIGURE 1-2. Comparative heat flow through air spaces. (Shirtliffe, C.J. 1972. Thermal resistance of building insulation. *CBD 149*, DBR NRCC, Fig.1.)

One way to control radiant heat transfer through a building envelope is by the use of reflective insulation, usually made of aluminum foil. It is very seldom used for three reasons:

- It works only while the surface remains bright and shiny.
- It only controls radiation and has practically no effect on conduction and convection (Handegord and Hutcheon 1952).
- Serious stratification occurs with the lower part of the cavity becoming filled with cold air (Handegord and Hutcheon 1952).

Instead of using reflective material, wall cavities are more often fitted with insulation. This makes the cavity almost opaque. As a result very little heat can radiate across it. Radiation is reduced more than conduction (see Figure 1–2).

1.2.3 Convection

In addition to the heat that is transferred by molecular collision (conduction) and that radiated like radio waves, heat is moved from one place to another by currents of air. Natural convection is a very simple process; when air is warmed it expands. The expanded air is lighter than air that has not been warmed. The lighter warm air rises and cooler air moves in to take its place. This circulation of air can take place in a space as small as a test tube. It also occurs when the warm air rises over North Dakota and cool air from the Northwest Territories moves in to take its place. In buildings the air that rises is usually heated by the heating system. The air that falls is cooled by cool wall and window surfaces. Frequently, the down current of cool air causes uncomfortable drafts. This is the principal reason that most convectors (radiators) are placed beneath the windows in a room.

Air is a good insulator if convection currents can be prevented. In fact most insulations do just that. Plastic foams hold the air in place by capturing it in tiny bubbles.

Fiber insulations hold the air in place because air molecules cling to solid surfaces so tenaciously that it is very difficult to move them. This is why it is so difficult to blow the dust off an automobile by driving fast. Glass fiber insulation and mineral wool present a lot of surface area. In all but the skimpiest densities, they hold the air in place so that their insulating value is not destroyed by convection currents within them. As described in 1.5.2, a lot of its insulating value will be lost if air currents can move behind the insulation.

Although glass fiber insulation will usually stop convection currents within it, it will not stop wind or other air currents blowing through it. Under such circumstances it is useless as insulation but it makes a great filter.

1.2.4 Summary

1. Conduction is the transfer of energy (heat) that occurs when warmer more active molecules collide with cooler, less active ones. It is the only way that heat can move through solid opaque materials. Thus it is the way most of the heat goes through the opaque parts of the building envelope. Insulations are poor conductors and are used to impede the flow of heat.
2. Nobody really knows what radiation is, but enough experiments have been performed to give a pretty good model. It is best described as the electromagnetic radiation of energy from a warm body to a cool one. What is thought of as heat is usually a fairly narrow band of this very broad spectrum, as illustrated in the graph in Figure 1–1. Radiation is controlled at windows by using reflective coatings. The temperatures of roofs exposed to direct sunlight can be lowered by using light colored membrane or ballast to reflect the sunlight. In wall cavities, radiation can be controlled by filling the cavities with insulation so that one surface of the cavity cannot "see" the other.
3. Convection transfers heat by air flow. In building envelopes, convection is minimized through proper installation of the various envelope elements.

1.3 HOW MUCH DIFFERENCE DOES INSULATION MAKE?

1.3.1 A Perspective on Energy Use

J.B. Findlay, formerly Chief Engineer, Planning and Construction, Carleton University, suggested that a good way to get a perspective on the heat flow in and out of a building is to look at the heating requirement for a reasonably well-designed office building—double glazing, about 2" (50 mm) of insulation in the walls and 3" (75 mm) or 4" (100 mm) of insulation on the roof. In such buildings, where winters are cold (8000 degree days F, 4500°C), the energy use per unit of floor area for one year is roughly as follows:

Loss through the building envelope	2–3 million BTU/ft² (230–300 MJ/m²)
Summer cooling	400,000 BTU/ft² (40 MJ/m²)
Fans and pumps	600,000 BTU/ft² (60 MJ/m²)
Total	3–4 million BTU/ft² (330–400 MJ/m²)

In this instance, the heat loss through the building envelope is about 75% of the total. A very poorly designed or poorly performing enclosure might raise the heat loss through the building envelope to five or six million BTU/ft².

On the other hand, before the energy crisis, there were heating and ventilating systems that consumed ten times as much energy as the example above. Because of this, many people still retain the thought that the loss through the envelope accounts for only 10% of the annual energy bill. It can be seen that, as the engineering of the mechanical systems improves, the importance of insulation and airtightness in the building envelope increases.

1.3.2   Comparison with Other Means of Energy Conservation

Increasing insulation in the walls of buildings can make a substantial difference but only after other more important energy conservation measures are taken; for example, reducing infiltration.

In very cold weather, a door with a 1/8" (3 mm) crack all around it will waste about 240,000 BTU (24 MJ/hr) when subject to a 20 mph (33 Kmph) wind. Almost any improvement here will be more beneficial than additional insulation.

When there are large areas of window, improving the performance of the walls provides less significant savings than improving window performance. For example, in a 1500 ft² (150 m²) building with double glazed windows making up 25% of the total wall area—that is 300 ft² (30 m²) of window to go with the 900 ft² (90 m²) of wall—the heat loss through the windows would be about twice that through even mediocre wall construction. (Window performance can be improved by better placement, better shading, shutters, low emissivity coatings, etc.)

1.4   CURRENTLY AVAILABLE INSULATIONS

1.4.1   Insulating Values

Table 1–2 lists the most popular of currently available building insulations.

1.4.2   Foamed Plastics

The plastic itself provides some resistance but the gas filling the cells provides most of the insulation. The cells "package" the gas so that it cannot move around. Convection is thus prevented, and the true conductive resistance of the gas is available. Freon gas is sometimes used to foam urethane. The high thermal resistance of freon gives foamed urethane a resistance that can be twice that of foamed polystyrene. However, unless great care is taken, the gas in the cells will escape by diffusion and be replaced by air. When this occurs, the resistance of the insulation is reduced about 50%. (Shirtliffe 1972)

Smoke from burning plastic foams presents a serious hazard for building occupants, particularly those in high-rise buildings where there is the potential for vertical spread of fire in cavity walls. Polystyrene and polyurethane decompose in a fire to produce toxic gases.

The freon used in many insulations presents an environmental hazard if it escapes.

Urea-formaldehyde foam insulation, as it was used in Canada and the United States, is subject to substantial shrinkage and disintegration. It emits irritating formaldehyde and other gases and supports allergenic fungal growth. Its use is now forbidden in Canada and in some states.

TABLE 1–2.   Characteristics of building insulations.

Materials	Rsi standard face to face resistance of one meter³	R value used in roofing based on the resistance of one inch thickness		Bearing strength		Rating	Density	
		SI units (m²)	Imperial (ft²)	kPa	lbs/ft²		lbs/ft³	Kg/m³
Glass fiber for roofing	27.72	0.68	3.87	47.9	10	1	9	144
Extruded poly-styrene (smooth surface)	34.65	0.876	5	143.6	30		2.2	35
Polystyrene (molded beads)	24.74	0.70	3.57	47.9	10		1.5	16
Glass fiber (blankets, batts)	23	0.58	3.3				0.3–2.0	4.8–32
Loose glass fiber fill	23	0.58	3.3				0.6–2.0	9.6–32
Cellulose fill	21.69	0.55	3.1				2.3	37
	25.64	0.65	3.7				3.2	51
Fiberboard (wood or cane)	17.3	0.44	2.5				18	288
Polyisocyanurate	48.53	0.90	6	96–172	20–36	1	2	
Phenolic foam (air filled)	29.11	0.74	4.2	96	20	1	3	
(gas filled)	56.2	1.43	8.1			1		
Polyurethane freon filled (partly aged)	43.82	1.11	6.32	165–225			2.5	40

Most of the foamed plastic insulations exhibit unexpected behavior that affects their use. The negative effects of polystyrene (extensive condensation in the boards, susceptibility to solvents, hard to bond to) are pretty well known and can be avoided or compensated for. Those of other foamed plastics are only being discovered. Such insulations should be used with caution. Let someone else do the experimental work.

1.4.3   Glass and Mineral Fiber Insulation

The tenacious bond between air and other surfaces was discussed in section 1.2.3. The bond between air and fibers holds the air in place and prevents convection currents. As a result, insulation made of fibers works in more or less the same way as the foam insulations; holding the air so that it is not subject to convection. The resistance of fibrous insulations is not greatly different from foamed plastics. Comparative values are given in Table 1–2.

1.4.4   Wood Fiber Insulation

For two decades after World War II, fiberboard made of milled wood pulp or cane was used extensively for roof insulation. It was largely replaced by dense glass fiber insulation, then by extruded polystyrene. There has been a great deal of difficulty fastening roof membranes down to polystyrene insulation. As a result, fiberboard is making a comeback as a cover for the polystyrene; in fact it is advised as a cover for most foamed plastic insulations.

1.4.5   Cellulose Insulation

Cellulose for insulation is made from milled pulpwood and paper, particularly recycled newspapers. It is treated to inhibit fungus growth and fire. It can be blown in place or poured in place by hand. Wherever it is used, care must be taken to get the recommended density. If it is put in place too loosely, air can circulate through it and drastically reduce its insulating value. Properly placed, it is an economical and effective insulation.

1.4.6   Expanded Mica Insulation

Mica granules are inert, fireproof and readily poured in place. They have slightly less insulating value than other poured-in-place insulations.

While the relatively small granules make it easy to pour in place, they also make it easy for the material to run out of little holes in walls and ceilings. There is also some thermographic evidence that it may settle in walls and leave open spaces at the top. For these reasons it is not used extensively.

1.5   WHERE AND HOW TO INSTALL INSULATION

1.5.1   Purposes and Location of Insulation

- Insulation in buildings should reduce heat loss in cold weather and heat gain in summer. If insulation were only required to control heat flow, it would not matter where the insulation is placed in the wall.
- Insulation will improve the mean radiant temperature of the interior. Cold walls or walls that are very warm cause discomfort to people sitting or standing nearby. Keeping the surfaces moderately warm increases one's sense of comfort. The position of insulation in the wall is not critical for this purpose.
- Insulation can reduce thermal movement in the structure. Many of the stresses and cracks in buildings are caused by movement due to temperature changes. Movements in the structure can be eliminated by placing the insulation outside the structure. Similarly, foundation walls can be kept warm by placing insulation outside of the foundation wall.
- Insulation can also prevent freeze-thaw cycles in roofing membranes. Freeze-thaw cycles, particularly in the presence of moisture, can be very destructive. When the insulation is placed outside the roof membrane, the membrane is protected from climatic changes.
- Small amounts of insulation can keep the air/vapor barrier above the dew point in cold weather, thus preventing condensation in the wall. When insulation must keep the air/vapor barrier warm, it must, perforce, be placed outside that barrier.

The air barrier is much more effective, more likely to be complete and better supported when it is placed within the wall construction but outside the building's structure. These two requirements lead to the arrangements shown in the details in Part 1.

1.5.2 Convection Around the Insulation

If insulation is applied to a wall in a way that allows air to circulate around it or behind it, convection currents will be set up that will reduce its insulating value. For example, any air between the insulation and warm masonry will be warmed by the warm masonry. If it can, it will rise, and cold outside air will move in to take its place. As this cold air is warmed, it rises and the cycle continues. Laboratory measurements show that if this kind of convection is allowed to occur through a 1/8" (3 mm) gap between an insulation board and its backup, it will, under severe conditions, reduce the value of the insulation by 40%. (Lorentzen and Nesje 1962).

The exterior walls to which insulation is applied are seldom flush or true to line. Thus the insulation board may touch in one place but be 3/8" to 3/4" (10 mm or 20 mm) away in another. As well as the wall being irregular, the seams in 1/8" (3 mm) air/vapor barrier material may be 3/8" (9 mm) thick and so hold much of the board 1/4" (6 mm) or more away from the rest of the membrane. Where adhesive alone is used to hold the insulation, it seldom has enough tensile strength, when first applied, to hold the boards tight to an irregular surface. Some insulations are too stiff to follow normal irregularities in the walls. Frequently in the past, board insulation was applied with daubs of adhesive that held the insulation 1/4" (6 mm) or more away from the air/vapor barrier. Many adhesives have failed prematurely. Some solvent based adhesives have eaten away the insulation.

Of course, if convection could be stopped in the cavity between the insulation and its backup, the dead air space would add to the insulation in the wall, as it does in sealed double glazing. Sometimes the joints in the insulation boards are sealed to keep out cold air. Sealing to prevent convection is very difficult to achieve and maintain. Have a look at one of these installations before using the technique. The problems are particularly easy to see where the cladding is being removed in an older building.

Convection is a serious problem if batt insulation is not fitted carefully to wood or metal studs. Thermographic investigation shows gross reduction of the insulating value if the batts are displaced by wiring or careless installation.

One interesting problem that came to light is the displacement of insulation caused by drywall screws that miss the studs, often resulting in the insulation twisting around the screws and pulling away from the studs.[1]

1.5.3 Heat Bridging

If a sheet of metal penetrates the insulation in a wall, it will act as a "heat bridge" carrying heat through the insulation. Very little metal is needed to drastically reduce the value of the insulation. For instance, if you placed ordinary 0.04" (0.9 mm) metal studs so that you had only one metal stud for each four feet (1200 mm) of wall, the metal stud would carry exactly the same amount of heat as the four feet

---

[1] These interesting discoveries were made during thermographic studies performed in 1979 by Peter Mill's Building Science group at Public Works Canada.

(1200 mm) width of wall. Thus there will be twice as much heat flow with the stud in the wall. When conductance is doubled, thermal resistance is halved. With the usual three studs in each four feet (1200 mm) of wall, one might be left with only a quarter of the nominal resistance of the insulation that was used.

To some extent, other components in the wall, such as the gypsum board, prevent metal studs from getting all the heat that they are capable of conducting; so the heat bridging phenomenon is less drastic than this calculation might indicate. Even so, metal studs at 16″ (400 mm) on center will reduce the value of any insulation batts between them by nearly 50%. Actual tests are described in NRCC document No. 13858.

1.5.4 Drainage

Some architects are reluctant to use glass fiber insulation in walls for fear it may get wet. To satisfy oneself about this, lay a slab of glass fiber insulation down on a flat surface, flood it with water (difficult enough), now stand the slab up on edge, and see what happens to the water.

1.5.5 Recommendations

For these reasons, it is recommended that a medium density, glass fiber cavity wall insulation be used in walls and that it be applied with rustproof mechanical fasteners that hold it tightly to the air/vapor barrier. Do not bridge the insulation with metal studs or continuous metal furring.

On foundation walls, apply waterproof polystyrene foam outside the waterproof membrane. Where it is exposed above grade, use cement coated polystyrene foam to protect it against sunlight, lawn mowers, snow shovels, etc. Some interesting experiments are being conducted using rigid roofing type Fiberglas as foundation insulation. It works quite well because the water runs out of it, leaving only the bottom inch or two saturated. In fact it makes an excellent drainage layer. It should probably not be used in silty soils for fear of plugging it up with silt.

On roofs, use waterproof extruded polystyrene foam in the protected membrane system. For conventionally insulated roofs, use the special high density glass fiber insulation made to be used as roof insulation.

1.6 IMPROVING THE THERMAL PERFORMANCE OF WINDOWS

Heat flow through windows can be controlled by the following:

- providing double or triple glazing,
- applying reflective coatings to control radiation,
- orientation,
- applying thermal shutters or drapes.

These matters are discussed more fully in Chapter 5, Windows.

[2]R.S. Merriweather, 3315 Outrider, San Antonio, Texas, 78247. Tel. (512)490 7081.

1.7 HOW MUCH INSULATION IS NEEDED

A sophisticated way of selecting insulation thickness is to use computer programs designed to minimize energy use. Steady state conditions, which are the basis for most heat loss calculations, never occur. External temperature fluctuations combined with erratic use of lights, elevators, hot water, and fans result in extremely variable energy use. Over the past ten or fifteen years a number of computer programs have been developed that are intended to give a truer picture of energy use. They use hour by hour weather data, including solar effects on the windows in a particular building. They give a vastly different picture of insulation requirements from those indicated by steady state calculations. With them, it is relatively easy to compare the cost and effectiveness of changing the resistance of building insulation. These programs are available from such firms as Merriweather.[2] One should be cautioned that NRCC retained a number of consulting engineers to use one of these programs on a hypothetical building. They got very erratic results. However, other government departments claim to be getting more consistent results.

In office towers, particularly where the area of the building envelope is small compared to the floor area, the heat generated by lighting, fans, pumps and equipment may be more than the heat loss through the walls. Under these circumstances, heat loss through the walls may not be too serious, unless you are planning to store or redistribute the heat. On the other hand, in residential buildings where the major energy use is for heating, it is wise to insulate the walls to a far greater extent.

Energy use also depends on the severity of the winter, so recommendations for thermal resistance are proportioned to the number of degree days. Any 24 hours in which the mean temperature is 1°F below an arbitrary 54°F is considered a one degree day. For those who use SI units, these temperatures are 1°C and 18°C.

Recommendations for energy conservation in colder climates are available in NRCC document No.22432, Measures for Energy Conservation in New Buildings.

REFERENCES

Handegord, G.O., and Hutcheon, N.B. 1952. "Thermal Performance of Frame Walls." *Research Paper No.5*. Ottawa: DBR NRCC.

Lorentzen, G. and Nesje, R. 1962. *Experimental and Theoretical Investigation of the Influence of Natural Convection in Walls with Slab Type Insulation*. Figure 6. Trondheim: Norges Tekniske Hagskole.

Shirtliffe, C.J. 1972. "Thermal Resistance of Building Insulation." *CBD 149*. Ottawa: DBR NRCC.

2

Airtightness and Vaportightness

2.1 INTRODUCTION

Today there are sophisticated and expensive mechanical systems to condition the air used in buildings. These systems distribute the air, add fresh air when needed and remove stale or contaminated air. They add moisture to the air or remove it and hold humidities within very close limits. Not only is particulate matter removed, but pathogens and even some unwanted molecules. Temperatures are controlled with great finesse. In response to external conditions and to occupancy, one room may receive a carefully metered amount of heat while its neighbor is being cooled.

Most architects will read the foregoing paragraph with a wry smile, recognizing it as a list of a mechanical engineer's intentions rather than a list of accomplishments. Yet one should realize that all of this sophisticated conditioning is bypassed by the air that leaks into the building and that the leaks are an architectural responsibility.

Air leakage is possibly the most pervasive and damaging fault in a building envelope (Handegord 1982). It is the cause of the following:

- major energy loss, winter and summer, and thus an important factor in the energy budget;
- contamination of inside air;
- malfunction of the mechanical control system;
- drafts;
- heating problems, not only in older buildings, where one might expect heating problems on cold windy days, but in many new buildings;
- freezing pipes, again not limited to older buildings but experienced in some buildings that were supposed to have "state of the art" insulation;
- damage to plaster, paint, and other water sensitive building materials; and
- stains, rot, and frost damage due to moisture in the building envelope.

The moisture mentioned in the last item has, as its source, water vapor which is carried into the walls on currents of air from the inside. When the vapor reaches cold parts of the wall, it condenses and may freeze.

When the air currents are reversed, as they will be in other parts of the building, these currents of air, and the forces that cause them, are quite capable of forcing rainwater into the building. Thus infiltration (air leakage into the building) is a contributing factor in rain penetration of the building envelope (see Chapter 3).

162

Because of the unpredictable nature of the forces that cause it, air leakage is an unreliable source of ventilation and a dangerously undependable source of combustion air.

It is curious that air leakage is not more widely recognized as a very serious problem, for few of its effects will come as a surprise to architects. Possibly it is because they have never had the occasion to tot them all up. More likely it is because they may not be aware of the great volumes of air leakage that are experienced in most buildings.

This chapter describes the mechanisms of air leakage and examines the effects of air leakage on the performance of buildings. It then describes measures to achieve airtightness and vaportightness.

The outward movement of large amounts of water vapor into the building envelope is often blamed on diffusion and vapor barriers are prescribed to stop it. This mistake leads to ineffective measures to control the moisture movement. This chapter examines both of the mechanisms: moisture migration by air leakage and moisture migration by diffusion.

2.2 MECHANISMS OF AIR LEAKAGE

First, it is interesting to realize that there are a number of ways that air can move in relation to a building envelope. It is not necessary to study them all, but it is important to realize that, in addition to infiltration and exfiltration (air leaking in and out through the building envelope), air can leak into one side of a wall then back out to that same side. It can also move around within a wall cavity without ever leaving the wall. Such movements are often responsible for carrying moisture into walls and for circumventing insulation in a wall.

Air moves from areas of high atmospheric pressure to areas where the pressure is lower. In buildings there are four mechanisms that change the air pressure and thus provide the power for air leakage. They are wind pressure, stack effect, mechanical pressures, and convection within a cavity.

2.2.1 Wind Pressure

Simply holding up one's hand in the wind gives a sense of the pressure developed. This pressure is made up of two components, a positive pressure on the windward side and a negative pressure on the back or lee side. What is not often realized is that, on a building, there is a large negative pressure along the sides that are parallel to the air flow. This negative pressure or suction is analogous to the lift of an airplane wing and, under some circumstances, may be several times the pressure on the face of the building. A similar negative pressure extends along a flat or low sloped roof. The windward face of a steeply sloped roof acts more like a wall.

Figure 2–1 shows the pressure distribution on a simple building. The total pressure that wind is capable of exerting on a surface is called the static pressure. The decimal fractions shown on the sketches are the proportions of that static pressure. Notice in the sketch that the positive pressure is not constant over the face of the building but is greatest somewhere below the center. The pressure diminishes toward the edges of the windward face. Notice too that there are large changes in pressure on the roof and other sides.

The aerodynamics of buildings is a fascinating subject but, for the author's purposes, there are only a few important things to remember. First, wind on buildings

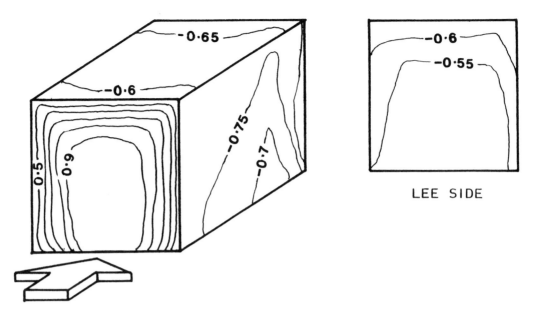

FIGURE 2-1. Pressure distributions on the faces of a cube in a constant velocity field. (Baines, W.D. 1965. Effects of velocity distribution on wind loads and flow patterns on buildings. *Proceedings, Symposium No.16*, Wind Effects on Buildings and Structures, held at the National Physical Laboratory, England, in 1963, published by HMSO London in 1965. Fig.4.6.4a.)

will develop air pressures that are capable of causing large amounts of air leakage if there are openings. People who occupy leaky buildings will hardly have to be reminded of this. Second, it goes without saying that these wind pressures only occur when the wind is blowing. They are positive on the windward side of the building and usually negative on the other sides and on the roof, if it is flat. If the pressure on the face of the building is positive compared to the pressure inside, air will leak in; if it is negative with respect to inside, it will leak out.

Finally, winds at the surface of the earth, particularly in cities, are extremely turbulent. This means that the wind is continually changing direction and speed. In turn the pressures generated by the wind are continually changing in position and intensity in a most unpredictable way.

2.2.2   Stack Effect

The second source of pressure that causes air to leak through a building envelope is stack effect. The name comes from the fact that this is the force that makes chimneys or smoke stacks work. The process is easily understood. In a cold environment, when the air in a building is heated it expands, and some of it is forced out of the building. Now there is less air in the building and, of course, it weighs less than it did before the heating took place. In other words, it weighs less than a similar column of air outside the building. It is easy to imagine what will happen. The lighter air in the building will attempt to rise (like a hot-air balloon) and will leak out through any holes that are available. The heavier, colder air from outside will move in to take its place. This movement inward will take place through any available holes toward the bottom of the building. The opposite effects occur when the air in the building is cooled in summer. The pressures developed by stack effect are remarkably similar to those generated by a moderate wind. The graph in Figure 2–2 shows the pressures that might be expected.

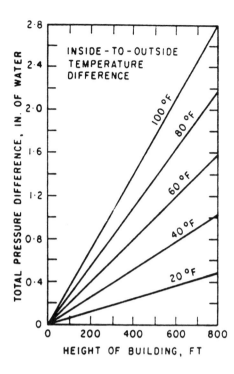

FIGURE 2-2. Pressures generated by stack effect for various differences between inside and outside temperatures. (Wilson, A.G. and Tamura, G.T. 1968. Stack effect and building design. CBD 107, DBR NRCC. Fig.2.)

In tall buildings, entrance doors present the largest holes for the movement inward of the heavier, colder air in winter. Most people have felt the inward pressure that makes these doors so difficult to open in winter and have heard the great whistling and hissing that the air makes as it leaks in around them. Revolving doors equalize this pressure.

The important thing about stack effect is its pervasiveness. It is very constant compared to wind, causing air to leak in and out of buildings any time that the temperature of the air in the building is different from outside. This means nearly all the time.

2.2.3 Mechanical Pressures

The third source of pressures that will cause air to leak in and out of buildings is the pressure difference created by fans. If there is an excess of air being exhausted from the building, as there might be in a laboratory building with a large number of fume hoods, then the pressure in the building will be lower than outside and air will try to leak into the building. Mechanical engineers like to have a positive pressure in the building to reduce drafts and pollution. Under these circumstances, air will leak out through the building envelope. In many large buildings the condition will be quite different at night, for many of the fans will be shut down to conserve energy. Pressure imbalances generated by mechanical systems are often about the same as those generated by wind or stack effect.

2.2.4 Convection Within a Space

It is possible for the air in a wall cavity to be warmed by the warm side of the wall and cooled by the cool side. As mentioned in Chapter 1, the warm air rises and the cooler air falls, thus setting up a convective cell.

Because unsealed concrete masonry is extremely leaky, air can enter the block cavities in one place and exit in another. An example of this was found in a major northeastern museum that behaved as though it was not insulated. Cold air was able to leak through the joints in the insulation and masonry and enter the block cavities. There it was warmed, rose and leaked out at the top, thus circumventing the insulation.

2.2.5   Summary of the Mechanisms of Air Leakage

The only things that can be said for certain are the following:

- The pressures that are developed across the envelope of a building are a complex summation of the positive and negative pressures generated by wind, stack effect and the building's mechanical systems.
- These three phenomena produce extremely variable pressures in terms of time, position and intensity. For instance, the lee side of a building near the top might have an air pressure that was made up of a positive stack effect pressure, a negative wind pressure and a mechanical system pressure that was negative by day and positive at night.
- The pressures produced are frequently in the order of 0.2 to 0.3 in. of water (50 to 75 Pa).
- They need to be addressed in order to control energy losses, maintain comfort and minimize building envelope deterioration.

2.3   HOLES IN THE BUILDING ENVELOPE

In the next few paragraphs, quantitative examples of air leakage are given. They are given in cubic feet ($0.028m^3$). Unless otherwise noted, the pressure difference that powers the leakage is taken at 0.3 in. of water (75 Pa). Although this pressure is widely used as a reference, it is a fairly high pressure. It is the velocity pressure (all the pressure available) in a 24 mph (40 kmph) wind. Since only a portion of the velocity pressure is developed on a building, it represents the pressure developed by a substantially stronger wind. In the case of stack effect, it represents the pressure developed at the top of a 20 story building on a very cold day.

2.3.1   Cracks and Holes Built Into the Building Envelope

Most buildings are assemblies of precise factory built components fitted to hand-crafted frames and walls. Windows are examples of the factory built components. They are built to very close tolerances. Concrete floors and columns are examples of hand crafting. In such work, inaccuracies of 1 in. (25 mm) are common. The large and variable gaps between the two are seldom properly sealed and thus form a large proportion of the holes through which air will leak.

Leakage can also occur through the joints in precise, factory built units. The leakage through an average weatherstripped window can be 14 ft³/h per foot of crack when the pressure difference is 0.1 in. of water, a very modest pressure difference (Sasaki and Wilson 1962). Under those conditions, in a room, 10′ × 10′ × 10′, fitted with two windows each 40″ wide by 48″ high, the window leakage alone would change the air in the room about once in a little over two hours. In SI units the leakage rate is 0.4386 l/s, the pressure is 25 Pa, the room 3 m × 3 m × 3 m, and the windows 1000 mm × 1200 mm.

Concrete block masonry leaks like a sieve, about 40 ft³/hr (3.4 l/s/m²) at 0.1 in. of water (25 Pa). In the same room and under the same conditions as above, 100 ft² (9 m²) of concrete block masonry wall with no window would leak 4000 ft³/hr (30.6 l/s), enough to change the air in the room in 15 min. Concrete block wall tests are reported in NRCC Technical Note 525. It is a useful pamphlet to have in one's technical library.

While on the subject of concrete block masonry, it should be remembered that in steel or concrete framed construction there must be a crack, usually 3/8″ (10 mm) or more, between concrete block walls and the structural beam or slab above them, to prevent the beams and slabs from loading the walls. Incredible amounts of air leak through these cracks unless counter measures are taken. Caulking is seldom adequate.

Brick veneer adds very little to the airtightness of walls, because the veneer is usually open at the top and usually fitted with weep holes at regular intervals. In some buildings there are also intentional openings, shielded against rain, that are actually meant to let air through.

2.3.2 Movement Cracks

The cracks and openings in the discussion so far have been those that are more or less "built-in". There is another set that occurs as the building ages. It includes the cracks that open as wooden members dry out in the normal seasoning process. Concrete and concrete masonry units undergo a similar kind of shrinkage. In the case of concrete, this shrinkage is related to a permanent deflection called "creep", which may be as large or larger than the elastic deflection. Some of the most difficult cracks to close occur where nonbearing masonry walls shrink away from the steel and concrete frames that surround them. There are also cracks that open and close as the adjoining materials expand or contract in response to changes in temperature and moisture content. It is also possible for cracks to open and close as the load changes on portions of the building.

What is important here is the fact that holes and cracks exist in great number and that they are of a size that allows very large quantities of air to leak through the building envelope. The air leakage through the envelopes of several large buildings has been measured. The leakage through one with masonry walls and operable aluminum windows amounted to almost 2 ft³/min. for each square foot of outside wall (9.84 l/s/m²) at 0.3 in. of water (75Pa). All architects should read Shaw, Sander and Tamura's (1973) surprising report of this test in NRCC Document 13951.

2.4 WATER VAPOR MIGRATION

2.4.1 Moisture Carried into Walls by Air Leakage

The leakage rate through a crack 1/8″ × 12″ is 25 ft³/min with a pressure of 0.3 in. of water (10 l/s through a crack 3 mm × 300 mm at 75 Pa). In 24 hours this would amount to 36000 ft³ (864 m²). At a very moderate 30% RH, this amount of air will carry over 1 gal. (5 kg) of water through the crack in 24 hr. At 50% RH, more than 2 gal. (7.6 l) would be carried through this crack.

2.4.2   Moisture Carried into the Wall by Diffusion

First a word or two about diffusion. Porous building materials, such as stone, bricks, concrete and plaster are really agglomerations of crystals or particles that do not fit together very well. The poor fit leaves a lot of empty space, in fact about 50% of the volume. Although these pores are microscopic in size, they are much, much larger than the molecules of water in humid air. Water molecules can move through these pores, moving from areas of high vapor pressure to areas of lower vapor pressure. Remember that vapor pressure depends only on the number of water molecules in a given volume of air.

It can be seen that the progress that they make through the pores depends on the size and continuity of the pore structure.

The rate of diffusion through many building materials is trifling. Even when outside conditions are cold and dry and when the building has a very humid interior (50% RH and 70°F or 21°C), the moisture diffusing through 100 ft^2 (10 m^2) of 6″ (150 mm) poured concrete would amount to 1/8 cup (30 grams) in 24 hours. One hundred square feet of vapor barrier made of 2 mil (0.05 mm) polyethylene would allow only 2 teaspoons (10 grams) to diffuse through the membrane in the same 24 hr.

The following are several important things to remember about vapor barriers:

- They are usually intended to stop or retard diffusion and are not often suitable to stop air leakage. Plastic films and aluminum foil, which are quite effective vapor barriers, are seldom strong enough to withstand wind loads. As a result they do not make good air barriers. The plastic films are very difficult to seal. Examining walls where these films have been adhered to concrete with acoustical caulking, showed that the film had been torn loose by wind pressure. In addition there have been some examples of premature aging, splitting, and disintegration of polyethylene film.
- A few holes in a vapor barrier intended to stop diffusion only are not terribly important. For instance, had the 1/8″ x 12″ (3 mm × 300 mm) crack previously discussed been in a vapor barrier intended only to stop diffusion and not air leakage, it would have increased diffusion by less than three percent since it represents only a small percentage of the area of the wall.
- Water vapor transferred into or through a building envelope by diffusion is only a small fraction of the amount transferred by air leakage. Until the air leakage problem is solved, vapor barriers will play a very insignificant role.
- One problem that can arise is caused by putting a layer of material with a good vapor resistance outside one that has low vapor resistance; for instance, putting a vaportight roof membrane outside of an imperfect vapor barrier. In such cases, the water molecules can go through the vapor barrier but be trapped by the roof membrane, thus creating the possibility of condensation.

2.4.3   Summary

All of the foregoing can be summarized by the following statements:

- Air leakage has a number of damaging effects on building performance and upon the building fabric. These damaging effects are serious.
- The air leakage is caused by air pressures developed by fans in the building, by wind, and by temperature differences inside and outside the building.

The leakage occurs through holes and cracks caused by the following:

- thermal movement;
- movement due to moisture changes;
- structural deflection;
- poorly filled vertical joints in masonry;
- poor fit between precise, factory made components and the handcrafted, on-site construction, such as concrete and masonry;
- poor fit between structural frames and the infilling panel walls; and
- an unwarranted faith in caulking.

2.5 ACHIEVING AIRTIGHTNESS

2.5.1 Caulking

Most attempts to achieve airtightness are made with caulking. This is very difficult to do, especially in the long term. First, the requirements for effective caulking are so onerous that they are not likely to be met on a building site. This is a complex subject and is discussed in detail in Chapter 4. The second reason why caulking fails, is that it is put in places where it would be ineffective even if it were perfect. One example is around the perimeter of masonry walls. In the first place, caulking around the perimeter of a block wall is like caulking around the perimeter of a sieve. In the second place, caulking at the inside face of the blockwork allows cold outside air to circulate within the cavities of the blockwork, thus circumventing the insulation, as discussed in Chapter 1.

2.5.2 Vapor Barriers

It has been explained in 2.4 that barriers against the diffusion of water vapor are seldom, if ever, needed, in spite of code requirements to the contrary. There is a real concern that they may be expected to serve as air barriers.

Under no circumstances should polyethylene film be expected to serve as an air barrier. Its useful life is uncertain, it is not strong enough to withstand wind loads, it cannot be sealed to the structural members that must penetrate it, and it cannot be made to adhere to other parts of the structure. Even acoustical caulkings extend and extrude like bubble gum when subject to moderate wind pressure.

A number of asphaltic coatings are sold as vapor barriers. In principle, a well formulated mastic should work, but they should not be used without the assurance of a realistic field test. As previously explained, their use to stop diffusion is likely unnecessary. Their use as air barriers is questionable, not so much because of the material itself but because of the surfaces to which it is applied. These surfaces, usually concrete block masonry, are so irregular and contain so many cracks and crevices that normal applications are not able to cover the flaws completely, particularly when they are sprayed on. They will not work in locations where movement may occur; movements such as thermal movement, moisture movement, deflections, creep in concrete, etc. In these locations an elastic membrane is required.

2.5.3 Parging

Parging turns masonry into an almost perfect air barrier, reducing its normal rate of leakage by a factor of 100. There are only two concerns about its use. First, it is not flexible and will fail wherever movement may occur. This still leaves the possibility that parging could be used in conjunction with strips of elastic membrane at the movement joints. The problem here is the need to wait until the parging cures, or at least dries, before the membrane strips can be applied. If a masonry cavity wall is being completed one story at a time, this would be unacceptable.

2.5.4 Membrane Air Barriers

At the moment the best results are obtained with modified asphalt membranes. They are available in formulations that can be fused onto the backup wall, whether it be masonry, concrete, gypsum board or metal. This is described in some detail in Chapter 4. There has been considerable experience with fused-on rubberized asphalt. It is a difficult application, particularly if the brick ties are already installed. In spite of that, it renders any surface airtight and, what is more, it is flexible wherever movement may occur. This is the system that is used in all the details in Part 1. Note that it makes an excellent connection between walls and properly chosen window frames. It only requires that the designer provide a surface to which it can be applied. This is readily achieved in most cases but there are a few places where it is difficult. For the most part these are worked out in the details.

Other very important attributes of these membranes are their watertightness and vaportightness. These are very useful characteristics, for it will be noted in Chapter 3 that some rainscreens, particularly brick masonry, are far from watertight.

REFERENCES

Handegord, G.O. 1982. "The Need for Improved Airtightness in Buildings." *Building Research Note No.151.* Ottawa: DBR NRCC.

Sasaki, J.R. and Wilson, A.G. 1962. "Window Air Leakage." *CBD 25.* Ottawa: DBR NRCC.

Shaw, C.Y., Sander, D.M., and Tamura, G.T. 1973. "Air Leakage Measurements of the Exterior Walls of Tall Buildings." *NRCC 13951.* Ottawa: DBR NRCC.

3

Preventing Rain Leakage

3.1 INTRODUCTION

In the 15th century, Alberti (1965) noted:

> For Rain is always prepared to do Mischief and wherever there is the least crack, never fails to get in and do some hurt or other. By its Subtlety it penetrates and makes its way, by its Humidity rots and destroys, by its Continuances loosens and unknits all the Nerves of the Building and in the End ruins and lays Waste.

It would be reasonable to expect that the intervening centuries have seen improvements in this most basic requirement for shelter. Unfortunately, failure is still quite common. The British Building Research Establishment recently tested 44 sample wall areas in new houses and found that all of them leaked (Newman et al. 1982). The results are illustrated in Figure 3–1 and Figure 3–2. These were cavity walls with the outer wythe of brick and the inner wythe of concrete block, a design intended to prevent rain penetration. Test conditions were not unusual and water was neither thrown at the walls with any force nor was any pressure difference established across the walls, yet an astounding 80% of the water applied to the outside of the wall reached the cavity and 2.5% reached the inside finish plaster.

Experience on this continent is not much different, for, as mentioned in the Prolegomenon, 75% of high rise condominiums leak water through the walls, as do 65% of our row houses. It may be that our expectations are too high. Thomas Jefferson is quoted as being satisfied, two hundred years ago, with walls that showed signs of moisture penetration only twice in twelve or fifteen years (Ritchie 1960). Surely something has been learned in the intervening years, particularly when automobiles can be driven at 60 mph (100 kmph) through the rain and not leak a drop.

This chapter will review what is known about rain leakage and will describe a wall system designed to resist rain penetration.

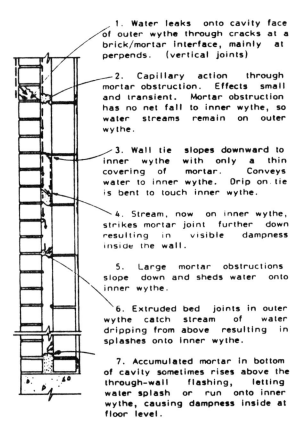

1. Water leaks onto cavity face of outer wythe through cracks at a brick/mortar interface, mainly at perpends. (vertical joints)

2. Capillary action through mortar obstruction. Effects small and transient. Mortar obstruction has no net fall to inner wythe, so water streams remain on outer wythe.

3. Wall tie slopes downward to inner wythe with only a thin covering of mortar. Conveys water to inner wythe. Drip on tie is bent to touch inner wythe.

4. Stream, now on inner wythe, strikes mortar joint further down resulting in visible dampness inside the wall.

5. Large mortar obstructions slope down and sheds water onto inner wythe.

6. Extruded bed joints in outer wythe catch stream of water dripping from above resulting in splashes onto inner wythe.

7. Accumulated mortar in bottom of cavity sometimes rises above the through-wall flashing, letting water splash or run onto inner wythe, causing dampness inside at floor level.

Open Cavity

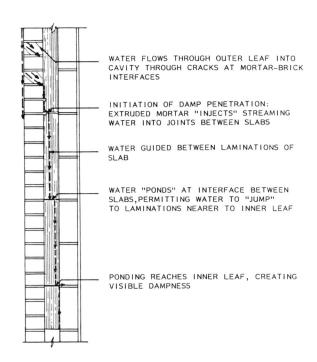

WATER FLOWS THROUGH OUTER LEAF INTO CAVITY THROUGH CRACKS AT MORTAR-BRICK INTERFACES

INITIATION OF DAMP PENETRATION: EXTRUDED MORTAR "INJECTS" STREAMING WATER INTO JOINTS BETWEEN SLABS

WATER GUIDED BETWEEN LAMINATIONS OF SLAB

WATER "PONDS" AT INTERFACE BETWEEN SLABS, PERMITTING WATER TO "JUMP" TO LAMINATIONS NEARER TO INNER LEAF

PONDING REACHES INNER LEAF, CREATING VISIBLE DAMPNESS

Cavity insulated with 50 mm laminated glass fibre insulation

FIGURE 3-1. (*Left*) Routes for water penetration across an unfilled cavity. (Newman, A.J. et al. 1982. Full-scale penetration tests on twelve cavity fills. Building and Environment 17(3) Fig.7.)

FIGURE 3-2. (*Right*) Routes for water penetration across a cavity containing fibre slabs. (Newman, A.J. et al. 1982. Full-scale penetration tests on twelve cavity fills. Building and Environment 17(3) Fig.9.)

3.2 EFFECTS OF WATER LEAKAGE

Water, leaking into wall construction, causes the following:

- dimensional changes, not only of wood and other cellulose materials but substantial changes in the dimension of bricks, concrete, and stone. Water may cause a 0.2% expansion in concrete (Baker 1968);
- rust and corrosion;
- decay due to molds and fungi;
- blistering of paint and other surface finishes;
- efflorescence—the whitish deposits on the surface of masonry;
- stains on the inside and outside of buildings;
- disintegration of porous building materials should the water freeze; and
- dislodging of stones, bricks, and other elements of a building when water freezes behind them.

3.2.1 Dimensional Changes

In *CBD 56*, "Thermal and Moisture Deformations in Building Materials," M.C. Baker explains the dimensional changes to be expected from thermal and moisture variations.

3.2.2 Fungal Growth

The same author has given an extensive explanation of the causes and prevention of rot and other fungal growth in *CBD 111*, "Decay of Wood," and *CBD 112*, "Designing Wood Roofs to Prevent Decay." Very briefly, he explains that fungal growth requires the following:

- a source of infection,
- suitable food,
- moisture,
- oxygen, and
- suitable temperature.

Its growth can be retarded or stopped by removing any one of the requirements or, of course, by poisoning the little creatures that cause the problem.

3.2.3 Efflorescence

There is an excellent treatise on efflorescence by Tom Ritchie in *CBD 2*, "Efflorescence." Persistent efflorescence is an indication that something else is wrong, usually ineffective flashings.

3.2.4 Phenomenon of Freezing

It will be easier to understand the damage caused by frost if the phenomenon of freezing in porous materials is understood. This theory has been put forward by Dr. Litvan (1980) of NRCC. Water has its maximum density at a few degrees above freezing. As it is cooled further it expands and, when frozen, it will have expanded almost 10%. The force of the expansion will distort or burst most containers. This freezing is often thought to be the cause of frost damage to porous building materials. However, similar frost damage occurs when the porous material contains benzene, a liquid which contracts, rather than expands, when it freezes.

It appears that moisture, clinging to the walls of the pores in fine porous materials, is held so tightly by the molecular bond that it cannot form ice crystals, even at temperatures well below freezing. Because the change of state (freezing) cannot take place, the supercooled liquid still has its heat of fusion. It is thus at a much higher energy level than any water that has frozen. If there are larger cracks or pores present where the bond is not so powerful, water in these cracks or pores will freeze. Thus we have supercooled water with a high energy level in one place and ice with a very low energy level in another. A migration of the supercooled water takes place, powered by its high energy. The migrating supercooled water freezes as soon as it is released from the powerful bond of the fine pores and becomes a target for more supercooled water. Ice continues to accumulate in pockets or "lenses". The forces developed in this process are large and are quite capable of fracturing bricks, stone and mortar. In clays the forces can exceed 290 000 lb/ft² (1400 KPa), quite large enough to heave foundations.

3.3 MECHANISMS OF WATER PENETRATION

There are three requirements if water is to leak through a wall:

- the presence of water,
- a hole, and
- a force to drive the water through the hole.

All three must be present at once. The removal of any one of them will prevent the leak. Kirby Garden, a famous building scientist, has used the analogy of drinking coffee to illustrate the phenomenon. He explains that you form an orifice with your mouth, span it with coffee, then arrange the pressure in your mouth so that atmospheric pressure forces the coffee in.

Many walls contain a cavity to interrupt the flow of water from one side of the wall to the other. If water is to cross this cavity, there must be a path for it, a bridge to conduct water across the cavity in much the same way that a hole conducts water through the solid part of the wall. As with the hole, water must be present at the bridge as well as a force to propel the water across the bridge.

3.3.1 Holes

The porous structure of bricks and mortar is not likely to cause leakage. In fact, there is evidence that porous brick walls are slower to leak than those built of dense bricks (Foster 1983). It is generally agreed that the holes principally responsible for leakage are those caused by an incomplete bond between bricks and mortar, particularly in the vertical joints. Others are caused by careless details and workmanship. Many cracks and holes are caused by movements in the building.

Briefly outlined, the reasons for such cracks and holes are the following:

- Poor fit between the hand crafted building shell and factory manufactured items such as windows.
- Deflections in the structure. Floors and roofs deflect under load. If the deflection is too great, such brittle materials as plaster and masonry may crack. In buildings with concrete slabs and frames, some of the deflection may be permanent and larger than the live load deflection. This kind of deflection is called plastic creep.
- Uneven settlement of the foundations.
- Warping caused because one side of an element is warm while another is cold.
- When two elements have different coefficients of thermal expansion, they will move at different rates. This is particularly evident where aluminum elements, such as window frames, are sealed to masonry or concrete. It also occurs where exposed structural frames containing infilling panels are exposed to large temperature swings. In this case the exposed frame may expand and contract differently from the panel walls.
- Changes in dimension caused by moisture gain or loss. Swelling, shrinkage, and warping in wood are examples. A similar case is the slight swelling in brick masonry when recently burned bricks begin to pick up moisture.
- Shrinkages that accompany the curing of concrete, particularly concrete masonry units. This is another cause of the cracks that appear between structural frames and their infilling panel walls.

Buildings using large prefabricated panels have fewer joints than those with smaller panels. However since there are fewer joints, there are larger movements in each joint.

3.3.2 Bridges

Just as holes provide paths for water through the solid parts of walls, so bridges provide the paths across the cavities. In masonry cavity walls, these bridges can be formed by ties that bind the two wythes. More often than not, mortar droppings accumulate on the ties to provide more effective bridges. Where the cavity is insulated, the insulation may become a bridge. Furthermore, mortar may be guided across the cavity by the joints in the insulation boards. Examples from actual observations are shown in Figure 3–1 and Figure 3–2.

3.3.3 Forces That Move Water Through Walls

Although they seldom work independently, there are four forces involved in the transfer of water through walls:

- gravity,
- capillary action,
- kinetic energy, and
- air pressure differentials.

Gravity

Gravity will draw water along holes, open joints or bridges that slope downward and inward, thus conducting water into or through a building wall.

Capillary Action

Most people have seen capillary action demonstrated. One experiment shows that water is drawn up against gravity into small tubes. The smaller the tube, the farther up the water will be drawn.

Similarly, the fine porous structure of most building materials draws water into the pores and is most reluctant to let it go. Because of the tight bond between water and the walls of the pores, these pores seldom contribute to leaking through walls. In larger capillaries, where the grip is less tenacious, water in the capillaries may be more readily dislodged by other forces. In fact, this seems to be the explanation for the large quantities of water that flow from one side of a brick wall to the other when water is gently applied to one face. Capillary action draws water into pores and crevices. Gravity then conducts it to the other side through channels that slope in that direction.

Kinetic Energy

In our case, this refers to the energy stored in raindrops because of their velocity. To penetrate a wall, the raindrops must be able to follow a direct path through the wall or must strike a surface and splash in a direction where a hole is open to them. Similarly, water flowing down a gutter or roof or some similar watercourse may pick up enough energy to reach a vulnerable area of the building that otherwise might not be wetted. An example of this is water rushing down a roof, across a valley and up under the shingles on the other side of the valley.

Air Pressure Differentials

If the air on one side of a wall is at a higher pressure than on the other, the pressure difference will force water through any holes that are present, much like drinking through a straw. Enough force to do this can be generated by wind or stack effect (see 3.4.2). As previously mentioned, it may work in combination with capillarity to cause leaking.

3.3.4   Presence of Water on the Surface

Some of the phenomena described require a sheet of water to cover the surface so as to span the holes. Others will function with less water. There are several circumstances that affect this accumulation. Most obvious is the quantity of rain.

If rain is being driven almost horizontally against the building, as it often is in maritime areas, very large amounts will be deposited on the walls. However, if the rain is coming straight down or if it is being blown away from the wall, even the heaviest rain will have little effect on the wall. Increased quantities of water may contribute much more to leakage than the pressure generated by the wind. (Newman, et al. 1982)

Water will drip onto walls from horizontal surfaces where snow has accumulated. Copings and sills constructed without drips are readily observable examples. Similar dripping often comes from plugged or leaking gutters. Often these sources are more pervasive than rain, for dripping may be present in the absence of rain, or continue long after the rain has stopped.

3.4   POSSIBLE SOLUTIONS

Obviously the best solution would employ details to neutralize as many as possible of the conditions that cause leaks. These conditions are now examined one by one and means of neutralizing them are discussed.

3.4.1   Plugging the Holes

Originally, efforts to control leaking in contemporary buildings concentrated on sealing the holes and joints. Good, long-life caulking materials became available about the same time that thinner, lighter wall construction became fashionable. It was expected that these new sealants would seal the holes and stop leaks.

After years of trying, most designers agree that it is almost impossible to seal the exterior cladding of a building for any length of time. The reasons for this will be examined in Chapter 4, Caulking and Sealing. There are, however, three reasons that stand out:

- The exposed elements of the building envelope are just that, "exposed," and are subject to cyclical heating and cooling. As a result, the cladding is continually expanding and contracting. Perhaps more important, different materials expand and contract at different rates so that "differential" expansion takes place. Such repeated movements are often well beyond the shear and elastic capacity of the sealant installation.

- Exposure to ultraviolet light eventually reduces the elasticity of most organic materials (including humans) and makes sealants even less capable of sustaining the tension and shear generated by movement, particularly if the movement is repeated over and over again.
- It is difficult to do a perfect job of caulking on-site. A faultless job takes a combination of skillful design, accurate construction, suitable materials, proper technique, good conditions, and a high degree of skill, concentration, and dedication on the part of the workman. It is unrealistic to expect this combination to be sustained in a reliable way.

When caulked joints on the surface of buildings form part of the rain barrier, these joints are often subjected to two of the conditions required for a leak; air pressure and water. With two of the three requirements for leaking present, all that is needed is a hole. It is for this reason that imperfections in face caulking are so vulnerable, much more so than if the flaws were farther back in a drier part of the wall.

The many joints in masonry are particularly hard to seal, for the appearance of the wall gives little evidence of the number of holes that may cause leaking. Frustration, caused by failure to seal these joints, explains why many stone buildings have been stuccoed or covered with weatherboard siding.

In *CBD 97*, "Look at Joint Performance," an interesting example is given of large panel construction where sealing the outer surface of the joints actually increased the amount of leakage.

3.4.2 Removing the Forces

Removing the forces that cause water penetration provides an attractive alternative to plugging the holes.

Gravity

As mentioned above, holes, orifices or bridges that slope downward and inward can conduct water into a building. The solution is to overlap panels of cladding so that water is channeled out instead of in. Shingles are a good example of this principle. Precast concrete panels can be formed with top and bottom joints sloping out in a similar way. In masonry walls where this is not possible, metal flashings and weep holes can be arranged to do the same thing.

Capillary Action

Improving the bond between masonry units and the mortar will reduce the unintentional cracks and crevices in walls. Intentional joints should be 3/8" (10 mm) or wider to avoid capillary action. Of course, these joints should slope down and out.

Kinetic Energy

Since kinetic energy will carry raindrops only through holes that they can "see" through, penetration can be prevented by a shield or by lapping the elements in an appropriate direction. Splashes from water falling within wall cavities account for a lot of water transfer across the cavity. They are not readily controllable, although ties and anchors that slope toward the outside might reduce the amount of dripping within the cavity.

Air Pressure Differentials

It was previously mentioned that air pressure differences can force water through any holes that are present. This fact has led many building scientists to suggest that equalizing the air pressure across the cladding might reduce rain penetration. They propose that this can be done by building adequate holes through the cladding.

Figure 2–1 in Chapter 2 shows the pressure differences on the faces of a building. It is not widely recognized that these pressure patterns are extremely irregular and change, second by second, as the wind changes speed and direction. If we are to equalize all these different pressures, the space behind the cladding must be divided into small and relatively airtight compartments.

Aside from the impracticality of this suggestion, there is a very real danger that the "partitioning" may provide bridges for the water to cross the wall cavity; a situation similar to that shown in Figure 3–2.

In the case of masonry, so much water leaks through brick cladding with no pressure difference across it (Newman, et al. 1982) that it is doubtful that pressure equalization would have much additional effect (see 3.1). A clean cavity behind the brickwork together with ties that do not aid water transfer would make a great difference to water migration through a masonry cavity wall.

It is reassuring to know that clean, well-designed cavity walls can control rain penetration without pressure equalization, for unless accidental bridges span the cavity, water will cling to the inner surface of the outer wythe and run down to a location where it can be drained toward the outside.

Pressure equalization can and does occur under some circumstances. Where it can be achieved without adverse effects, it is certainly beneficial. It seems to work in joints in well designed precast concrete and in such spaces as hollow window frames where the volume is small.

3.4.3 Removing Water, Two-Stage Waterproofing

With many types of cladding, water can be excluded from those parts of a wall where leaking may occur. With other materials, brick for instance, it cannot be excluded, but the quantities of water reaching those vital areas can be reduced to a manageable amount. Two-stage waterproofing refers to a system in which an outer rainscreen prevents or reduces water penetration that might reach any holes in the air barrier.

All building envelopes should include an air barrier. This is the line where the outside stops and the inside begins. As a result it is the line where all the air pressure differences occur whether caused by wind, stack effect or mechanical systems.

If there are flaws in the air barrier and water is present at the flaws, the pressures mentioned above will drive water through the holes. The amount of water reaching the air barrier can be reduced to a very small quantity by placing a rainscreen to protect the air barrier. The rainscreen is usually open, that is, it is not sealed. The most effective rainscreens are made of overlapping units that act like shingles. This system has been described by Kirby Garden in *CBD 40*, "Rain Penetration and Its Control."

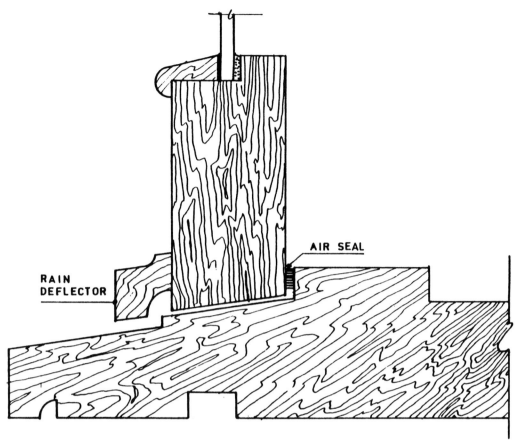

FIGURE 3-3. Two-stage waterproofing of a casement sash.

Three examples will illustrate this process. In Figure 3-3, the drip over the crack at the sill of a casement sash throws the water clear of the crack where an opening for water penetration exists and where, in all likelihood, a pressure difference exists.

In Figure 3-4, the cladding is a wythe of brick. Since the brick wythe is not water-tight, water can be expected to stream down the back of the brick. However, weep holes and flashings can be used to carry it out of the wall. Unfortunately brick ties, mortar droppings, and insulation frequently form bridges that carry water across the cavity from the back of the bricks to the air barrier. Cavities can be kept clean by placing a board on the brick ties to catch the mortar droppings. It is drawn up the cavity before the next row of ties is placed. The process is then repeated. As Figure 3-1 and Figure 3-2 show, ties formed with a drip in the middle simply allow drops of water to splash on the bottom of the cavity, wetting the bottom of the inner wall. The answer is to slope the ties toward the outside; a very difficult thing to get done consistently on the job. So, for that matter, is a clean cavity. Because of these difficulties it is essential to have a continuous and watertight air barrier to serve as a second line of defense.

Figure 3-4 also shows an accidental hole through the air barrier. At this stage it is well to remember that the purpose of the air barrier is to stop air movement. This is where the wind stops and where the resulting static pressure is developed. We now have a hole and the pressure to drive water through it. However, if our brick rainscreen works, no water will reach this hole and water leakage will be prevented.

Figure 3–5 shows an example of a well designed window frame. Here the outer gasket deflects most of the rain. Some does penetrate, and it is led out through weep holes. These weep holes may provide some pressure equalization. This effect can probably be increased by additional, appropriately spaced holes. The inner tape seal is the air barrier. If there are flaws in it, they are up out of the water that might otherwise be forced through them.

Except in windows, the sealed joint is away from ultraviolet radiation. It is also on the warm side of the insulation which will isolate it from the effects of thermal

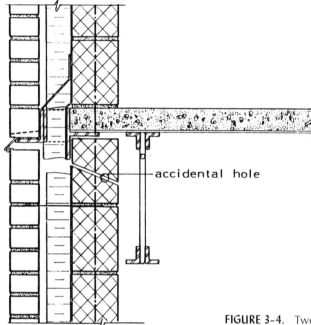

—accidental hole

FIGURE 3-4. Two-stage waterproofing in a masonry wall.

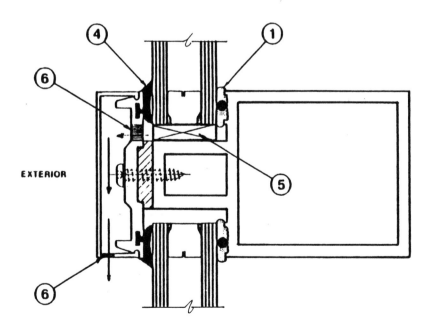

EXTERIOR

LEGEND

1. PRE-SHIM TAPE

4. GLAZING GASKET OR SPLINE OF EPDM, NEOPRENE OR PVC

5. SETTING BLOCKS OF EPDM OR NEOPRENE, SHORE "A"

6. HOLES FOR DRAINAGE AND VENTING

FIGURE 3-5. A WELL DESIGNED WINDOW FRAME—ALUMINUM CURTAIN WALL (Insulated Glass Manufacturers of Canada, Brantford, Ontario. 1986. Glazing Recommendations for Sealed Insulating Glass Units. Revised November 1986. p.10.)

movement and, as has been said, it is also away from any water which might be forced through flaws in the seal.

3.5 CONCLUSIONS

Water entering the construction that forms a building envelope can cause a variety of disfiguring stains, blisters and disintegrations inside and outside the building. It can cause dangerous structural failure in wood, steel, concrete, and masonry. The adverse effects on masonry and concrete are aggravated by freezing.

It is theoretically possible to seal joints at the face of a building. Indeed, such surface sealing seems relatively successful for some window installations, but it takes meticulous preparation, great care and skill. Generally, surface sealing or caulking is not very successful, especially over a period of years.

Instead, water access can be controlled by interposing a series of overlapping, sloped elements such as shingles to form a rainscreen. A well designed rainscreen can tolerate some water penetration for it will include a system to drain this water to the outside.

A masonry rainscreen will not exclude water entirely from the wall cavity. Debris, fasteners, and insulation will also, in all probability, conduct water across the cavity to the surface of the air barrier. In such cases the air barrier should be built to accept some wetting and also to form a second defense against water penetration.

3.6 RECOMMENDATIONS

1. Two-Stage Waterproofing

Design walls and windows to incorporate two-stage waterproofing. The principles for such walls are illustrated in Figure 3–4. The principles for windows are illustrated in Figure 3–5. This system also forms the basis for all of the details in this book. There is a brief, illustrated explanation of the use of two-stage waterproofing in connection with insulated airtight walls in the Prolegomenon. The application of two-stage waterproofing to windows is described in detail in Chapter 5.

2. The First Stage, a Rainscreen

The rainscreen for a wall should be built from elements that overlap like shingles. These elements can be built from wood, sheet metal, concrete, tiles, asbestos board or masonry. Figure 3–6 shows only the rainscreen.

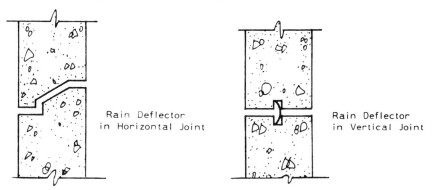

Rain Deflector in Horizontal Joint

Rain Deflector in Vertical Joint

FIGURE 3-6. Joints for precast concrete rainscreens.

Rainscreens of Wood

This book does not address itself to rainscreens of combustible construction, but most traditional wood cladding is satisfactory. Such construction is described in "Canadian Wood-Frame House Construction" published by Canada Mortgage and Housing Corporation, Ottawa, Canada.

Rainscreens of Precast Concrete

Precast concrete rainscreen panels should overlap at the horizontal joints and have metal rain deflectors in the vertical joints as illustrated in Figure 3–6. Joints should not be narrower than 10 mm. In both cases, a gasket (not shown here) at the inside face of the joint will further reduce rain penetration.

Rainscreens of Asbestos Board

Although asbestos board has been used successfully for this purpose, it is hard to recommend it because the asbestos fibers, which are liberated when sawing the material, are a serious health hazard.

Rainscreens of Brick and Rubble Stone

Although brick cladding can be made quite waterproof, typical single wythes of brick leak very badly; so badly in fact that they can hardly be described as rain-screens. In addition, mortar droppings, brick ties and cavity insulations all form bridges to transport water across the cavity. It is important, therefore, to provide a "second line of defense" against water leakage in walls with brick cladding. This can be done best by using a continuous, waterproof air barrier membrane such as rubberized asphalt sheet material. It is described in 4.2. The same remarks apply to rubble stone work.

Water leakage through brick clad walls can be reduced by keeping the cavity clean and by careful installation of the ties.

3. The Second Stage, an Air Barrier

Airtightness and air barriers are described in Chapters 2 and 4. The best air barrier seems to be a "torched-on" membrane of rubberized asphalt, as described in Chapter 4. This is the system shown in most of the details in Part 1. It easily covers the flaws in most backup walls, it provides flexible movement joints and a waterproof second line of defense against leaky rainscreens, such as those built of masonry.

British experiments, mentioned earlier in this chapter, showed that enormous amounts of water may penetrate a brick wythe and that, subsequently, large amounts may cross the wall cavity. Under these circumstances, the membrane air barrier may be all that stands in the way of water penetration into the building. From a waterproofing point of view, there is nothing wrong with considering that the air barrier membrane may also serve as the "raincoat" that prevents water penetration into the building. In this position it should give excellent service, for it is protected against sunlight, large temperature swings and mechanical damage.

4. Wall Cavity Flashings

These flashings are so difficult to install properly that they should be used only where absolutely necessary. They are difficult because they must maintain a proper slope while avoiding such obstructions as brick ties and while being threaded through cuts or joints in the insulation. Since water may get well back into the wall cavity, the best flashings will be made from strips of rubberized asphalt, adhered to the air barrier membrane. Because the rubberized asphalt cannot be exposed to view or sunlight, it should be used in combination with a strip of copper, stainless steel or monel, as shown in the details. Copper should not be used against a galvanized shelf angle (see 7.4.11 for more about through-wall flashings).

5. Cladding Supports as Heat Bridges

Some heat loss through cladding supports is beneficial for it tends to dry the supports in what may be a very damp environment. Excessive heat loss should be avoided. This is done by reducing the area of steel that penetrates the insulation. There is a limit to how small the members should be, however, for small sections corrode through more readily and the sections must, of course, be large enough to be structurally sound. The best arrangement is to use short, adjustable, cantilever supports rather than continuous sections penetrating the insulation.

6. Adjustable Cladding Supports

The structural frames of buildings are not likely to be built within close tolerances. Floor edges are frequently 1'' to 2'' (25 mm to 50 mm) out of line and similar amounts out of plumb (from floor to floor). Not only that, but bolts and anchors for cladding supports are seldom where they are expected to be.

For these reasons cladding supports must be three-way adjustable. One way of doing this is shown in Figure 3–7. The amount of adjustment available will be about 1 1/4'' (30 mm), depending on the bolt size, usually 3/4'' (20 mm), and the minimum end distance that must be left between the slotted holes and the edge of the steel members.

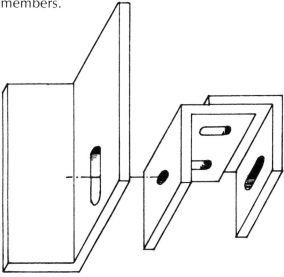

FIGURE 3-7. Three-way adjustable shelf angle support.

If this adjustment is not provided, shelf angles and other supports will be cut and shimmed on the job. Not only does this burn off any rustproofing but frequently it is structurally hazardous.

7.   Insulation

A close fit between insulation and its backup is important, as explained in Chapter 1. For this reason, glass fiber insulation is preferred because it can be drawn up tighter to the irregularities of the average backup wall than can the rigid polystyrene foams.

REFERENCES

Alberti, Leon Batista. 1965. *Ten Books on Architecture.* London: Alec Tiranti.

Baker, M.C. 1968. "Thermal and Moisture Deformations in Building Materials." *CBD 56.* Ottawa: DBR NRCC.

Foster, D. 1983. "Water Off a Duck's Back." *Building Design, Structural Clay Products,* Brick Supplement.

Litvan, G.G. 1980. "Freeze-Thaw Durability of Porous Building Materials and Components." *A.S.T.M. Special Publication 691:* pp. 455–463.

Newman, A.J., Whiteside, D., Kloss, P.B., and Willis, W. 1982. "Full-scale Water Penetration Tests on Twelve Cavity Fills—Parts I and II." *Building and Environment* 17(3): pp. 175–191.

4

Sealing Joints

4.1 INTRODUCTION

This chapter looks at the reasons why some joints are sealed and some are not. It also looks at the demands placed upon the materials used to seal them. It goes on to review a few of the most effective sealants currently available and to summarize their characteristics. Application methods are given, along with additional requirements for dependable caulking. Proper application and the other related issues combine to make up such an extensive list of requirements that one can question the feasibility of meeting them all.

Two membranes are described which can be applied to walls where they serve both as air barriers and flexible joint seals. These membranes are recommended in place of caulking in two-stage weatherproofing.

This chapter deals only with walls, for if the recommended style of window frame is used, no caulking will be required between glass and frame or between the frame and the air barrier. Caulking will be needed only in glass roofs, frame joints and perhaps where the window trim meets the cladding (see Chapter 5). The roofing and flashing details presented in Part 1 are sealed with a membrane rather than caulking and are described in Chapter 7. Recommendations are given both for caulking and for membranes.

4.2 WHICH JOINTS TO SEAL

Buildings are assemblies of components and wherever one piece meets another there is a junction to think about. Sometimes these joints can be left open, as they are between shingles; other times they should be sealed. A review of the requirements for a building envelope, which are listed in Figure 4–1, will help to sort out whether or not the joints should be sealed.

Going through this list, it is clear that the effectiveness of joint sealing might affect the control of the following:

- heat flow,
- air flow,
- vapor flow,
- rain penetration,
- noise penetration, and
- fire.

```
     1.   Control heat flow;

     2.   Control air flow;

     3.   Control water vapour flow;

     4.   Contol rain penetration;

     5.   Control light, solar and other radiation;

     6.   Control noise;

     7.   Control fire;

     8.   Provide strength and rigidity;

     9.   Be durable;

    10.   Be aesthetically pleasing;

    11.   Be economical.
```

FIGURE 4-1.   Principal requirements of a wall. (Hutcheon, N.B. 1963. Requirements for exterior walls. CBD 48, DBR NRCC, pp.1,2.)

Many designers respond to these requirements by caulking every joint in sight (as well as those that are hidden). This is not always a good idea. The reasons for saying so are developed in Chapter 3. The conclusions reached in that chapter lead to two fairly simple answers:

• Sealing the joints at the exterior face of a cavity wall is not necessary, and is often unwise.
• Air, water, heat, vapor, and sound can best be controlled by sealing the building just inside the insulation.

4.3   CHARACTERISTICS REQUIRED IN SEALANTS

Where no perceptible movement is expected, a nonelastic material such as mortar is used to close joints.

On the other hand, there are many joints in buildings that should be sealed and where the materials on either side of the joint may be expected to move with respect to one another. If the movement is to be repeated, as it might be if it were due to expansion and contraction caused by daily temperature changes, then the sealing material should be elastic so that it can recover its original shape once the movement is over. If the movement occurs only once, for instance the shrinkage of concrete masonry, then the seal should be flexible enough to accept the change in shape, but, since it will never be required to recover, elasticity is unimportant.

Thus the requirements for sealants range through the following:

- Materials that need little capacity for movement.
- Materials that must have good flexibility with little need for recovery.
- Materials that must have good flexibility and be elastic enough to recover.

There are other requirements that these materials must have. These are the following:

- Good adhesive qualities so they can stick to the materials they are joining.
- Reasonable curing time, for they are often expected to perform as soon as they are applied.
- Good cohesive qualities, neither given to sagging out of shape nor to being easily torn apart.
- Excellent durability, for in many installations they can never be reached for repair.

4.4 MATERIALS AVAILABLE TO SEAL JOINTS

4.4.1 Categories of Sealants

There are four generally accepted categories of sealants, classified by their ability to absorb movement. As can be seen, their ability to move and recover varies widely:

- Linseed oil putties, where the allowable movement is about 3%.
- Butyl rubbers, where the allowable movement in the joint is ±7%.
- Solvent curing acrylics that can tolerate a movement of plus or minus 10% of the joint width.
- Polysulphides, silicones and polyurethanes, flexible enough that they can tolerate joint movement of 25% of the joint width without damaging the seal. With low modulus silicone, the allowable movement rises to plus or minus 50% of the joint width.

The first three categories are seldom used in the construction of high quality building envelopes. Seven, more effective, sealants from the fourth category are described in Table 4–1.

High performance sealants have been used extensively for the following:

- exterior joints in metal and concrete curtain wall panels,
- metal-to-glass sealing,
- control joints,
- expansion joints,
- sealing hairline cracks, and
- flexible junctions between air/vapor barrier components.

TABLE 4-1. Summary of properties, high performance sealants.*

TYPE OF SEALANT	ACRYLIC (SOLVENT)	POLYSULFIDE 1-PART	POLYSULFIDE 2-PART	URETHANE 1 PART	URETHANE 2 PART	SILICONE 1 PART
Movement capacity, %.	10–15	15	25–40%	25	25 to 40	25 (50)
Theoretical joint width as a multiple of expected movement.	8X	4X	4X	4X	4X	4X
Maximum joint width.	3/4" (20 mm)	1" (25 mm)	1" + (25 mm)	3/4"(20 mm)	2"(50 mm)	2"(50 mm)
Life expectancy, years.	10–20	10–20	10–20	10–20	10–20	10–30
Service temperature range, °F.	−30 to 70	−40 to 80	−50 to 80	−40 to 80	−40 to 80	−55 to 120
Application temperature range, °F	40 to 80	40 to 80	40 to 80	40 to 80	40 to 80	40 to 80
Tack free cure time, hours.	36	24	35–48	12–36	24	1
Cure time for spec. performance	14	30–45	7	8–14	3–5	5–14
Shrinkage, percent.	12–15	8–12	10 min	nil-5	nil-5	nil-5
A scale hardness, new at 75°F(24°C.)	0–25	20–45	20–45	20–45	10–45	20–45
A scale hardness, 5 years, 75°F(24°C.)	30–55	30–55	35 +	30–55	20–55	20–45
Resistance to extension at low temperatures.	high	low to high	low to moderate	low to high	low to high	low
Primer required for bond to: Masonry	no	yes	yes	no	usually	usually
Metal	no	possibly	possibly	no	usually	usually
Glass	no	possibly	possibly	no	usually	no
Clean up solvent. (before cure)	xylol MEK	xylol MEK	xylol MEK	toluol MEK	xylol toluol	xylol MEK
Price range, $ per U.S. gal.	15–20	15–30	15–25	12–30	12–18	15–40
Canadian specification.	19-GP-5M	19-GP-13M	24 M 80	19-GP-16 CGSB19-13-M82	19-GP-15 CGSB24M80	19-GP-9 19-GP-18
U.S.A. specifications	TTS 00230 AMMA 8030	ASTM C920 TTS 000 230C	ASTM C920 TTS 000 227E	ASTM 920-79 TTS 00230C Type 2 class A	TTS 00227E Type 2 class A	TTS 00230C Type 2 class A

*Adapted from: Baldwin, Bob. 1976. Selecting high performance building sealants. Plant Engineering 5008, Table 1.

4.5 REQUIREMENTS FOR SATISFACTORY CAULKING

The requirements for dependable, long life, airtight, watertight caulking are now summarized. If they are used with an understanding of their characteristics and if the requirements for good caulking are observed, sealants can function very well. However, these requirements are so onerous that it is unrealistic to expect all of them to be met in a reliable way.

4.5.1 Designing the Joint

The expected movement at the joint must be calculated and the joint then designed to function within the safe, long-term adhesive and cohesive limits of the material, bearing in mind whether the sealant is likely to be applied in cold or hot weather; i.e., whether the joint will be at its greatest or least width respectively (see 4.5.11). Usually the manufacturer of the sealant will assist with this design.

4.5.2 Related Sealant Characteristics

In choosing a sealant, the designer must consider the position and exposure of the joint and whether the movement is periodic or progressive so that one can decide on such structurally related sealant characteristics as material creep, recovery capability, abrasion resistance, tear resistance, self healing capability, curing time, shrinkage, and the effects of fatigue.

4.5.3 Material Substitution

Because the design will be based on specific sealant characteristics, great care must be taken in allowing substitutions for the selected sealant.

4.5.4 Handling, Storing, and Mixing

Materials must be handled, stored, and mixed in strict accordance with the manufacturers' requirements.

4.5.5 Preparing Joints for Caulking

It is important to clean the joint surface on both new and old work. Because new materials are often covered with a protective film, wash all nonporous surface materials with an oil-free solvent, such as xylol, toluol, or methyl ethyl ketone (MEK). Lacquer coatings are best removed with lacquer thinner. When applying sealant over a concrete surface, remove weak concrete and loose aggregate by sawing, sand blasting, grinding, or wire brushing.

For remedial work, workmen should remove all old caulking and oily residues, cut at least 3/8" (10 mm) deep into the joint, sandblast or wire brush surfaces, remove dust with an air blast, solvent-wash the surface, and remove paint. Although these tasks (often not done even when specified) seem extreme for remedial work, they are important determinants of how long the joint will subsequently remain sealed. Neglect of these tasks initially is probably the reason that the seals fail.

Apply surface conditioner or primer, if required, and allow to dry. These materials are not cleaning agents and should be applied only to clean, dry surfaces. Handle according to manufacturer's instructions. Occasionally, primers are omitted without serious consequences. Only the user can decide whether or not it is worth the risk.

The caulking bead in Figure 4–3 has a backup rod that is usually made of a plastic foam that will not bond to the sealant. The rods are used to control sealant depth and shape, important elements in joint design.

Use masking tape, if bead lines of exact shapes are required. It should also be used if porous surfaces make cleanup difficult. Apply masking tape after surface conditioner has been applied.

4.5.6   Shaping the Joints

The shape of a caulked joint is very important. Figure 4–2 shows a shape frequently found in joints. The sealant bead is thick and strong in the middle and has only a small area in contact with the sides. When the joint expands, the thick center section resists the movement and, since there is only a small area sticking to the sides, the caulking bead breaks loose.

Figure 4–3 and Figure 4–4 on the other hand, show sealant beads with comparatively large areas in contact with the sides of the joints, so it is difficult to tear them loose. The center portion is concave and thinner and thus exerts less stress on the bond. This shape is achieved by forcing the sealant into the joint over an ethafoam rod of the proper size, then tooling the top of the joint into a similar concave shape. The caulking must not stick to the rod in the bottom of the joint. The area in contact with the sides of the joint and the depth at the neck of the concave bead are important design factors. The sealant manufacturer will usually assist with this aspect of design.

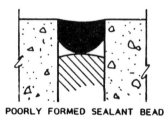

POORLY FORMED SEALANT BEAD

FIGURE 4–2. Poorly formed sealant bead. (Garden, G.K. 1967. Use of sealants. CBD 96, DBR NRCC, Fig.1f.)

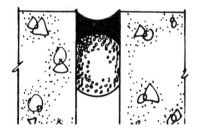

WELL FORMED SEALANT BEAD

FIGURE 4–3. Well formed sealant bead. (Garden, G.K. 1967. Use of sealants. CBD 96, DBR NRCC, Fig.1d.)

WELL FORMED CORNER BEA

FIGURE 4–4. Well formed corner bead. (Garden, G.K. 1967. Use of sealants. CBD 96, DBR NRCC, Fig.1e.)

4.5.7 Application and Tooling

Apply sealant carefully according to instructions. Try to force the sealant bead into the joint to eliminate voids as shown in Figure 4–5.

Do not break the cartridge seal until just before use. Two part materials should not be mixed too far ahead of use. Tool joints immediately after the sealant is applied and before a skin begins to form. Tooling forces the sealant against the sides of joints, eliminates voids, and gives the required concave shape to the exposed surface. Remove masking tape immediately after tooling is completed.

4.5.8 Skill and Concentration

The preparation, filling, and shaping just described must be carried out perfectly and consistently by a skilled applicator. It requires remarkable skill, knowledge, and concentration to perform this demanding task hour by hour, day by day.

4.5.9 Joint Condition

The architect's design drawings will show the joints at their median width, with corners neatly formed and all surfaces plumb, level, and true to line. Nothing could be farther from reality. Corners will be chipped, chamfered, and honeycombed. Joints will be out of line and of changing width. Frequently, the width will be outside the specified tolerance.

The surfaces to which sealants are to be applied may not be sound and suitable for caulking. For example:

• Gypsum board is cut by scoring the surface, then breaking the gypsum core. This shattered surface is seldom satisfactory for caulking.
• In exposed aggregate precast concrete panels, unsound or improperly embedded aggregate frequently interferes with a tight joint.
• Very few sealants will make a permanent bond to polyethelene film.

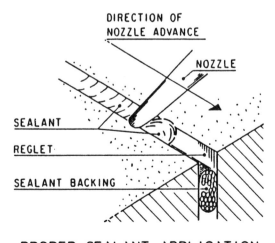

PROPER SEALANT APPLICATION

FIGURE 4–5. Proper sealant application. (Garden, G.K. 1967. Use of sealants. CBD 96, DBR NRCC, Fig.2.)

4.5.10 Changing Joint Width

Frequently, joints will vary in width by 100%. Changing width will require a different bead thickness and an enlarged area in contact with the edges; in other words, redesign. The applicator may not have the knowledge or supplies to resolve the problem.

4.5.11 Temperature Effects

The temperature must be within the range shown in the tables. If the temperature is quite warm, the materials that are being joined may be near their maximum size due to thermal expansion. As a result, the joints between them will be at or near their minimum size. Sealants applied under these conditions will be over extended when the panels cool. Similarly, caulking done in cold weather may be subject to excessive compressive stresses. Temperature changes from day to night may also put too much stress on sealant material that has not had time to completely cure.

4.5.12 Access to Work

The applicator must have easy access to the work. Good workmanship cannot be expected if the joint is difficult or impossible to reach.

4.6 MEMBRANE AIR BARRIERS

Where airtightness MUST be achieved, a membrane air barrier should be considered. Currently, a number of buildings are being constructed with membrane air barriers adhered to back-up walls of concrete, concrete blockwork, and drywall. The material used is rubberized asphalt: asphalt modified with polymers to improve its elasticity.

4.6.1 Materials

Basically, there are two types of rubberized asphalt. One is self-adhering. It has a very tacky surface that will adhere to most clean, dry building materials. It is supplied with a protective paper layer that is removed to expose the tacky surface. There is some evidence that it does not stick well to damp concrete blockwork. Insist on new material. Old stock does not bond well at all.

The other material is about 3 mm thick and is reinforced with a nonwoven mat of polyester. This sheet material is applied by melting the surface with propane torches. The concrete blockwork is heated with the same torches at the same time. The molten surface of the membrane is then pressed against the warm masonry surface and the two are welded together.

4.6.2 Characteristics

Because the material will elongate about 70% and is somewhat elastic. It can run across joints in the construction where small movements may occur; joints that would otherwise have to be caulked. Special materials with more elastic reinforcements are available for those joints that are designed to accommodate building movement.

On buildings with concrete frames and concrete block infilling panel walls, this material provides an airtight, watertight, highly vapor-resistant layer on the concrete blockwork, which is notoriously porous. It also provides flexible seals at the joints between the concrete framing members (columns, beams, etc.) and the concrete blockwork.

4.6.3 Polymers Used to Modify Asphalt

The polymers, styrene butadiene styrene (SBS) and actactic polypropylene (APP), that are used to modify the asphalts have different characteristics and thus impart different characteristics to the membranes. The SBS modified asphalts seem to be giving good service and are developing an enviable reputation. As a result, everybody is getting into the act and there are many new modified asphalts coming on the market. It would be wise to have them analyzed and tested before allowing them on a job. Compare them with materials that have performed well over a long period in a similar climate.

Asphalts modified with SBS polymers are claimed to have the following:

- superior elasticity and thus better fatigue resistance,
- superior compatibility with other asphalts, and
- somewhat better high temperature resistance.

4.6.4 Application to Gypsum Board and Metal

Gypsum board can be damaged by the heat from propane torches. Rubberized asphalt material has been successfully applied to gypsum board by heating only the membrane. To do this, the work was enclosed with a temporary shelter so that the gypsum board was dry. Do not attempt to apply the membrane to damp gypsum board.

Difficulty has also been experienced applying the membrane to metal. If this difficulty is encountered, use pieces of compatible self-adhering membrane to seal the membrane to the metal.

4.6.5 Fitting the Membrane Around Brick Ties

Fitting the membrane around brick ties is a difficult and tedious job. It must be done by skilled craftsmen. Consideration should be given to applying brick ties after the membrane is in place.

4.6.6 Insulation Fasteners

When a torched-on membrane is used, it is possible to heat the perforated heads of the fasteners and fuse them to the membrane.

4.7 RECOMMENDATIONS

Effective sealants with remarkable properties are available. Properly designed and prepared joints can be sealed as well and as consistently as good craftsmanship allows. However, a brief perusal of the essential requirements will show that it is extremely difficult to meet all of these conditions consistently. This is the reasoning that lies behind the recommendations that follow.

4.7.1 Face Caulking

Caulking to the faces of buildings cannot be relied upon to remain watertight or airtight. However, caulking can be used to close the joints on the face of a building as long as there is adequate cavity drainage to get rid of the water that penetrates flaws in the caulking and as long as there is an air seal farther back in the wall. Such face sealing is sometimes used because it is thought to improve the appearance of the building.

4.7.2 Glass Roofs

At the NRCC Window Seminar in 1979, Claude Perreault remarked "no self-respecting architect can design a building today without a glass roof." These are very demanding structures, particularly where sealants are concerned. The ideal arrangement would be to design in accordance with the principles of two-stage waterproofing. However, at the current state of the art, some surface caulking must be used. Fortunately, the components can be accurately formed and installed. Acceptable results can be obtained if the joints are properly designed, prepared, and accessible for repair.

4.7.3 Two-Stage Waterproofing

In insulated buildings where two-stage waterproofing is used, the air seal is in a less demanding environment. In typical construction, the exposed surface temperature may vary 145°F (83°C), while the temperature just inboard of the insulation will vary only 25°F (14°C). Not only will the temperature swings be reduced to one-sixth of those in an exposed location, but a seal in this position will be protected from ultraviolet light and mechanical damage. A design such as this increases the expectations for effective caulking. However, many requirements remain to be met and since some are beyond the designer's control, failures are to be expected. A rubberized asphalt membrane is preferred. When it is used, it also provides a dependable, sealed "raincoat" for the building that is quite forgiving of flaws in the cladding (see 3.2.4).

4.7.4 Accessibility for Repair

It should be clear that perfect caulking may not be achieved and that even well caulked joints will fail in time. Therefore, it is necessary that joints be accessible for repair. Unfortunately, two-stage waterproofing often results in air seals being placed in a location which makes them inaccessible. A solution to this problem requires great inventiveness on the part of the designer.

One solution anticipates such failures. Joints in the cladding are aligned with those in the insulated precast concrete backup as shown in Figure 4–6. These joints are wide enough to allow the joints between the inner precast panels to be repaired or recaulked. A small section of insulation would be removed and replaced to permit this repair.

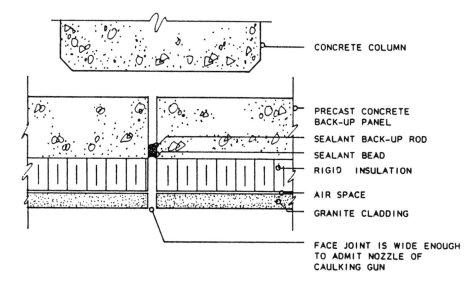

FIGURE 4-6. Caulking for airtightness in prefabricated panel assembly.

4.7.5 Recaulking

Recaulking requires special attention. Because the original caulking may have failed prematurely or because it is no longer available or more likely because some salesman has been leaning on the buyer, one may wish to change sealants. If so, be aware of the following:

- Make sure the new material is compatible with the old: get it in writing.
- Alternatively saw or grind off the old caulking. Even this may leave some traces of the old sealant.
- Assure that the criteria in section 4.5 are observed.
- Read and observe the manufacturer's written instructions.

4.7.6 Up-to-Date Information

Because manufacturers are constantly developing new sealants and reformulating the old ones, new products may exceed current standards. It is recommended that up-to-date, written design information be sought from reputable manufacturers who have shown concern for their long term reputation.

5

Windows

5.1 INTRODUCTION

This chapter deals with windows in aluminum frames. Because aluminum frames require no painting, are not subject to rot and are not affected by the presence of moisture, they are used almost exclusively in commercial, institutional, and industrial buildings.

Windows are a rather special part of the building envelope. In addition to complying with all the requirements of the rest of the wall (Figure 5–1), they involve architectural issues such as scale, meaning, imagery, context, and mood; to say nothing of space and the spatial effects of light, daylighting for vision, ambient and radiant temperatures, heat storage, dirt and insects; ease of operation, maintenance and cleaning; thermal breakage and the possibility of etching, and so on.

This chapter examines how windows meet these requirements. The major issues are reviewed again in respect to a well designed window frame.

5.2 CONTROL OF HEAT FLOW

It is true that, because of solar heating, a properly placed window can gain more heat than it loses, even in cold winters. This is seldom the case in practice, simply because of the number of other issues that must be resolved (see 5.1).

Good windows have only 1/20 or 1/30 the insulating value of an equivalent area of insulated wall or roof (Figure 5–2). Because of solar heating and because they are such poor insulators, the sizing and positioning of windows and the selection of the type of glazing are principal factors in heating and cooling the building. They affect not only the cost of heating and cooling equipment but also the cost of operating this equipment. Air leakage, a major cause of heat loss is described in 5.3.

Heat flow by radiation is perhaps the most important aspect of heat flow through windows. It is discussed in detail in Chapter 1.

5.2.1 Multiple Glazing

Almost all of the insulation provided by windows comes from the still air layer that clings to each surface. Unless there is a wind, these layers have a thermal resistance of R 0.68 (Rsi 0.12). A 15 mph (25 kmph) wind reduces the thickness of the air film and its resistance drops to R 0.17 (Rsi 0.03).

1.   Control heat flow;

2.   Control air flow;

3.   Control water vapour flow;

4.   Contol rain penetration;

5.   Control light, solar and other radiation;

6.   Control noise;

7.   Control fire;

8.   Provide strength and rigidity;

9.   Be durable;

10.   Be aesthetically pleasing;

11.   Be economical.

FIGURE 5-l. Principal requirements for a wall. (Hutcheon, N.B. 1963. Requirements for exterior walls. CBD 48, DBR NRCC, pp.1,2.)

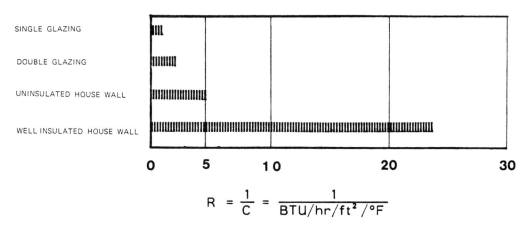

FIGURE 5-2. Thermal resistance of windows and other construction.

The optimum gap between panes is 5/8″ (15 mm to 16 mm). Reducing the gap to 1/4″ (4.8 mm) reduces the insulating value of double glazing by 21%. Increasing the gap to 100 mm (4 in.) reduces the insulating value only slightly, 2%. Triple glazing adds two more still air layers and brings the resistance to R 3 (Rsi 0.52).

It is also possible to reduce the conductive portion of heat transfer through double glazing by filling the space between the panes with a gas less conductive than air.

5.2.2   Reflective Films

Kirchhoff's law states that the ability of a surface to absorb heat (absorptance) is the same as its ability to radiate heat (emittance). It is possible to use coatings or films to change the emittance and thus the absorptance of windows. Low "e" glass is glass with a film or coating that reduces its emittance, thus reducing the amount of heat that it loses by radiation. Adding a low emissivity film within the cavity or to one glass surface of double glazing can increase the insulating value by over 50% in summer and winter. Glass can be supplied with a wide range of reflective coatings.

5.2.3   Orientation

Double glazed windows that face south, southeast, or southwest have the potential to gain more heat from the sun than they lose through conduction to the exterior. With triple glazing there is a possibility of a net heat gain with vertical windows facing the sky in any direction as far north as 45 degrees latitude. Although windows receive heat while the sun is shining through the window, they lose a lot of it at night when the temperature is coldest outside. To be useful, a good part of the heat must be stored. There are a number of good articles and books on the collection and storage of solar heat.

Also unless proper care is taken, rooms may be overheated by solar radiation. The effects of south facing shading overhangs is shown in Figure 5–7.

There is some solar gain from blue sky and through cloud cover. Except for this, however, the sun must be shining through the window to provide solar gain. Trees, other buildings, and orientation may prevent sunlight from reaching windows. Conversely, unexpected solar reflection may be received from snow cover, water surfaces, decks, and adjacent buildings. As mentioned in 5.2, solar heating will be a mixed blessing unless the windows are properly placed and shaded and unless they are oriented correctly. There must either be adequate heat storage capacity in the building or a means of using some of the heat from the sunny side of the building to heat the cooler side.

5.2.4   Thermal Shutters and Drapes

Convection currents will make any loose-fitting drape or shutter less effective than a tight one. The subject of convection currents circumventing insulation is discussed in Section 1.2.3.

When shutters are placed on the room side of windows they will, if they are at all effective, reduce the heat reaching the window. In winter this will result in the window surfaces becoming very cold. If warm moist interior air can reach this cold surface it will condense there. Thus interior shutters must be tightly sealed to prevent the passage of interior air. Blinds and drapes do not provide much insulation, but they do cut down radiation to the cold window surface and, as a result, increase comfort. Shutters on the outside do not create a condensation problem and are to be preferred. With both kinds of shutters, there is a thermal shock to the glazing when the shutters are closed or opened. Such shocks are likely to shorten the life of sealed glazing units.

5.2.5 Cold Surfaces

Because windows are such poor insulators, they are cold when it is cold outside. Even the inside surface of double glazing can be close to the freezing point (Figure 5–3). Most people are probably aware that sitting close to a cold window can be quite uncomfortable, even when the air temperature is warm.

In northern climates, window surfaces are frequently below the dewpoint of the air in the room. The cool surface temperature of windows is often the factor that limits the humidity that can be carried in a room.

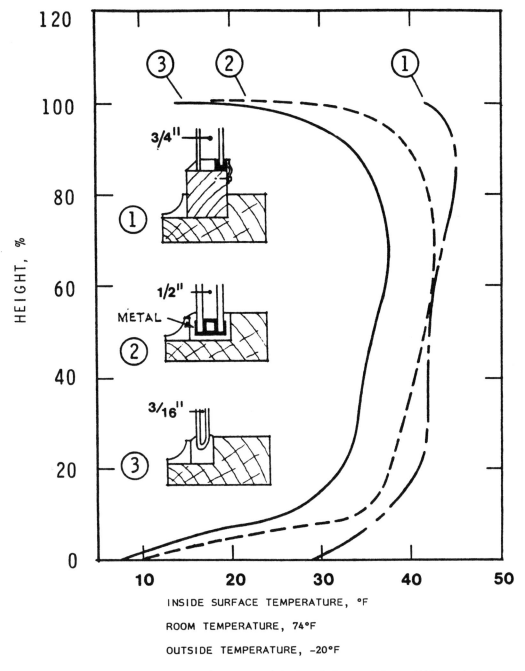

FIGURE 5–3. Surface temperatures on three types of glazing. (Solvason, K.R., and Wilson, A.G. 1963. Factory-sealed double-glazing units. CBD 46, DBR NRCC, Fig.2.)

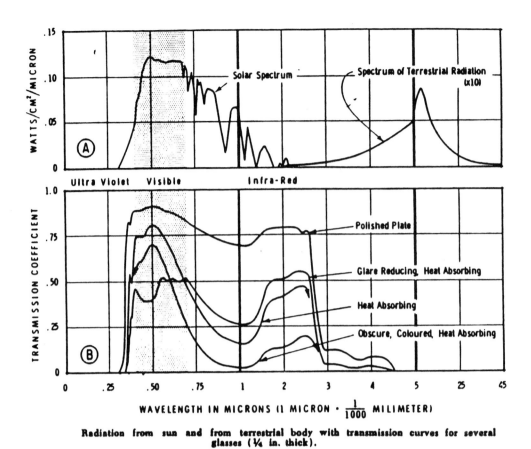

Radiation from sun and from terrestrial body with transmission curves for several glasses (¼ in. thick).

FIGURE 5-4. Radiation from sun and from terrestrial body with transmission curves for several glasses. (Garden, G.K. 1964. Characteristics of window glass. CBD 60, DBR NRCC, Fig.1.)

There are a number of phenomena that are associated with these cold surfaces. The first depends on air coming in contact with the cold surface. The air is cooled, becomes denser and falls to the floor. These convection currents cause drafts along the floor. The condition can be quite serious and is the reason that most heating units are placed underneath windows.

The point has been made that glazing has poor resistance to the flow of heat. It has much less resistance to the flow of heat in the form of daylight and sunlight. As a matter of fact, glass is chosen for windows simply because it is transparent to visible light. The coincidence can be seen in Figure 5–4.

5.2.6 Radiation Through Windows

As described in Chapter 1, as daylight and sunlight pass through windows to fall on objects and surfaces, these surfaces are immediately warmed as some of the heat is absorbed. The rest of it is re-radiated into the space and even back to the window, where it has trouble getting out. This "greenhouse" effect is very desirable if we are trying to heat the room with solar energy. It may be very undesirable if we are not.

Thus, in buildings where it is desirable to get optimum benefit from solar heating, the size of the windows and their placing are controlling design decisions.

5.3 CONTROL OF AIR FLOW

Ventilation through a window is perhaps the oldest of requirements. The word "window" is thought to be derived from the Nordic word meaning "wind-eye" which suggests that its earliest purpose was to ventilate (Quirouette 1979). The openable window has taken on many forms. The ventilating characteristics of even the commonest forms are quite different. It is obvious which windows can be left open during the rain, which windows deflect drafts away from the occupants of the room, what percentage of the total window can be opened, which models should be easiest to operate, and which ones can be closed most tightly.

Even with the ventilators closed, many windows leak a great deal more air than most people expect. This air leakage occurs because of the following:

- The glass is not sealed tightly into the sash.
- The sash does not close tightly to the frame.
- The window frame is not properly and permanently sealed into the airtight part of the wall. Amounts are shown in Figure 5–5.

While the air leakage around windows is normally associated with older buildings, there are many newer buildings where no one wants to sit close to the windows on a windy day. The design of windows that will resist air leakage is a remarkably difficult task and reasonable solutions have only been found in the last few years.

One of the most difficult joints to close properly is the one between the window and the wall. There is a sizeable crack between the window and the wall. It comes about because the window is made in a factory and is usually very accurately sized and shaped. The hole into which it fits, on the other hand, is hand crafted by masons or other tradesmen. Under normal circumstances it may vary 3/8" to 1/2" (10 mm to 15 mm) in dimension and it may be out-of-square or warped an equivalent

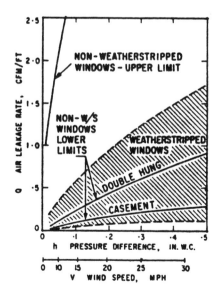

FIGURE 5–5. Window air leakage characteristics. J. R. Sasaki and A. G. Wilson 1962. Window air leakage C.B.D. 25, D.B.R. N.R.C.C. FIGURE 1

amount. As a result, the opening for the window is usually made 3/8″ to 1/2″ (10 mm to 15 mm) bigger in both directions than the window it is to receive.

Sealing this crack is difficult for many reasons, not the least of which is the fact that the window frame and the opening are made of different materials that have different coefficients of expansion. Methods of sealing this crack are shown in the details in Part 1. It should be noted that the space between the window frame and the wall opening, at the head of the window, can be used to take up deflection that might damage the window.

5.4   CONTROL OF WATER VAPOR FLOW

To understand the implications of water vapor flow on windows one should understand how it moves around. There are two mechanisms. The first is diffusion. This simply means that water vapor molecules in the air are able to move through a number of building materials. They cannot penetrate glass or metal, so this mechanism is of no concern in windows.

For practical purposes, there are always water molecules floating around in the air, so that when the air moves, the water molecules move with it. This mechanism, vapor carried by air leakage, is the one to be concerned about.

The most common evidence of moisture carried by air leakage through window assemblies is the buildup of condensation and frost between double windows. Because the glass and frames are vaportight, the only source for this frost and condensation is the air that leaks through cracks in the assembly from the room into the space between the double windows. In most instances this buildup of frost is just a nuisance because it obscures our vision through the windows. In some buildings however where the air inside is highly humidified, 1″ to 2″ (25 mm to 50 mm) of ice and frost can be built up between the panes. The results can be disastrous when it finally melts. One of the chief virtues of sealed double glazing is that moisture cannot leak into the space between the panes of glass and so these windows are free of condensation, at least as long as the seals last.

5.5   CONTROL OF RAIN PENETRATION

The control of rain leakage at windows is a very poorly understood science.

The rational approach to weather-tightness of window frames is the two-stage method, described in Chapter 3, which tolerates some imperfections in the air seal (see Figure 5–6). Two-stage water control in a well designed aluminum window frame is achieved by having a rain deflector on the outside of the frame and an air seal near the inside of the frame. There is a drain in the air space between the rain deflector and the air seal. If any rain does get past the first stage (rain deflector) it will not reach the air seal. This is very important for it is at the air seal that pressures exist that might drive moisture into the building; all that is needed is a flaw in the air seal.

The effectiveness of the outer gasket or spline would be greatly improved if there were no air-pressure difference across it to force water in. It is thought that the pressure difference across the spline can be reduced by providing pressure equalizing openings between the air space and the outside. The drainage holes will usually suffice.

To achieve two-stage water resistance, the following features have been incorporated into the design of the frame shown in Figure 5–6.

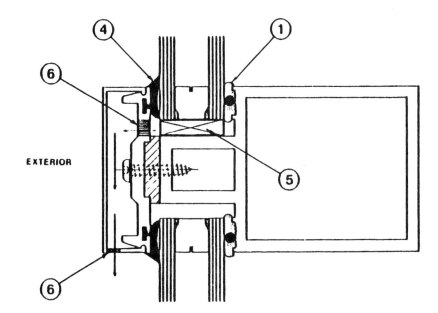

FIGURE 5-6. A WELL DESIGNED WINDOW FRAME—ALUMINUM CURTAIN WALL (Insulated Glass Manufacturers of Canada, Brantford, Ontario. 1986. Glazing Recommendations for Sealed Insulating Glass Units. Revised November 1986. p.10.)

- The frame, sash, glass assembly must provide a continuous line of airtightness. This line of airtightness must connect with the airtightness line in the supporting wall.
- According to the rules that were established in the Prolegomenon, this air barrier must be kept warm. This is done with insulation in the wall, a thermal break in the window frame and an outer sheet of glass, and an air space in the glazing.
- The air seal must be protected from wetting by an outer water deterrent (usually a spline or gasket) and an air space that cannot be bridged by water. Horizontal window frame members should slope outwards from the air seal, and water stops should be located wherever water can migrate inwards by gravity.
- Some outside air should be allowed to enter the cavity between the outer water deterrent and the air seal. This can be achieved by making the pressure-equalizing openings to the outside much larger than the equivalent orifice area of the air seal, and by ensuring that these openings, approximately 3/8" (10 mm) minimum diameter, cannot be blocked by water flowing over the outer face or draining outwards.

The theory of pressure equalization is discussed in Chapter 3. There is little agreement on whether or not it actually works, but holes are required for drainage in any case.

When dealing with rain leakage through and around windows, it is well to remember that there are three sets of joints in windows that must be made watertight:

- joints between the glass and the frame or opening sash,
- joints between the opening sash and the window frame, and
- joints between the frame and the wall.

If the window is to perform properly, each of these joints must be designed with two-stage waterproofing.

The cracks at joints to be waterproofed may be quite large because considerable clearance is required between the factory made frame and the hand crafted wall. Openings may deviate from right angles at the corners. Similar small clearances are required between the glass and the frame. There must also be some clearance between the frame and any operating sash to allow the sash to operate. Not only must these clearances accommodate the manufacturing tolerances but must also accommodate the differential expansion between such materials as glass, aluminum and masonry.

5.6 CONTROL OF LIGHT AND OTHER RADIATION

Along with the provision of ventilation and a view, the provision of daylight is one of the most important purposes of a window. Because of its continuous variability, hourly, daily and seasonally, daylighting design is a complicated task but it does produce rewarding results and often a delightful visual environment. Both the desire to use less energy and general dissatisfaction with environments that are dependent entirely on artificial light have fostered a great deal of research in the science of daylighting. There are several simple useful methods for its design. On the simplest level, there are three or four rules that can be applied.

The first rules are based on the fact that a bright window in a dark wall causes an uncomfortable glare. This contrast can be alleviated by having windows in more than one wall so that each wall receives some light from other windows, by painting the walls a light color to reduce the contrast and by splaying the inside reveals of the window opening.

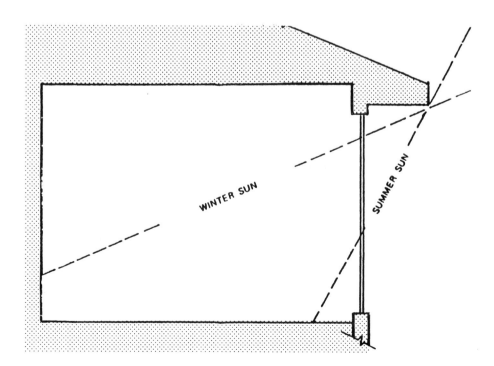

FIGURE 5-7. Shading from south facing overhang.

The orientation of the windows has a great effect on the amount and quality of daylighting. Windows facing north are lit mainly by the north sky and the light has a tendency to be cool and blue. Windows facing east and west get direct sunlight in the morning or the afternoon, unless they are shaded by trees. This direct sunlight can be quite uncomfortable and is difficult to control.

As mentioned in Chapter 1, the most controllable sunlight is that which comes from the south. The higher altitude of the sun in summer makes it possible to control it with overhangs of various designs. The difference shows in Figure 5–7, where the low winter sun floods across the room, and summer sun is almost excluded.

5.7 CONTROL OF NOISE

In cities and in urban areas, noise has been increasing steadily, due to road and air traffic and to some extent the process of construction. How windows control the flow of such noise is governed by four factors: the weight of the glass, the distance between panes in multiple glazed units, orientation of the window, and airtightness.

Multiple pane assemblies provide better sound insulation value than the equivalent weight of a single pane of glass. For instance, two single panes of glass, spaced approximately 4" (100 mm) apart, would give about the same noise insulation value as a single light of glass weighing two and a half times as much as the pair of panes. A spacing of 4" to 6" (100 mm to 150 mm) is the practical optimum for double glass windows designed to reduce air-borne noise transmission. However, improvement can be obtained from even a 2" (50 mm) cavity. Because of the very narrow spacing in sealed units, these units offer negligible increase in sound insulation value over single glazing of the same total weight.

Orientation is the single most cost-effective solution to noise control for windows. Considering that a wall component is only as good as its weakest element, windows should be oriented away from the noise source whenever possible.

A conflict arises when it is desired to ventilate through a window while trying to control noise entry. However, some window arrangements will achieve acceptable performance. For example, a double horizontal slider, with the opening staggered to either side, is effective in controlling noise while permitting ventilation. Tests show that a double horizontal slider, with a spacing of 4" (100 mm) between the lights and an opening of 2" (50 mm) at each end, is as effective in reducing noise entry as a factory sealed double glazed unit which is fully closed (Olynyk 1968).

Sound entering a building through a wide open window will be attenuated some 5 to 10 decibels. This depends on a proportion of the window area to the full wall area. Ordinary single windows provide a sound transmission classification (stc) of about 25 (sound insulation value). Well-fitted double windows can attain an stc of about 35, depending on the surface weight and air space depth (Olynyk 1968). In summary, there may be design occasions when noise is the critical factor governing the selection of the most appropriate type of openable window.

The science of sound control and its implications are discussed in many texts.

5.8 CONTROL OF FIRE

Windows are very important elements in the control of the spread of fire from one building to another. A fire in one building will soon break the windows facing it in adjacent buildings. The heat of the fire then radiates into the rooms of the adjacent building and quickly raises the contents of the room to combustion temperatures.

This happens long before the fire can do any damage to the cladding of the building. However, the cladding may have an effect on the spread of fire from one floor to the floor above.

Building regulations usually state that buildings adjacent to one another must not have any windows facing each other, unless they are separated by a predetermined distance. Generally, any building 4 ft (1200 mm) or less from a property line is not permitted to have windows in a wall abutting the property line. Beyond the 4 foot limit, tables guide the maximum percentage of unprotected openings in each of the walls of the building.

Another option is to use sprinklers at the windows (see *CBD 248*).

5.9   PROVISION OF STRENGTH AND RIGIDITY

High winds, particularly if they are gusty, generate large pressures on the face of buildings. On the windward side, pressure is positive. On the other three sides, it is a suction force. Tall buildings in windy areas may be subject to pressures of 80 lb/ft² (0.4 kPa). It is clear that windows must be securely and permanently anchored into walls or frames that are capable of withstanding these forces. Wind may also carry roofing gravel and other debris that will endanger windows.

Thermal and other structural movements in buildings may affect window anchors and also distort the window frames so that the glass is no longer well secured. For instance, Figure 5–8 shows the distortion induced when the floor structure sags or creeps. This is a very common phenomenon. The amount of distortion shown is exaggerated, of course. A gust of wind can, and has, sent large panes of glass sailing across the countryside. These are lethal projectiles.

Nowhere is the provision of strength and rigidity more obvious than in glass roofs and skylights. Sloped glazing is subject to the same snow and wind loads as any other roof. Additionally, for glass roofs adjacent to higher buildings, the impact load of falling snow and ice from roofs above must also be considered.

Glass roofs are prone to increased thermal breakage because they are often turned towards the sun. They also pose a particular problem with respect to fire protection. Such roofs usually have an outer light of heat-strengthened or heat-tempered glass and an inner light composed of wire glass. The wire reduces the strength of the glass but it keeps the pieces from falling if the glass should break.

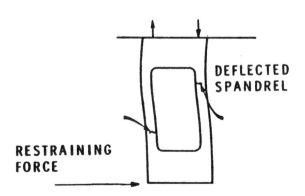

FIGURE 5-8.   Panel distortion due to creep in concrete frame. (Plewes, W.G. 1970. Cladding problems due to frame movements. CBD 125. DBR NRCC, Fig.3.)

5.10 DURABILITY

Except for its brittle nature, glass is a very durable substance. The weak link in a window assembly is usually the sealing material. Some of these sealants, like the old-fashioned putty, harden, crack and shrink in a relatively few years. Others are degraded by sunlight or actually squeezed out of the joint by wind pressure. In most windows, the seals are now a combination of rubber gaskets and "glazing tapes". The glazing tapes usually include a rubber shim that prevents the tape from being squeezed out.

Many windows today are glazed with "sealed double glazing". These are composed of two sheets of glass spaced 1/4" to 1/2" (6 mm to 12 mm) apart and sealed around the edges. The air filling the cavity between the two sheets of glass is especially dried, so that condensation will not occur.

Breakage of single glazing and the outer pane of double glazed units may be caused by absorption of solar radiation by the center while the edges of the glass remain cool. Thus glazing units with a high solar absorptance are more susceptible to solar breakage than clear glazing.

Solar breakage is also affected by interior and exterior shading devices as well as by the edge strength of the glass. Solar breakage can be minimized by reducing the heat build-up in the glass, by using strong glass, and by avoiding shading configurations that increase the stress in the glass.

The inside pane of a sealed double-glazing unit is also susceptible to breakage, but in this case breakage is caused by differences in heat loss between the edge and center of the glazing unit in cold weather. Breakage can be minimized by avoiding localized heating of the inner pane, by minimizing thermal contact between glazing unit and the cold parts of the glazing surround, and by using glass with edges free from flaws that may initiate a crack (Sasaki 1970).

As mentioned in the introduction to this chapter, the popularity of aluminum frames is due in no small part to the fact that they require very little maintenance.

5.11 AESTHETIC CONSIDERATIONS

Resolving the architect's wishes for meaning, scale, order, proportion, etc., with all the other issues that have been mentioned is always very difficult.

5.12 ECONOMY

It is easy to see that a cheap window might be economical in the short term but that maintenance or replacement could make it quite expensive in the long term. If you know the initial cost of the window, how long it should last, what the maintenance costs might be and what its effect might be on the energy consumption of the building, you should be able to calculate its cost in the long term. Quite often people do try to provide an estimate of "life cycle costing". You should bear in mind that the whole business is not nearly so scientific as it sounds, for it is very difficult to predict what is going to happen to a building in the long term, to say nothing of predicting the cost of fuel. Most major occupancies are in a continual state of flux and quite often these changes affect the use and operation of the building that houses them. It is certainly a good idea to take a look at costs over the long term. The point being made here is that it should be done with some skepticism.

Windows often have more effect than anything else on the initial cost and the operating cost of equipment for heating and cooling buildings. This is due to the fact that windows are poor insulators and that they provide access for solar heating. It was mentioned in 5.2 that solar heating is just fine when needed but only increases air conditioning costs if not required.

Most frames are now made of anodized aluminum. Actually, while bare aluminum discolors rather badly, the gradual greying and blackening may be quite acceptable if it is anticipated in the design.

The view out from a building is certainly enhanced by clean windows, so that if the view through windows is to be enjoyed, windows must be kept reasonably clean. This is a costly business in large buildings with many windows. The view into a show window is also enhanced by clean glass. In both cases, dirty windows not only affect the view but, more subjectively, affect our perception of the efficiency, cleanliness and tidiness of those who occupy the building. Grubby windows do little for a corporate image. So, in the design of windows, it is necessary to take account of how they can be cleaned, from where and by whom.

5.13   RECOMMENDATIONS

There are many kinds of windows on the market. Of these, there is one kind in particular where the design has evolved to the point where they perform very well. These are the windows and frames designed for curtain wall systems. They are not the particular property of any one manufacturer. Almost all large window manufacturers make window frames that follow this pattern. A typical section is shown in Figure 5–6. The following recommendations are based on the use of such frames.

5.13.1   Air Leakage

Use a flexible membrane such as rubberized asphalt to span the gap between the frame and the wall. Notice that one edge of this membrane can be clamped into the frame and the other sealed to the wall. Within the frame itself, seal between the frame and the glass with a shimmed tape. These tapes are made in the correct thicknesses to accommodate the frame construction. They have tiny rubber rods or ''shims'' embedded in them to keep wind pressures from squeezing out the adhesive material from the joint. Place the seal on the warm side of the frame and away from wet and cold that might affect its performance. The seals on the opening sash are similarly placed, back on the warm side of the frame.

5.13.2   Rain Leakage

Between the window frame and the wall, between the sash and the frame and between the glass and the sash, employ a two-stage waterproofing system with an outer gasket to act as a rain deterrent and airtight inner seal.

5.13.3   Easy Operation

First, there should be some means of holding the sash in any open position. Double hung windows usually have a counter balancing arrangement of some sort to allow the sash to be held in their partially open position. These seldom operate very well for very long. Horizontal sliders by their very nature will stay in any position desired.

Projected sash have a friction shoe that works quite well.

It should be possible to draw the window up tightly to its seals. This is best done by a cam handle arrangement. On large windows, more than one will be required. Some casement windows close with a crank arrangement. This should not be used to draw the opening sash up tightly to the seal, if the crank operates on one corner of the window. Pulling forcefully on one corner can distort the sash and break the seals.

5.13.4 Accumulation of Frost and Condensation

Frost and condensation on the glass itself is a function of the glass surface temperature. Raise this critical inside temperature of the glass by using double or triple glazing or by using low emissivity coatings on the glass.

Condensation and frost on the window frames can be controlled in several ways. The trick is, of course, to keep the inside surfaces of the frame warm, at least above the dew point of the air in the room. Do this by following these rules:

* Put an effective thermal break in the frame.
* Place the bulk of the frame in the warm part of the wall.
* Keep the parts outside the thermal break as small as possible.
* Do not allow cold air to circumvent the thermal break. It is surprising how many window installations allow this to occur. It invariably happens if the frame is allowed to span the cavity in a cavity wall. Do not try to span the wall cavity with the window frame.
* Where high humidities must be maintained within the building in cold climates, heating cables will be needed to warm the frames.
* Keep the frame warm by having a very thin seal between the large warm part of the frame and the glass, and a thicker, insulating gasket between the glass and the cold outside part of the frame.
* Put the window above a convector or other source of heat.

Condensation on windows is also a function of the humidity of the air in the room. Condensation increases noticeably in houses when the humidity is raised by cooking or laundry.

Humidity is higher in today's tighter buildings, because it is not diluted by air leakage. Persistent condensation on windows can be cured by a simple increase in fresh air, by dehumidifiers or by heat exchangers.

In such buildings as hospitals and art galleries, high humidity is a requirement. In others, such as car washes and paper mills, it is a consequence of the process. In all cases, solutions require multiple glazing and some system to keep the inner surfaces as warm as possible.

5.13.5 Prevention of Cracking and Breaking

Glass is very strong in compression and very weak in tension. Knowing this, it makes sense to keep glass in compression as much as possible to protect it from tensile forces. Tensile forces in windows come most frequently from heating the center of a pane of glass and chilling its edges. The center tries to expand but the edges are cool and will try to shrink. The expansion of the center of the pane will stretch the cool edges of the glass and put them in tension. As mentioned above, glass cannot stand much tensile stress. The heating of the center of the glass comes either from solar heating from outside or from the heat of the building inside.

5.13.6 Preventing Cold Glass Edges

Preventing cool edges will not only remove one cause of window breakage but will also reduce frost and condensation. Cool edges can be prevented in a number of ways (Sasaki 1970):

- Keep the bulk of the frame in the warm part of the wall, inside the insulation.
- Keep the part outside the thermal break as small as possible so that comparatively little heat will be lost.
- Make the outer spline a poor conductor of heat.
- Make the inner glazing tape relatively thin to improve its thermal conductivity.
- The frame may be warmed by connecting the sill directly to a convector enclosure.
- Use a good thermal break.
- Design the pressure plate in conjunction with the best possible insulator.

5.13.7 Allowance for Movement

Windows are not likely to fall out of a well-constructed frame, unless the frame is badly distorted by building movement. It was mentioned earlier that there must be some clearance all around the glass between the glass and the frame. This allows the frame and the glass to expand and contract at different rates and take up minor discrepancies in the size and shape of the glass and the frames. It is important that this clearance is distributed as evenly as possible all around the window, for if the glass is pushed to one side or can work its way to one side, there may be inadequate "bite," or overlap, to hold one side of the glass in place.

REFERENCES

Olynyk, D. 1968. "Sound Insulation of Some Window Construction." *Technical Note 526.* Ottawa: DBR NRCC.

Quirouette, R.L. 1979. "Requirements for Windows." *Proceedings: NRCC Seminar on Windows.* Ottawa.

Sasaki, J.R. 1970. "Potential for Thermal Breakage of Sealed Double-Glazing Units." *CBD 129.* Ottawa: DBR NRCC.

6

Watertight Roofing

6.1 INTRODUCTION

Roofing systems are divided into two broad categories; watertight and watershedding. Shingles are a good example of watershedding roofing. Using a combination of sloping surfaces and overlapping units, these roofs are able to stop rain penetration even though they are far from "watertight". The subject of this chapter is watertight roofing, made from membranes with sealed joints. These sealed membranes are used to waterproof relatively flat surfaces; in fact, they are often called flat roofs.

Flat or watertight roofing has not been very dependable. Premature failures probably affect at least half of the installations. The high failure rate is due, primarily, to poor edge design, but inappropriate materials and poor application techniques also take their toll. The high failure rate of conventional roofing encourages the use of new systems, but these have an even higher failure rate. Of the hundreds of new roofing materials and systems that have been offered over the last thirty years, only a few are still in use. This sad history should make the prudent designer look for gradual improvements in well known systems rather than a revolutionary cure-all. In this respect 2-stage waterproofing has not yet been incorporated into roofing with any great success (see 6.6.3).

6.2 PROFILES OF WATERTIGHT ROOFS

Many watertight roofs are intended to be level, drainage being provided either at the edge(s) or where the designer thinks that the low spots will be. These roofs are never really flat, as anyone knows who has ever seen one after a few hours of rain. It is obvious, at such times, that the surface is a series of humps and valleys; the humps rising out of the water that accumulates in the valleys. Observing these roofs after rain also shows how seldom the designer has been able to guess where the low spots will be.

In spite of this and other problems that are discussed in this chapter, thousands of roofs are built this way: first of all, because it is cheaper than providing slopes to drains; second, because even the gentle slopes that are used are hard to deal with aesthetically; and thirdly, because many designers believe (with some justification) that, if the membrane is watertight when applied, sloping it will not make it more so.

Since water lying on the roof is thought to cause premature aging of the membrane, NRCC and the Canadian Roofing Contractors Association advise that roof membrane surfaces should slope to drains. Sloping the membrane about 1:50 will overcome most construction inaccuracies and thus drain most of the water from the roof surface. Certainly, water lying in depressions in a roof surface will exacerbate any leaks that are present. However, sloping the roof for this reason does not seem to be going to the heart of the matter, which is a waterproof membrane. Also, in many climates snow may be followed by rain followed by freezing weather. The result is a buildup of ice on the roof that will defy any drainage system.

A small, well designed roof is turned up at the edges to form a shallow bowl in which the bottom is gently sloped to the roof drain (Figure 6–1). Where the area is large, the roof may be divided into a number of such "bowls", each with its own drain. The turned-up edges are not always carried around each bowl but are most often reserved for the roof edges (Figure 6–2). The size of these individually drained areas depends primarily on the amount of slope the designer can accommodate. Even at the minimum slope of 1:50, a rise of one foot (300 mm) accumulates over a horizontal distance of 50 ft (15 m).

Often the turned-up edge of the roof membrane rests against a parapet and the joint between the two must be protected by flashings. Most of them are designed to act more or less like an umbrella (Figure 6–3).

In northern climates ice and snow will build up to pond water against parapets, enough sometimes to a depth that may rise above the turned up edge. For this reason it is strongly recommended that the roof membrane be carried over the parapet (Figure 6–4). This is done with flexible membrane flashings, which is discussed in Chapter 7 and is shown in all of the parapet details in Part 1.

Even in warm climates the membrane should carry out over the parapet. Simply flashing the roofing to the face of the parapet is never successful (see Chapter 7).

It should be noted here that many successful roofs, usually on low buildings, have slopes to an edge where the water is carried away by a gutter or simply allowed to fall to the ground (Figure 6–5). There are two problems associated with this system. First, the drained edge is rather unsightly and usually is reserved for the alley side of low rise commercial buildings. In parts of the country where snow accumulates

FIGURE 6-1. Typical low sloped roof profile.

FIGURE 6-3. Parapet flashing functions.

FIGURE 6-2. Low sloped roof profile with multiple drains.

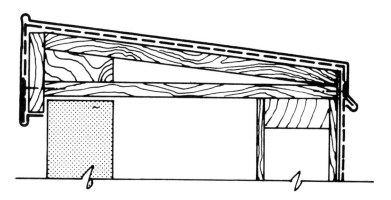

FIGURE 6-4. Rubberized asphalt base flashing carried up and over the parapet.

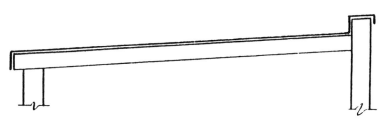

FIGURE 6-5. Watertight roof sloped to one edge.

on the roof surface, a more serious problem is caused by icicle formation. Accumulated snow insulates the roof surface and allows the heat from the building to melt some of the under surface of the snow. The resulting trickle of water freezes as it reaches the roof edge and loses the protection of the snow. These icicles can be large and hazardous.

In buildings that are heated, it is more sensible to collect the water from roof drains into rain-water leaders that run down through the building, thence into storm drains on the owner's property and into storm sewers in the street. In unheated or scarcely heated buildings where the temperatures are sufficiently low for rainwater leaders to freeze, they can be warmed, when necessary, with heating cables.

6.3 INSULATION SYSTEMS

Because the arrangement and performance of roofing membranes are determined primarily by the insulation method used, the methods of insulation are examined first.

Most roofs are insulated. Recommendations for optimum insulation in colder climates are given in NRCC document "Measures for Energy Conservation in New Buildings." There are three insulation systems in use today:

1. Conventional system where the insulation is placed beneath the roof membrane.
2. Protected membrane system where the membrane is protected by waterproof insulation.
3. Double drained system where the insulation is placed between two waterproof membranes, each of which is drained.

No matter which of these systems is used it will be necessary to hold the components down against wind uplift.

Manufacturers suggest that components in some systems may be held down with mechanical fasteners. This book does not recommend such systems, especially where the systems are severely tried by high winds and low temperatures. Continuous and dependable adhesion is the recommended method of assembly. It is hard to beat hot asphalt if it is compatible with the other materials being used. No matter what the assembly, CHECK FOR COMPATIBILITY between all components and insist on everything being well adhered, starting from the deck up. There is one exception to these cautions. Styrofoam should not be adhered to the membrane in the protected membrane system.

6.3.1   Conventional System

The conventional system is shown diagramatically in Figure 6–6. Because this system does not lend itself to the criteria laid down in the Introduction, it is not used in any of the details in Part 1. However, conventionally insulated roofs can give years of satisfactory service. To do so, they must be detailed and applied with great care and understanding. Proper installation is described in 6.4. The important considerations are outlined below.

Air/Vapor Barriers in the Conventionally Insulated System

Use an air/vapor barrier whenever the roof membrane will be below the dew point of the inside air for prolonged periods. In humidified buildings find the dew point on a pyschrometric chart. As a rough check, inside air at 70°F (21°C) and 30% RH will condense on the membrane when the membrane is cooled to about the freezing point.

To be of any use, the air/vapor barrier must be put on just like a roof. Two plies of felt mopped with hot asphalt works well. Be sure that it is continuously sealed to the roof membrane around the edges of the roof and around all openings, vents, etc. There may be hundreds of these. The membrane must be well adhered to the deck.

Insulation in the Conventional System

Glass fiber roof insulation is the preferred insulation in conventionally insulated roofs. Be sure that it is well adhered to the air/vapor barrier. If one is talked into using one of the foamed plastic insulations in a conventionally insulated roof:

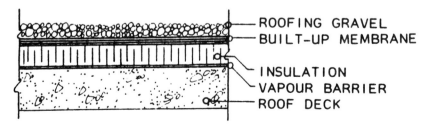

FIGURE 6-6.   Conventionally insulated roof assembly.(Baker, M.C., and Hedlin, C.P. 1972. Protected-membrane roofs. CBD 150, DBR NRCC. Fig.1c.)

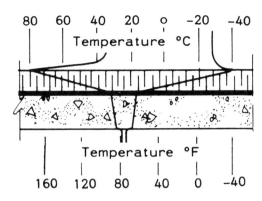

FIGURE 6-7. Temperature gradients through a conventionally insulated roof assembly. (Garden,G.K. 1965. Thermal considerations in roof design. CBD 70, DBR NRCC, Fig.1.)

- Check the insurance rates.
- Be sure that it can be adhered to the air/vapor barrier.
- Be sure that it is chemically compatible with other elements of the assembly.
- The manufacturers will likely ask you to cover it with fiberboard. Be sure they are well stuck together. Usually hot asphalt is the only satisfactory adhesive. Contact adhesives should work but it is awfully hard to get them properly applied. CHECK FOR COMPATIBILITY. Remember that fiberboard will not hold anything if it gets wet.

Whether it gets into the insulation through leaks in the membrane or from condensation of vapor, glass fiber insulation can store large quantities of water. Water in the insulation will damage the roof membrane by attacking it from its vulnerable underside. It is vitally important to have a good air/vapor barrier and to periodically examine the roof for leaks. Such examinations can be performed readily and economically using infrared thermography.

The use of combustible roof insulation will usually affect insurance rates.

Membranes for Conventionally Insulated Roofs

Membranes are examined in detail in 6.4, but it should be noted here that the roofing membrane in a conventionally insulated system is exposed to wind scouring, wind uplift, rain, snow and ice, ultra-violet light, flying debris (including gravel), mechanical damage from workmen, tools and ladders, and, most important, to the broad temperature swings illustrated in the graph in Figure 6–7. Note that the roof surface is hotter than the air temperature when the sun is shining on it. It is colder than the air temperature when it can radiate to the night sky. Until recently, most of the membranes in these conventionally insulated systems were built-up from bitumens and felts. Now, rubberized asphalt and elasto-plastic membranes are also used.

6.3.2 Protected Membrane Roofing

This system, which is illustrated in Figure 6–8, has the membrane covered by a layer of insulation. Thus the membrane is protected against large temperature swings, against ice, snow, mechanical damage and ultra violet rays; in fact from most of the destructive forces that act on a roof. It also conforms to many of the criteria laid

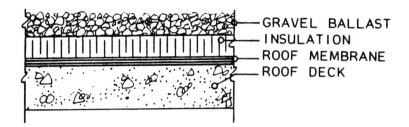

FIGURE 6-8. Protected membrane roof assembly. (Baker, M.C., and Hedlin, C.P. 1972. Protected-membrane roofs. CBD 150, DBR NRCC, Fig.1e.)

down in the Prolegomenon. For these reasons it is the recommended system and has been used in all the roof details in Part 1.

Membranes for the Protected Membrane System

Any good membrane should be satisfactory, for, once the insulation has been placed, the only destructive forces on the membrane are time and water. Membranes and their characteristics are described in section 6.4.

Insulations for the Protected System

The system was patented in 1968 by the Dow Chemical Company, makers of Roofmate, the insulation used in this system. One could wish for a system open to other suppliers. However, with a few exceptions, Roofmate is an ideal insulation for the purpose, being light and easily handled, waterproof and having a relatively high thermal resistance of R 5/in. (34.65m·K/W), compared, for instance, to high density glass fiber roof insulation which has a thermal resistance of R 4 (27.72m·K/W).

Because the material is very light, it will float on water that may accumulate on the roof. The usual cure for this is to ballast the insulation with gravel, crushed stone or concrete paving stones. This adds substantially to the load on the roof structure. Dow recommends 20 lb/ft² (105 Kg/m² for 100 mm) of Roofmate. If a roof floods and the insulation is inadequately ballasted, it is a sad sight indeed. Gravel falls beneath the insulation boards and the boards are scattered around like sheets of ice after a spring flood in a Canadian river. At drains where water may accumulate and flood the gravel ballast, more gravel will be needed since gravel weighs only 40% as much under water. In high wind areas this gravel may be blown about and constitute a safety hazard.

Dow suggests two other ways of handling this problem. The first is to apply a plastic scrim over the insulation boards. Roof flooding may lift the boards but the scrim holds them in place so that they settle back into their proper position. Recently Roofmate insulation boards have become available with a cement coating and tongue and groove edges. The interlocking edges serve the same purpose as the scrim. With these "floating" systems it is important that the insulation is not partially adhered to the membrane, for it may tear the membrane as it lifts. A polyethylene parting sheet is placed below the insulation to prevent partial adhesion.

Polystyrene insulation is eroded rapidly by ultraviolet light. In the ballasted system, the ballast keeps sunlight away from the insulation. When a scrim is used, two or three centimeters of gravel are used to prevent ultraviolet light from reaching the insulation and to prevent wind uplift. The tongue and groove boards have a cement coating which serves the same purposes.

When the insulation is not completely adhered to the roof membrane, water will be held between the two by capillarity. This poses another problem because, although the insulation boards are waterproof, they are not vaportight. Although the roof membrane forms a perfect barrier to vapor from within the building, water held under the insulation boards is warm and evaporates readily. This vapor diffuses through the walls of the cells in the insulation at the rate of 1.2 grains/hr/ft^2/in. of mercury pressure difference (1.75 ng/s·m·Pa). During winter months when the top of the insulation is cold, vapor may condense in the insulation boards. Water in the cells is a much better conductor than the gas it replaces and results in a lowered thermal resistance. Fortunately, this condition is often accompanied by a snow cover which will make up for some of the reduced thermal resistance of the insulation. There are conditions of course when vapor can evaporate from the insulation. Since concrete pavers may impede this drying, it is just as well to hold the pavers a few millimeters clear of the top surface of the insulation. This is best done with some simple shims cut from the edge of an insulation board. Roofmate has a bearing capacity of 30 psi (210 KPa), so that only a small area of shim is required.

One of the chief concerns about the effectiveness of the insulation in the protected membrane system stems from the fact that rainwater and melting snow can run beneath the insulation. To some degree, this increases heat loss from the building. It also causes concern, in buildings containing highly humidified air, that at times the deck temperature may be lowered to the dew point. The former problem has been studied extensively by the U.S. Army Cold Regions Research and Engineering Laboratory, and it is generally agreed that there is a 10% loss in insulation value over a heating season. Calculations indicate that concrete decks are not likely to be chilled below 50°F (10°C), but there may be a problem with metal decks. The calculation is relatively simple and should be done for any building where the relative humidity is maintained at 50% or above during the winter.

6.3.3 Double-Drained System

This system was introduced in CBD 99. It is arranged as shown in Figure 6–9 with the principle membrane beneath the insulation and another membrane, important but not vital, above the insulation. Both membranes are drained.

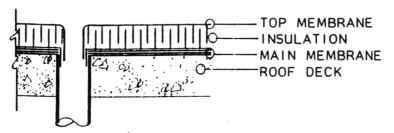

FIGURE 6–9. Double-drained roof assembly. (Baker, M.C., and Hedlin, C.P. 1972. Protected-membrane roofs. CBD 150, DBR NRCC, Fig.1d.)

It was designed to provide the following advantages:

- Any kind of roof insulation could be used.
- A leak in the upper membrane would not affect the watertightness of the lower membrane. Thus the upper membrane and insulation could be repaired without endangering the building and its contents.
- No ballast is needed to hold down the insulation.
  The system is not recommended for the following reasons:

- If a built-up membrane is used for the top surface, it must be well adhered to a strong substrate and must be restrained around the edges to avoid shrinkage. Adhesion directly to plastic foams is not advised, so the insulation choice is narrowed to glass fiber or wood fiber. Since the system is supposed to be able to survive for some time with wet insulation, wood fiber is not a good choice for insulation.
- Wood blocking is required to provide edge restraint for the top membrane. This blocking must be fastened through the lower membrane. The blocking must then be sealed off with a flexible membrane.
- The insulation in the system will not really drain very well. Capillarity will hold water in the insulation. There it can attack the vulnerable underside of built-up roofing. Venting has not been effective in drying damp insulation.
- There is a danger that any stoppage in the rain-water drainage system could flood the insulated layer between the membranes.

6.4 MEMBRANES FOR WATERTIGHT ROOFS

There are three categories of roof membrane presently in use:

- Membranes built-up from plies of roofing felt embedded in hot bitumen.
- Single plies of elasto-plastic membrane.
- Two plies of modified (rubberized) asphalt reinforced with polyester or glass fiber fabric, either woven or arranged isotropically, that is with fibers matted together in every direction. Although not advised, this material can be used as a single ply.

6.4.1 Built-up Membranes

The term "built-up membrane" refers to membranes built-up from alternate layers of "felts" and bitumen. The felts are usually made from cellulose (wood pulp), although glass fiber, asbestos and polyester are used. Asphalt has almost replaced pitch as the bitumen, although some pitch is still used. The bitumen is heated to melt it, then mopped onto the felts as a liquid.[1] The felts, which come in rolls 36" (914 mm) wide, are rolled into this hot mopping. Four is the usual number of plies. Each ply covers three-quarters of the ply beneath plus one inch (25 mm), so that when the roofer is finished he has 4 layers as shown in Figure 6–10. Figure 6–11 shows the four layers laid up 2 plus 2; a system to prevent leaks from running from top to bottom of the built up membrane.

---

[1]The author, after several sad experiences, refuses to allow felt laying machines on roofs for which he is responsible.

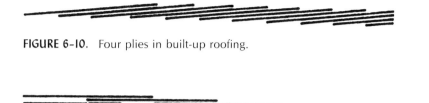

FIGURE 6-10. Four plies in built-up roofing.

FIGURE 6-11. Four plies laid 2 plus 2.

Built-up membranes have traditionally been used to cover the insulation in conventionally insulated roofs. A tremendous amount of information is available on these membranes, much of it in the documents listed at the end of this chapter. In spite of that, they suffer many failures. They fare somewhat better in the protected membrane system because they are protected from the violent temperature swings. Anyone using them should study the problems and the possible solutions.

When discussing membranes for conventionally insulated roofs, it was mentioned that the membranes in these systems are exposed to wind scouring, wind uplift, rain, snow and ice, mechanical damage from workmen, tools and ladders, large temperature swings and possibly ultraviolet light.

Wind uplift is countered by having the membrane well adhered to the roof and also, to some extent, by a layer of gravel. The main purpose of the gravel layer is to protect the membrane from the destructive effects of ultraviolet light. Wind often displaces this gravel layer, particularly at the windward corner of the building. It is customary to replace it at windward corners and in other high wind areas with concrete paving stones.

A well applied built-up roof membrane is proof against rain, snow and ice. At moderate temperatures, a thick tough built-up membrane is only equalled by two ply rubberized asphalt.

Severe temperature swings are very hard on roof membranes. There are two phenomena involved. First is the loss of flexibility that accompanies extreme cooling of the membrane. As mentioned above, it is quite serious in built-up membranes, so it is important not to abuse them when they are cold. Some but not all of the newer membranes are quite flexible at very low temperatures. This characteristic is usually given in the manufacturers' literature.

Secondly, the combination of felts and roofing asphalt produces a plastic, rather than elastic, membrane. As a result, when the membrane contracts in cold weather, its plastic nature allows it to relax in that condition. Furthermore, when the temperature rises, the compressive forces generated in the membrane are more likely to cause wrinkling than to restore the membrane to its initial dimension. It now behaves as though this were its original shape and it is ready to contract again during the next cold cycle. Cumulative shrinkages of 4″ (100 mm) or more, have been noted. The cure for shrinkage is proper restraint of the membrane either by good edge fastening, or better still, by good adhesion to a strong substrate.

R.G. Turenne (1980) of NRCC has done some interesting research on wrinkling. He has found that the excess material required for wrinkles to form has come from interply slippage. He attributes this interply slippage to an excess of asphalt between the plies. It comes from moppings that are too heavy, a common condition when asphalt is applied in cold weather. Other causes of an excess of asphalt are the use of 40 lb base sheets and too heavy a mopping for temporary protection of felts.

Finish the roof or use a squeegee to avoid this problem. Roofs applied with the felts in a 2 + 2 configuration may also result in too much asphalt.

The four plies and their moppings are not particularly waterproof. Watertightness comes from a flood coat of hot asphalt over the surface. The asphalt flood coat is then covered with a few centimeters of gravel, which protect it from sunlight and mechanical damage. The mineral aggregate reduces the maximum surface temperature, the seasonal range of temperatures and the short term fluctuations at the black surface. Thus it inhibits weathering of the membrane.

Roofing Asphalt for Built-Up Membranes

Roofing asphalt is a residue from the distillation of crude oil. The residue is heated in a still, then oxidized by blowing bubbles of air through it. This process gradually raises its viscosity and softening point. Depending on where the process is stopped, it produces the following:

- Type 1 asphalt, which softens about 140°F (60°C);
- Type 2 asphalt, which softens about 165°F (75°C); and
- Type 3 asphalt, which softens about 195°F (90°C).

Type 3 with its higher viscosity and melting point is suitable for steep slopes, such as those in flashings. This property is achieved at the sacrifice of elasticity, "stickiness," self-healing power, watertightness and long life. On the other hand, Type 1 asphalt softens at such low temperatures that it is thought to act as a lubricant and allow interply slippage. Previously in this section such slippage was described as the cause of wrinkles. For that reason, Type 2 is used wherever possible. It is recommended that it should not be used on slopes over 1:8.

Roofing Felts for Built-Up Membranes

No.15 Saturated Rag Felts—the "15" comes from the fact that the felts weigh about 15 lbs. per square (100 ft²). The term has no meaning in the SI, since it weighs 0.6 Kg/m². "Rag" refers to the partial rag content that was used in the fibers. Now, the "felts" are composed almost entirely of wood pulp fibers, felted together and bound with asphalt.

They are not completely saturated with asphalt, nor are they waterproof. This is very important to note. Rolls of felt that have been exposed to rain, snow or even very humid conditions are useless for roofing and will inevitably cause problems. The main problem is the foaming caused by escaping steam as the moisture is raised above the boiling point by the hot asphalt. The bubbles so formed eventually contain a mixture of water and air that causes blistering and leaking.

Unless they are embedded in bitumen, wood-pulp felts when wetted will wrinkle, shrink and lose their strength. Shrinkage is discussed in *CBD 181*. Ridging, shrinking and splitting are discussed in NRCC *Document No. 112*. Shrinking, ridging, and splitting are all too well known to the practicing architect.

Felts that have been laid and not covered with a flood coat will absorb water from rain or dew with the same results. On the other hand if the felts in an incomplete roof are mopped as a temporary protection against moisture one is just asking for wrinkling. Any damp felts or insulation should be removed and replaced. Asphalt-saturated roofing felt standards are contained in C.S.A. Standard A123.6.

Glass Fiber Felts for Built-Up Membranes

A new kind of glass fiber felt is now on the market. Those introduced 20 or 30 years ago were not successful. It appears, from a limited number of applications, that the new felts perform quite well, providing great strength and reduced water sensitivity. It is worth monitoring their performance. They display a remarkable springiness and cannot be walked on while the asphalt is soft. Neither can fishmouths be closed by stepping on them.

6.4.2 Elasto-Plastic Membranes

For about 10 years, Max Baker at NRCC had a small area on the Council grounds where manufacturers of new, improved roofing systems were invited to apply samples of their wares. The sample yard was removed, unfortunately, but at the time of its removal, not one of the 20 or so "improved" systems was intact. Some were in tatters; others, like their manufacturers, had disappeared.

In spite of this poor performance, there is no question that dependable new roofing systems will be developed. Until they have a history of successful performance, skepticism is advised.

Many of the following descriptions come from NRCC *BPN No. 50,* "New Roofing Materials" (Baker 1984).

Most of the elasto-plastic membranes are remarkably flimsy and can be punctured easily with an ordinary lead pencil. Others are easily burned by butting a cigarette on them. Cleaners, solvents, and adhesives used during installation often are extremely combustible and will dissolve many foam insulations that may be present. Dust, age, contaminants, and moisture can affect the self-adhesive materials. Underheating or overheating adversely affects the torched-on systems. If laps are not sealed or are easily separated, the roof will leak.

EPDM: Ethylene Propylene Diene Monomer Roof Membrane System

A single-ply sheet composed of synthetic rubber, similar to butyl rubber, it is especially resistant to ozone and ultraviolet light, which give it good weather resistance. It is not compatible with asphalt. Thickness varies from 1/32" to 1/16" (0.76 mm to 1.42 mm). It is not usually reinforced, but can be reinforced with woven or isotropic fibers. The formulation of extenders and oils contributes to its performance. EPDM sheets cannot be solvent or heat welded. The sheet laps are joined together by contact splicing cement. Most failures have been attributed to field spliced seams, so very large single sheets, factory fabricated, are available. Application can be loose laid and ballasted, or fully adhered.

Polychloroprene (Neoprene) Roof Membrane System

A roof membrane composed of single ply sheets of synthetic rubber, Neoprene is the generic name for polymers of chloroprene. This particular synthetic rubber has good resistance to petroleum oils, solvents and weathering. Some formulations require a protective coating of Hypalon to retard weathering. Thickness varies from 1/32" to 1/8" (0.76 mm to 3 mm), with 1.5 mm material usually used for roofing.

Application can be loose laid and ballasted, or fully adhered. Contact cement is used for joining and adhering. Uncured material is used for flashings because it is more flexible than the cured material: it will cure with aging.

CPE: Chlorinated Polyethylene

A cured material that has outstanding resistance to ozone, heat, acids and weathering, it also has good resistance to mineral oils and general chemical attack, but will swell in aromatic and chlorinated solvents. Chlorinated polyethylene is available in both sheet and liquid applied systems. It is compatible with bitumen, so that it can be applied over bituminous materials and can be used as base flashings for bituminous roofing and sealed to bituminous air barrier membranes. The sheet material sometimes contains an asbestos backing to facilitate handling. Total membrane thickness is approximately 0.04" to 0.087" (1 mm to 2.2 mm), depending on the manufacturer. Applications can be fully adhered with hot asphalt or contact adhesive. Seams are usually heat welded.

P.V.C.: Polyvinyl Chloride

Polyvinyl chloride is produced in Europe and the United States in rolled sheet form, 0.04" to 0.06" (1 mm to 1.5 mm) thick, usually 0.048" (1.2 mm), and is sold in the U.S. and Canada by a number of companies. Some products are reinforced with glass fiber or polyester, but other products are nonreinforced. The material has good resistance to creep and can be solvent- or heat-welded to itself, making it practical for field fabrication of a roofing membrane. The solvent is tetrahydrofuran.

PVC is often applied as a loose-laid system with no attachment to the roof deck or insulation. It is kept in place only by attachments at the roofing terminations and around penetrations through the roof, and by a layer of rounded gravel or other ballast. The ballast also protects the underlying membrane from ultra violet radiation and other weathering. Partially attached systems have been used where roof slope or the structure prevents the use of heavy gravel ballast. Attachment is usually by mechanical fastenings. For the reasons outlined below, these are not recommended in this book. For some systems special fasteners are driven into the deck through plates or discs set on top of the insulation. The discs are PVC coated and the PVC membrane can be solvent welded to them. This allows for some membrane movement, but secures the membrane and insulation against uplift and slippage down slopes.

Metal bars can also be placed on top of the membrane with fasteners passing through them and through the membrane and insulation to the deck. The bars and fasteners are then covered with a strip of PVC that is adhered or welded to the membrane. Both of the mechanically fastened systems described may allow the membrane to flutter between the fasteners when wind is blowing over the roof. This fluttering may also pump humid inside air into the insulation. Mechanical fasteners are prone to corrosion and may also puncture the air/vapor barrier. Where this cannot be tolerated it may be necessary to provide full adherence. In this case the entire membrane is bonded with adhesive to its substrate. The fully adhered system functions like a fully adhered conventional built-up roofing system, and is limited in the amount of substrate movement that it can accommodate.

Nonreinforced PVC is subject to shrinkage and, in loose laid systems, this can result in pulling in at roof edges to cause disruption of edge flashing details. Reinforced PVC is much less likely to have any shrinkage problems. However it is wise to use material from a manufacturer with a proven record.

R.G. Turenne has recorded a number of failures of nonreinforced PVC in cold climates. Shrinkage is certainly a problem. Loss of flexibility seems to be another, whether due to the gradual loss of plasticizers or to the cold weather.

It is claimed that drying through the membrane is possible, since PVC membranes have a permeance several hundred times that of built-up roofing. Such drying however is likely to be insignificant.

The workable temperature range for the material is claimed to extend down to 5°F (-15°C). Even if the material is flexible at such low temperatures and can stand the rigors of the cold application, there is no doubt that application at higher temperatures is more desirable. Where human discomfort is involved at the lower temperatures, the level of careful workmanship required for the assembly of such materials is unlikely to be present, unless the work can be carried out under shelter.

PVC has good resistance to weather and chemicals generally, but is adversely affected by coal tar, asphalt, oils and animal fats. When used over old bituminous roofs, it must be isolated from the old bitumen by a separation layer. It must be protected from the tracking of asphalt or tar from an old roof, the flow of bitumen onto it from a higher roof, and fumes from built-up roofing below. Oils used for servicing heating, ventilation and air conditioning equipment may also damage the material. PVC cannot be sealed directly to bituminous air barrier membranes.

6.4.3   Rubberized or Modified Asphalts

In North America efforts have been concentrated on understanding and accommodating the idiosyncrasies of built-up bituminous membranes. In Europe, and to an increasing extent in the U.S. and Canada, the properties of the bitumens and the felts have been improved. Bitumens are modified with the addition of polymers which improve the elasticity of the membranes, thus avoiding the problems discussed in the section on built-up membranes. Some of these modified materials have better resistance to flow, high permissible strains (movement) and better fatigue resistance. The two principal modifiers are styrene butadiene styrene (SBS) and atactic polypropylene (APP). They are quite different and produce quite different products. SBS seems to be superior, providing greater elasticity.

At the same time, strong water-resistant mats of polyester or glass fiber replace the water-sensitive wood pulp felt. The modified asphalt is best applied to the mats in a factory, where quality control is obviously better than on a roof.

The Europeans have had inconsistent results with single ply applications, so they advise two plies. The two plies are welded to the deck and to each other, either with a heavy coat of hot asphalt or by melting the asphalt layer on the membrane with propane torches. The material seems to be elastic enough that it is not split by normal roof movement or small cracks.

Some manufacturers supply this material as a liquid, to be applied to the deck in thickness of 0.15″ to 0.2″ (4mm to 5mm). Such applications are subject to all of the problems of on-site fabrication. Many single ply applications have not performed well because of the difficulty of judging (and applying) adequate thickness. Others have failed because of pinholes formed by foaming. The foaming is caused by applying the material to damp roof decks. Two layers would provide some relief from both of these problems.

Modified asphalts, like other asphalts, are damaged by sunlight. They must be protected. This is achieved with an integral metal surface layer (copper or aluminum), by mineral chips embedded in the surface (like asphalt shingles), by separately applied sunscreening mastic, or by applying gravel ballast.

Rubberized asphalt is the material used for the air barrier and roof membranes in the details in Part 1.

6.5 MAINTENANCE PROGRAM

Because watertight roofs have an abnormally high failure rate, a regular program of inspection and maintenance will be needed.

6.6 RECOMMENDED READING FROM NATIONAL RESEARCH COUNCIL OF CANADA DOCUMENTS[2]

- *Building Research Note 63,* "Unusual Deterioration of Bituminous Roofing Materials."
- *B.R. Note 69,* "Exposure of Some Roofing Systems."
- *B.R. Note 89,* "Protected Membrane Roofs in Canada."
- *B.R. Note 112,* "Ridging, Shrinkage and Splitting."
- *B.R. Note 124,* "Polyurethane Foam as a Thermal Insulation."
- *Canadian Building Digest 67,* "Fundamentals of Roof Design."
- *CBD 69,* "Flashings for Membrane Roofs."
- *CBD 70,* "Thermal Considerations in Roof Design."
- *CBD 73,* "Moisture Considerations in Roof Design."
- *CBD 75,* "Roof Terraces."
- *CBD 89,* "Ice on Roofs."
- *CBD 99,* "Application of Roof Design Principles."
- *CBD 150,* "Protected Membrane Roofs."
- *CBD 151,* "Drainage from Roofs."
- *BPN No. 50,* "New Roofing Materials."
- Baker, M.C. 1980. "Roofs." Montreal: Multiscience Publications.

One other paper by R. Turenne is not yet published. It will deal with the problems of wind uplift on single ply membranes.

REFERENCES

Baker, M.C. 1984. "New Roofing Materials." *BPN No. 50.* Ottawa: DBR NRCC.
Turenne, R.G. 1980. "Bituminous Roofing Membranes—Practical Considerations." *CBD 211.* Ottawa: DBR NRCC.

[2]These documents are available either free or at a nominal cost from Publications Sales and Distribution, National Research Council Canada, Montreal Road, Ottawa, Canada K1A 0R6.

7

Flashings

7.1 INTRODUCTION

Studies done by a number of thermographers have shown that a very high percentage of roof failures, perhaps higher than 80%, is associated with roof flashings. There are two main causes. First is a lack of understanding of how flashings work. This is unfortunate, for the principles are remarkably simple. The second cause stems from the fact that many of the vertical surfaces to which flashings are built are not waterproof themselves. Under these circumstances, even the best conventional flashings are of little use.

The following paragraphs discuss in some detail the design of effective flashings. These flashings always consist of a base flashing and counterflashing. The base flashings are continuous, flexible, waterproof extensions of the roof membrane. These extensions are protected by counterflashings, which are often metal. It is impossible to make these metal counterflashings watertight.

7.2 BASE FLASHINGS

It was mentioned in Chapter 6 that properly designed "flat" roofs are best shaped like shallow bowls. The turned up edges of the bowl are hard to apply at the same time as the "flat" part, so usually they are done separately. The name for these separately applied turned up edges is "base flashings."

When the materials are bituminous, they are called "bituminous flashings". When they are built-up from strips of felt and asphalt, the operation is called "stripping". The correct method is described in 7.4.1.

7.3 COUNTERFLASHINGS

Base flashings are most often protected from sunlight and mechanical damage[1] by metal "counterflashings". The only other purpose for counterflashings is decorative. They can never be watertight, so efforts to caulk or solder the joints are a waste of time. The metal expands and contracts with changes in temperature. A 10 ft (3 m) length of aluminum will change dimension by 0.3″ (8 mm) on most roofs. When this much movement must be accommodated at each joint, joints are not likely to

---

[1]This is a tenuous point, for metal counterflashings are readily disfigured by ladders, etc.

remain watertight. If metal counterflashings were designed with the same slope as a copper roof, they might act as small water shedding roofs, but this is hardly ever done.

The most important aspect of the design of counterflashings is to design them so they can be applied without damaging the waterproof base flashings. Although they can protect the base flashings to some extent, think of them as mere decoration.

Frequently, architects show metal counterflashing extending down to the roof surface, usually with no means of holding it there. This is a great mistake, for it will be only a matter of time before some fool nails the lower edge through the membrane near the roof surface where it is sure to leak. The holding clips for metal counterflashings must be as high as possible on the parapet or wall.

Failure to recognize these fundamental aspects of flashing design has led many designers to attempt to join metal to the bituminous roof membrane; an entirely unnecessary and doomed procedure. Bitumen to metal joints have been successfully made and maintained when the area of metal is small, for instance the flange of a pipe flashing. The limiting dimension is probably less than 3 ft (1 m).

7.4 DESIGN OF FLASHINGS

7.4.1 Parapet Flashings

Look at Figure 7–1. Begin the base flashings out on the roof surface. A flexible waterproof membrane, compatible with the roofing, should be used. Take the membrane up and over the top of the parapet and fasten it along the outside face of the coping. There will be strong wind forces trying to peel the base flashings from the parapet. Ensure that the material is well adhered to the backup. Welding rubberized asphalt with propane torches is a good system.

Snow, lying on the coping, will gradually melt, and if it can find any holes, it will find its way into the parapet, thence into the roofing. Thus it is vitally important that the coping be covered with a waterproof membrane and that it is built with a slope. It should slope toward the roof so that dripping water will not stain the face of the building. The reason that masonry caps always fail in cold climates is that, so far, no one seems to be able to build an unpunctured, sloping, waterproof membrane between the parapet and the coping.

Although they are frequently specified for such use, stripping and bituminous flashings cannot be run over the top of a parapet. The reason is simple. Since the felts themselves are not waterproof, they must be mopped with hot asphalt, up and over the parapet. No sane roofer wants to do this for fear of dripping asphalt on the face of the building, so they are left dry with the hope that the metal counterflashing will keep water off them. It doesn't because it is never designed with enough slope to shed water effectively.

Don't use that system. As suggested before, use one of the elastoplastic, factory fabricated, waterproof membranes. Use one that is compatible with the roof membrane. In this document, rubberized asphalt is advised. It is available with either a mineral or metal surface as a sunscreen and so needs metal counterflashing only as a decoration. Base flashings are the real flashings and provide all the watertightness that will ever be achieved.

7.4.2 Metal Counterflashing

Assure that the base flashings are complete, sloped and waterproof in themselves before applying metal counterflashing. The counterflashings must be applied in a way that does not destroy this watertightness. Figure 7–1 and Figure 7–2 show how this is done. Use clips to hold the metal down. These allow the metal to expand and contract. As well, they avoid unsightly surface nailing. Use ''s'' locked end joints as shown in Figure 7–3. Note that the fastening clips are on the sides of the

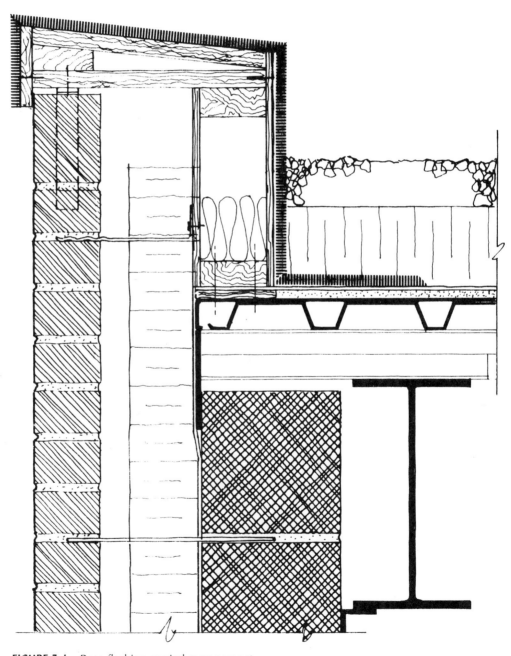

FIGURE 7-I. Base flashing carried over parapet.

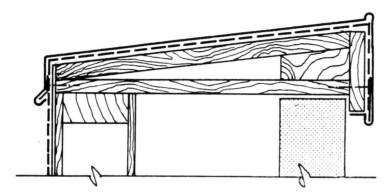

FIGURE 7-2. Clips hold down the edge of metal flashings.

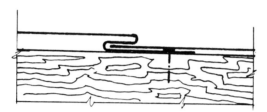

FIGURE 7-3. "S-lock" end joints allow for expansion in the metal flashing.

wood coping to reduce the chance of leaking. Note also that they are high above the roof surface where water might be ponded. It is too dangerous to take metal counterflashing down any farther than shown here. Use mineral surfaced rubberized asphalt or other material with an integral sunscreen to go the rest of the way. The mineral surfacing will provide the necessary sunscreen. The details show it nailed to the outer face of the wood coping. If there is still concern about slippage, nail it as well along the vertical face of the coping on the roof side.

7.4.3   Where a Wall Rises Above a Roof

Look at Figure 7–4. To get a complete, waterproof flashing where walls rise above a roof, for instance at an elevator penthouse, the base flashings should run from the roof surface up the wall to be sealed tightly to the air barrier in the wall. This is the detail that is used in the details in Part 1.

It is a mistake to finish flashings to wall cladding, for water will always get behind the cladding whether it be brick, concrete, or metal.

Furthermore, attempts to waterproof this joint by joining base flashings to the through-wall flashing of a cavity wall are almost always futile. The sequence of the trades makes it impractical. This is the most common cause of roof failure. The detail in Figure 7–5 has never been built in a satisfactory way. The reasons become clear as one follows the sequence of trades.

The masonry, air barrier, insulation and membrane through-wall flashing are installed first, by the mason. Usually specifications call for this flashing to be cut off so as not to show at the face of the joint. Later, the roofer applies the roofing felts and base flashings as shown in the drawing. He then routs out the mortar joint and installs the metal counterflashing. Because the through-wall flashing does not lap

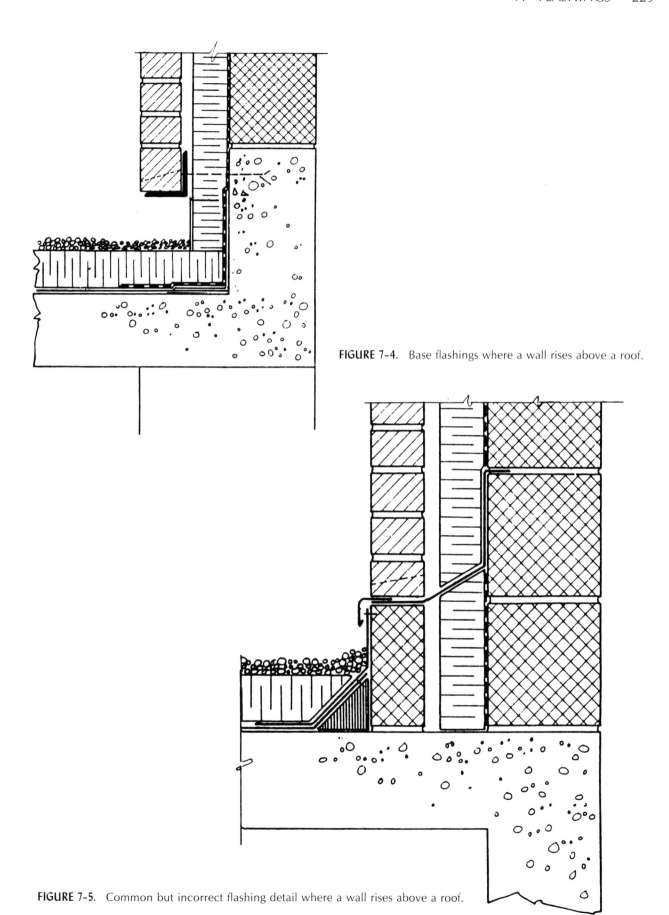

FIGURE 7-4. Base flashings where a wall rises above a roof.

FIGURE 7-5. Common but incorrect flashing detail where a wall rises above a roof.

and turn down over the metal counterflashing, water that is conducted into the joint by the through-wall flashing, can find its way behind the base flashing and thence to the deck. This is particularly serious in conventionally insulated roofs. Through wall flashings are usually such a mess that they do more harm than good.

7.4.4 Where Movement May Occur

Base flashings must always be designed to take into account deflection of the roof. Designing a watertight, airtight base flashing where the roof can move independently of the wall rising above it is the most difficult detail in architecture. Where at all possible, the wall and roof should be joined so that there can be no independent movement. Unfortunately in most buildings with structural frames, there will be a beam or joist that runs parallel to the wall. Usually this beam or joist will be free to deflect independently of the wall. These junctions are seldom detailed. The correct approach is shown in the details.

7.4.5 Sealing Metal to Roofing Membranes

Except for flanges less than a meter square, it is impractical to seal bituminous and other membranes to metal counterflashing; the coefficient of expansion of the metals is just too great. When a membrane is sealed to a strip of metal, the joints look as if they are sealed forever. However there is considerable movement at the end of each strip. This end movement will break the bond. There are a number of patented contrivances that attempt to overcome this problem. They generally consist of a strip of rubber or plastic, clamped in a bent or extruded metal flashing. The clamped joint may work quite well. The ends will not.

7.4.6 Gravel Stops

Gravel stops, shown in Figure 7-6, are used in details made necessary by architectural detailing in the International Style, where thin roof edges were highly prized. It is a silly detail and, as normally built, can be expected to leak. Where this detail is present in existing buildings to be re-roofed, it should be replaced with a curb. There are some alternate suggestions in *CBD 69*, "Flashings for Membrane Roofs."

7.4.7 Pipes Through a Roof

Pipes through roofs, particularly vent pipes, are often supported by a column, floor or by some part of the building other than the roof deck. As a result, when the roof

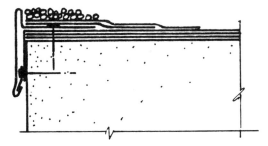

FIGURE 7-6. Gravel stop.

deck deflects, the pipe will not. For this reason it is very important to separate the flashing from the pipe. Figure 7-7 shows two methods that will allow differential movement. Any sealing or caulking between the sleeve and the pipe will be torn or ruptured by deflection of the roof deck.

Another approach is to put accordion type flexible sections in the rainwater leaders near the roof. First check the expected creep and deflection. If the flexible connections can accommodate the movement, then the vent pipes and flashings can be sealed together.

7.4.8 Modified Asphalt Flashings

See Figure 7-8. Eliminating the cant strip allows easily fitted square edges to the perimeter of the insulation and less displacement of the insulation, for installations of Roofmate have a tendency to "grow." The two plies of roof membrane are inter-

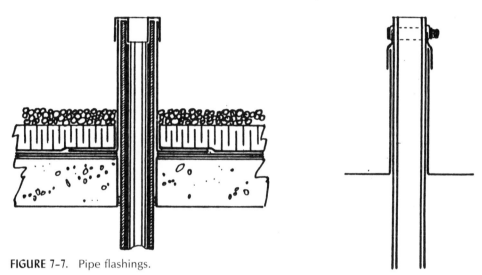

FIGURE 7-7. Pipe flashings.

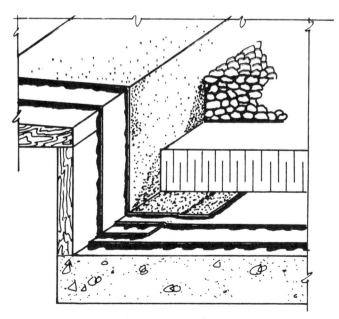

FIGURE 7-8. Modified asphalt base flashings.

leaved with the two plies of the base flashings. The first roofing ply can be reinforced with glass fiber, the top ply is reinforced with the stronger polyester mats. Note the mineral surface on the top flashing ply.

It should be mentioned here that cant strips are used in built-up roofing to ease the 90° turn from roof to wall.

7.4.9 Curbs

Look at Figure 7–9. Where expansion joints, skylights or mechanical platforms are to be placed on the roof, use a curb at least 8″ (200 mm) high, preferably 12″ (300 mm). Using rubberized asphalt or one of the elasto-plastic membranes, run base flashing up and over the curb as illustrated. Use mineral surfaced material for counterflashing. The only metal that should be used will come as part of the device being mounted. Fastening any metal counterflashing will surely puncture the membrane.

Expansion joints are made with two such curbs. A flexible waterproof membrane joins the two. Metal counterflashing may be used if it does NOT extend closer than 8″ (200 mm) to the roof. In Figure 7–10, note the air barrier membrane. It is essential.

7.4.10 Control Joints

Do not use control joints. Expansion joints are described in Figure 7–10. As mentioned in the paragraphs on bituminous membranes, shrinkage of built-up membranes is controlled by good adhesion to a strong substrate and by well fastened wood blocking around the perimeter. Interrupting the membrane is both unnecessary and dangerous. The control of shrinkage in bituminous membranes is discussed in *CBD 181* (Turenne 1976).

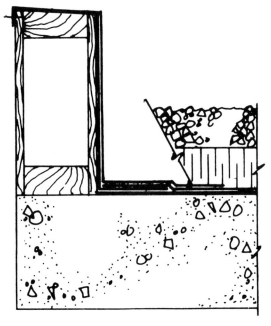

FIGURE 7-9. Curb detail.

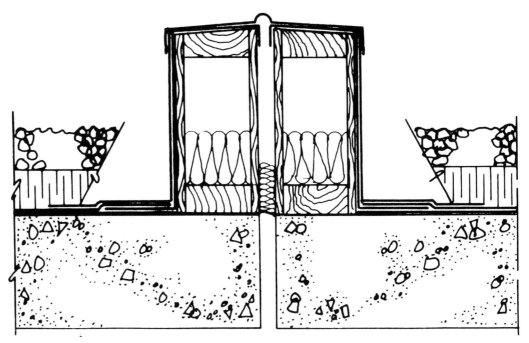

FIGURE 7-10. Expansion joint.

7.4.11 Through-Wall Flashings

The author now departs from roof flashings for remarks on the use of through-wall or wall cavity flashings. (Where a wall rises above a roof, see 7.4.3.)

One of the principles of two-stage waterproofing is that any water that penetrates beyond the cladding is drained out to the exterior face of the building. Usually this is done with through-wall or cavity flashings. In their simplest form, these flashings are waterproof membranes that drain water from the wall cavity. As simple as they appear (see Detail A5), there are factors that conspire against their proper installation.

- It is difficult to assure that the membrane will slope in the right direction. The membrane is run through a cut or joint in the insulation. Sometimes the position of that joint will turn the membrane up a bit so that it actually runs water in the wrong direction.
- Copper coated membranes have been removed from masonry walls that were only 16 years old. They had deteriorated to a remarkable degree and were completely useless.
- Water can run horizontally along through-wall flashing until it finds a joint in the membrane, thus allowing water to leak into the building.
- Heat sealed or solvent sealed membranes cannot be sealed in the presence of polystyrene cavity wall insulation.
- Copper or copper coated membranes cannot be used in the presence of galvanized shelf angles, brick ties, etc.

Because of these problems and because water running down the back of the cladding does no harm, it is recommended that through-wall flashings be placed

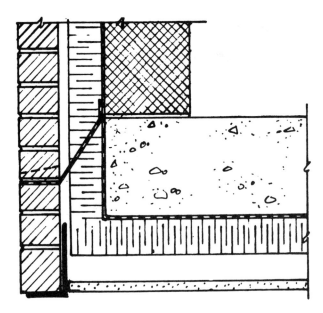

FIGURE 7-II.   Through-wall flashing.

only where absolutely necessary. They will be needed over windows and above soffits (see Figure 7–11). Other than these locations they may not be needed at all in buildings up to three stories that are constructed according to the details in Part 1. In tall buildings, the number of such flashings will depend on the effectiveness of the rainscreen and its exposure. Many of the details in Part 1 show how to install them. Use them only where needed and demand the utmost care in their design and installation.

Rubberized asphalt or one of the materials described as single ply roofing in Chapter 6 should work well, providing they are compatible with adjacent materials. Where metal is required, use sheet zinc in the presence of galvanized steel. Otherwise use copper, or terne plated stainless steel.

7.5   SUMMARY OF FLASHING DESIGN GUIDELINES

1. Base flashings at parapets must begin on the roof surface and be taken up and over the parapet. A flexible waterproof membrane, such as rubberized asphalt, should be used. Compatiblity is important.
2. At an elevator penthouse or other locations where a wall rises above a roof, the base flashings should run from the roof surface and be sealed tightly to the air barrier in the wall. This is very difficult when repairing existing buildings. There one might consider using the walls of the penthouse as an air barrier and applying new insulation and rainscreen.
3. Base flashings must always be designed to take into account any deflection of the roof deck. Places where deflection may occur are not always obvious. This is because details that show the structure are most often drawn to show connections and not at mid-span where deflection is usually greatest. Look at all edges of a roof, penthouse, skylight, etc.

4. Except for flanges less than three feet square, never try to seal membranes to metal.
5. Be sure that base flashings are complete and waterproof in themselves, then apply metal counterflashing in a way that does not destroy this watertightness.
6. Through-wall flashing should never be depended upon to join wall and roof.
7. Gravel stops can be expected to leak. Install a curb instead.
8. It will do absolutely no good to seal flashings to wall cladding, for water will always get behind the cladding whether it be brick, concrete or metal.
9. Never try to seal or caulk a pipe to its flashing sleeve unless there is an adequate flexible joint in the pipe.
10. Where compatible, use two-ply modified asphalt flashings. Both plies are reinforced. Often the bottom ply is reinforced with glass fiber and the top ply with polyester mat. The top ply must include a sunscreen of mineral granules, or copper or aluminum foil. The membranes are joined by ''torching''.

7.6 RECOMMENDED READING

CBD 69, ''Flashings for Membrane Roofs.'' DBR NRCC.
CBD 181, ''Shrinkage of Bituminous Roofing Membranes.'' DBR NRCC.
No. 84 Series Manuals, Soprema S.A. Canada, 1984.
Baker, M.C. 1980. *Roofs*. Montreal: Multiscience Publications.

REFERENCES

Turenne, R.G. 1976. ''Shrinkage of Bituminous Roof Membranes.'' *CBD 181*. Ottawa: DBR NRCC.

Index